SPLITTING THE DIFFERENCE

SPLITTING
THE DIFFERENCE

Compromise and Integrity in Ethics and Politics

Martin Benjamin

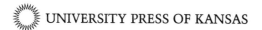 UNIVERSITY PRESS OF KANSAS

Published by the University Press of Kansas (Lawrence, Kansas 66045), which was organized by the Kansas Board of Regents and is operated and funded by Emporia State University, Fort Hays State University, Kansas State University, Pittsburg State University,
the University of Kansas, and Wichita State University.

Library of Congress Cataloging-in-Publication Data

Benjamin, Martin.
    Splitting the difference: compromise and integrity in ethics and
politics / Martin Benjamin.
        p.   cm.
    Includes bibliographical references.
    ISBN 0-7006-0414-6 (alk. paper) — ISBN 0-7006-0455-3
(pbk. : alk. paper)
        1. Compromise (Ethics)   2. Integrity.   I. Title.
    BJ1431.B46 1990
    170—dc20   89-39224
                                                          CIP

British Library Cataloguing in Publication Data is available.

Printed in the United States of America
10 9 8 7 6 5 4 3 2 1

The paper used in this publication meets the minimum requirements of the American
National Standard for Permanence of Paper for Printed Library Materials Z39.48-1984.

For Ronna, Kirsten, and David

Contents

There is something to be said, my lord, for his point of view,
And for yours as well; there is much to be said on both sides.
—*Sophocles*, Antigone

Preface

Can we ever compromise on matters of ethical principle without compromising our integrity? If so, when—and how? Is political accommodation compatible with ethical conviction? Can men and women who value their integrity commit themselves to the vocation of politics if, as a matter of course, it requires compromise on ethical issues?

I come to these questions as one who was, for many years, blind to them. They were never mentioned in my ethics courses when I was a graduate student in philosophy, nor are they addressed in the vast majority of books or articles in ethics or ethical theory. My appreciation of their importance grew as I became more involved in practical ethics and the making of public policy—going on rounds with physicians, participating in hospital case conferences, teaching medical and nursing ethics, and serving on a legislative task force on death and dying and a statewide committee examining ethical issues in organ transplantation. The result was a deeper understanding, first, of the limits of philosophical reason in resolving many ethical disagreements and, second, of its undeniable power in helping, through compromise, to contain them. This book represents my reflections on these and related matters.

Many individuals and institutions provided invaluable assistance as the project developed. Explicit awareness of the importance of compromise dawned through teaching and writing about ethical issues in nursing with my colleague Joy Curtis. A National Endowment for the Humanities (NEH) Fellowship at the Hastings Center in 1983–84 then permitted me to focus my reading and writing on the subject. The resources and atmosphere of the center were invaluable. I am especially grateful for the encouragement and suggestions of the center director, Daniel Callahan, and associates Ronald Bayer, Arthur Caplan, Bruce

Jennings, and Thomas Murray. James Muyskens and John Paris, also NEH Fellows at the Hastings Center, helped me to develop my thoughts through conversation and thoughtful criticism of an initial draft of the first half of the manuscript.

I was able to present what I had written at the Hastings Center to a graduate philosophy seminar at Michigan State University in the fall of 1984. I am indebted to those enrolled, as well as to a number of faculty members, for indulging my obsessions and for their useful comments and suggestions. Special thanks are due to Louise Blackledge, Howard Brody, Eugenio Echeverria, Bruce Miller, Paul Reitemeier, James Roper, Phil Shepard, Tim Tessin, and Tom Tomlinson.

Parts of the manuscript were presented at various times as colloquia or lectures at Union College (Schenectady), the University of New England, Miami University (Ohio), the Center for Christian Scholarship at Calvin College, and the University of Illinois at Chicago Medical Center. I am grateful to members of these audiences for their thoughtful and stimulating questions.

A research award from the Department of Philosophy and the College of Arts and Letters at Michigan State University permitted me to devote winter term 1988 to research and writing. For this I am grateful to my colleagues and to the dean of the college, John W. Eadie.

During the later stages, a number of people read and commented on parts or all of the manuscript. I would like to thank Ronna Benjamin, Gene Cline, Howard M. Ducharme, Richard J. Hall, Donald Koch, Michael Pritchard, and Bruce Omundson for their suggestions. Four whose thorough comments on the entire manuscript were especially acute and generous deserve special mention: Stephen L. Esquith, Mike W. Martin, Ronald Suter, and a reader for the University Press of Kansas who prefers to remain anonymous. Their critical suggestions during the later stages of my work led to a number of significant changes both in substance and in style.

Finally, I want to thank Kate D. Torrey of the University Press of Kansas for her continued encouragement and astute editorial advice.

Introduction

Politics is often characterized as the "art of compromise." The implication is that compromise is desirable and that devising a satisfactory compromise is in part a matter of insight, imagination, discipline, and skill. The same does not seem to be true, however, when we turn to ethics. In ethics, compromise is usually regarded as a sign of weakness or lack of integrity. Although history books may honor a politician like Henry Clay as "the great compromiser," our moral exemplars are usually men and women who have been steadfast in resisting pressures or temptations to compromise. Socrates, Sir Thomas More, Elizabeth Cady Stanton, Gandhi, Martin Luther King, Jr., and the like are admired not only for the nature of their convictions but also for their refusal to compromise them.

Does this point to an important difference between politics and ethics? Should democratic politicians adept at compromise be unconcerned with ethics in their professional roles? Should individuals deeply concerned about ethics refrain from entering the rough and tumble world of pluralistic politics? Or does compromise mean one thing in the political sphere and another in the ethical? An examination of the nature, value, and limitations of compromise in ethics and politics will throw light on these and related questions.

The notion of compromise is surprisingly rich and complex; we cannot hope to further our understanding without careful attention to its many dimensions. Thus in Chapter 1 I examine various related and overlapping uses of the term. Having developed a number of useful distinctions, we will then be able to formulate more specific questions about the relationships between compromise and integrity in ethics and politics. One of the most basic of these questions is whether two (or more) parties to a disagreement rooted in highly cherished but conflicting ethical convictions can compromise without sacrificing their integrity. Many believe that on matters of ethical significance there

1

can be no compromise—no compromise, one might say, without somehow being compromised. After showing, in Chapter 2, how integrity-preserving compromise is in fact possible, I turn, in Chapter 3, to a more thorough examination of the nature and value of individual integrity and its relationship to compromise. I conclude that, properly understood, integrity is not only compatible with a certain amount of compromise but that in the modern world the preservation of integrity will occasionally require compromises of a certain sort.

In dealing with concrete and particular moral conflicts I will be doing practical ethics; that is, my reasoning and analyses will focus on contexts and questions requiring more or less immediate and consequential moral choice and judgment even if some of these contexts are fictional or hypothetical. I will also, however, trace the connections between these concerns and more general questions about the nature of ethics. Among these questions are: What conception of the status of moral knowledge and principles is presupposed by the notion of integrity-preserving compromise? Is this a plausible or defensible conception? And is integrity-preserving compromise a temporary expedient—a stopgap until we discover the true comprehensive universal ethical theory that will enable us to resolve all disagreements without remainder—or is the need for such compromise likely to remain a feature of the human condition?

In addressing these and related matters I will, in Chapter 4, explore some of the relationships between practical and theoretical ethics. I will also show how insights acquired in practical contexts can inform and deepen theoretical understanding. In particular, an appreciation of the ineliminability of rationally irreconcilable moral conflict will accord greater importance to the notion of compromise than one generally finds among ethical theorists. This in turn leads us to a renewed theoretical interest in the notion of judgment; for we cannot, I argue, specify an interesting set of necessary and sufficient conditions that will dictate when we should compromise and when we should not.

In Chapter 5 I will focus on judgment and its relationship to practical questions of compromise and integrity. I also address the question of ethics in compromise. To what extent do ordinary moral precepts apply in attempting to negotiate a compromise to an ethical disagreement? In selling a house or a car, for example, people often ask for more than they are willing to accept. May we do similar things in attempting to reach some sort of accommodation in an ethical dispute?

May I, for example, deliberately overstate the intensity or scope of my ethical convictions in the hope of settling on a compromise more favorable to my actual views? Or does such misrepresentation border on, or count as, lying?

In Chapter 6 I return to the relationships between ethics and politics. Construing politics quite broadly, I focus upon whether, and to what extent, men and women who value their integrity can devise political compromises involving matters of great ethical significance. How, for example, can a legislator who is personally opposed to abortion on moral grounds agree to a more permissive legislative compromise? Here, as in the preceding discussions, little will be gained by simple prescriptions. Like fire, compromise is both necessary and dangerous to human life. Were we never to accept political compromise on matters of ethical conviction, we would cut ourselves off from large numbers of our fellow humans; were we always to accept it, we would become alienated from ourselves.

It may be fairly easy to identify cases around either pole—cases in which such compromises seem unproblematic and cases in which they seem intolerable. In between, however, we will find a broad middle region where matters are less clear and the tension between the individual and social dimensions of human existence less tractable. There is simply no set of determinate rules and principles that the opposing parties can methodically apply to arrive at mutually satisfactory resolutions. Yet the matter isn't entirely hopeless; it is not as if, lacking such rules and principles, the parties can do nothing but resort to force, manipulation, or other nonrational means of imposing their "merely subjective" viewpoints on those who disagree. The faculty of judgment—specifically moral and political judgment—occupies a middle ground between the mechanical application of universal rules and principles, on the one hand, and expressions of mere individual preference, on the other. I will therefore conclude by showing how moral and political judgment may, when sensitively and skillfully employed, contribute to devising and maintaining well-grounded, integrity-preserving compromises in an avowedly (and inescapably) pluralistic polity.

1
The Meanings of Compromise

Compromise, when reached honorably and in a spirit of honesty by all concerned, is the only fair and rational way of reaching a reasonable agreement between two differing points of view.
                                                 —*Edward Stettinius*, Roosevelt and the Russians

There can be no compromise on basic principles or on fundamental issues. . . . [w]hen people speak of "compromise" what they mean is not a legitimate mutual concession or a trade, but precisely the betrayal of their principles.
                                                 —*Ayn Rand*, The Virtue of Selfishness

We may at the outset distinguish three significantly different uses of the term "compromise": compromise as outcome; compromise as process; and compromise as betrayal. The words of Edward Stettinius, an American diplomat, exemplify the first two uses; those of the popular novelist and philosopher Ayn Rand the third.

THE STANDARD SENSE: COMPROMISE
AS OUTCOME AND PROCESS

Compromise is both something "reached" and a "way of reaching." As something reached, a compromise is a certain type of outcome of a conflict or disagreement; as a way of reaching, it is a process for resolving conflict or disagreement.

Consider, first, compromise as outcome. In 1983 President Reagan defended the decision to prohibit news reporters from observing the initial stages of the U.S. invasion of Grenada by claiming that troop security was, in this setting, incompatible with freedom of the press. But as columnist James Reston subsequently pointed out, the president was ignoring "a sensible compromise between security and freedom, used by General Eisenhower during the invasion of Normandy, and by every other President and theater commander since then in the Korean and Vietnam Wars" (*New York Times*, 9 November 1983). Reston was referring to the "pool system," in which a small number of reporters are permitted to observe what is going on and then to "pool" their notes and film with their colleagues. In this context the pool system seems to balance the wish of the military for total security and the desires of the press for complete access. Such an outcome—one that appears to more or less split the difference between opposing positions—is called a compromise.[1]

The process by which such outcomes are usually achieved is also labeled compromise. As a rule, parties to this process try to see matters from the other's point of view, engage in various forms of give-and-take discussion, and are prepared, at least in principle, to make concessions for the sake of coming to terms. In so doing they acknowledge each other's viewpoints as having some claim to equal respect and consideration. In contrast to certain other forms of bargaining and negotiation, the emphasis is on rational persuasion, mutual trust, and reciprocal concession rather than on force, threat, or intimidation. Thus Stettinius suggests that the process is "fair and rational" only when outcomes are "reached honorably and in a spirit of honesty by all concerned."

In what I will call the standard case, an outcome characterized as a compromise is reached as a result of the contending parties' participating in a procedure, also called a compromise. And it is the standard case that grounds the central dictionary definition: "a settlement of differences by mutual concessions." Corresponding to the standard case, I will call this use of the term compromise in the standard sense.

Yet an outcome may be characterized as a compromise even if it is not reached through compromise, and the process of compromise need not result in its intended outcome. Outcomes characterized as compromises may be imposed when the contending parties are unable to engage in the process of compromise, the situation requires a decision, and a powerful third party is able to impose a solution that seems to split the difference between them. Parents of two or more young children, for example, often find themselves in this position, as do labor mediators or judges in divorce proceedings. On the other hand, procedures appropriately characterized as compromise may fail to yield a similarly characterized outcome when no agreement is reached or when, for various reasons including mental lapse or ineptitude, one party unwittingly agrees to an apparently inequitable resolution. Such a lopsided outcome—one that could hardly be characterized as "splitting the difference"—should not be called a compromise. Thus although the standard case involves compromise as both procedure and outcome, we cannot assume that the one will invariably be accompanied by the other.

A further complication arises when the process of compromise results in a mutually satisfactory decision to abide by the outcome of a subsequent process. The immediate outcome, in other words, is agreement on a decision procedure that will generate a more substantive outcome—for example, an election, binding arbitration, or in some instances simply flipping a coin. There is no guarantee in such cases that the final or substantive outcome will split the difference between the contending parties. In some situations the nature of the dispute may permit no outcome other than "winner take all": one party wins the election, the other loses; the arbitrator awards a nondivisible good to A and not to B; tails wins, heads loses; and so on. Moreover, even if the process yields more proportionate outcomes—for example, an election in which the extent of a party's overall victory reflects the percentage of votes received—the result may be far from "splitting the difference." One party may receive 90 percent of the votes and the other only 10 percent

Should these be considered compromises in the standard sense? There are, I believe, circumstances in which the answer is yes. Certainly if the parties are contending over a nondivisible, nonshareable good, there is no way of substantively splitting the difference. Where the number of legitimate claimants for a certain nondivisible good greatly exceeds supply and "half a loaf" is of no more value than none, a compromise, it seems, must be purely procedural. Under certain conditions, then, the notion of compromise in the standard sense ought to be extended to cases in which the process of compromise among two (or more) contending parties results in a mutually satisfactory decision to abide by the outcome of a subsequent process, regardless of the balance or parity of the substantive result. The conditions are these: (1) the disagreement is over a more or less indivisible or nonshareable good; and (2) the initial procedure results in an agreement to abide by the outcome of a subsequent procedure that gives equal respect and consideration to the interests of all of the contending parties. An agreement in these circumstances to abide by the outcome of such a procedure can therefore be regarded figuratively, if not literally, as "splitting the difference" between contending parties. It is thus a special case of compromise in the standard sense.[2]

We must at this point note an important difference between a strict and a loose sense of "compromise." If two parties initially holding opposing positions (A and B, respectively) come to regard a third position (S, a synthesis that combines the strongest features of both A and B while avoiding their agreed-upon drawbacks) as superior to both initial positions and then embrace it, we do not, strictly speaking, have a compromise outcome. There has been no compromise—that is, no concession—by either party. In adopting S each has relinquished what is now regarded as a less correct view for one that is, on its own terms, much better. The result is one form of rational resolution of the initial conflict but not, at bottom, a compromise. Neither party has conceded anything to the other, no differences remain to be split, and each side has everything it now wants. The outcome may be a compromise in a loose sense of the term—that is "something intermediate between different things"—but to avoid confusion I will characterize the result as a synthesis or middle-of-the-road position, not as a compromise.

Suppose, however, that the party holding A and the party holding B remain wedded to their respective positions but find themselves in circumstances requiring a nondeferrable, joint decision on the matter. Efforts to persuade each other of the superiority of their respective views are unsuccessful, yet a mutually respectful give-and-take discussion eventually leads each to acknowledge the difficulties with her own position and the strengths of the opposing one. The parties may then begin to look for a compromise, C, which splits the difference between A and B. Each party will, in this event, make certain concessions to the other for the sake of agreement on a single course of action that seems both to have some independent validity and to capture as much of the spirit of A as it does of B. The matter is not, however, fully settled; there is no closure, no final harmony. Strictly speaking, a compromise does not end the disagreement. It makes the best of what both parties regard as a bad situation; each may subsequently try to persuade the other of the superiority of either A or B or to see that the same situation does not arise again. It is the discrepancy between one's belief in the superiority of either *A* or *B* and acting in accord with *C* that raises philosophical difficulties. If one's attachment to *A* or *B* is a matter of ethical conviction, how can one compromise without compromising one's integrity?

COMPROMISE AS BETRAYAL

For Ayn Rand, compromise as outcome and compromise as process are legitimate only when the opposing parties agree on basic principles but disagree over how these principles are to be implemented in particular cases. As an example she cites a buyer and a seller who agree on the principle of free trade but disagree about the price of a certain product or service (1964, p. 68). There is nothing wrong in this instance, she argues, if they finally compromise on a price that falls somewhere in between the seller's initial demand and the buyer's initial offer. But she is quick to add, "There can be no compromise on basic principles or on fundamental issues" (1964, p. 69). To compromise on basic principles, Rand maintains, is to betray them and to betray oneself; it is to compromise one's integrity as a moral person.

One need not subscribe to Ayn Rand's particular brand of libertarian egoism to understand what she means by "compromise on basic principles." It is this sense of compromise as betrayal that inclines us to regard compromise as morally questionable and to regard as exemplars those who have resisted various pressures or temptations to compromise. Even if we disagree with one or more of a person's basic principles, we often think more of her if she conscientiously tries to act in accord with them than if she is too willing to compromise them. Indeed, if she is always prepared to compromise, we may question whether she has any principles at all. Whatever her present position or principle, she is likely to alter it the moment she encounters significant opposition; the direction as well as the degree of change will vary with the nature and strength of the newly opposing view. Such a person, whom we might characterize as a "moral chameleon," is ultimately unreliable and untrustworthy. If we count on her too heavily she is liable to betray us as she betrays herself.

Related to this use of compromise as betrayal is a family of uses that often take the passive voice. To be compromised is to be exposed or revealed or to have significant limits placed on one's future actions. Thus in reviewing a book on occupied France, Anatole Broyard writes that "at a secret school for Jewish children, a young French teacher says that the children were grotesquely silent and secretive, having been taught that to talk about anyone was to compromise them" (1983). To compromise others in this sense is to betray them, to make them vulnerable.

Those who are compromised may in turn become preoccupied with their own survival or well-being. They may then become dangerous to others and unable to be trusted fully; having been compromised themselves, they are often vulnerable to pressures to compromise others. Examples can be found in Thomas Keneally's account of the remarkable efforts of the Austrian industrialist Oskar Schindler to save a large number of Jews from the Nazi death camps. At one point Schindler is asked by a courier for a Zionist rescue organization about the advisability of seeking additional assistance from a particular dentist. " 'No,' said Herr Schindler. 'Don't visit this man. He's been compromised by the S.S.' " (1982, p. 149). To have been compromised by the SS was to have somehow become beholden to them. Someone in this position could not be relied upon; the dentist's understandable concern for his survival and that of his family would in such circumstances strongly tempt him to betray the Jews' trust.

We may be compromised not only by the deliberate or inadvertent actions of others but also by our own failings or indiscretions. Thus in concluding its discussion of life or death treatment decisions for seriously ill newborns, the President's Commission for the Study of Ethical Problems in Medicine and Biomedical and Behavioral Research noted that "to the extent that society fails to ensure that seriously ill newborns have the opportunity for an adequate level of continuing care, its moral authority to intervene on behalf of a newborn whose life is in jeopardy is compromised" (1983, p. 229). Similarly, a public figure who is the standard bearer for a particular cause may be said to be compromised if prior indiscretions restrict her effectiveness. Consider, for example, a "law-and-order" legislator who is revealed as a tax cheat, or a highly censorious moralistic member of the clergy whose adulterous affairs are made public.

Despite differences among these particular uses of the term "compromise," they are nonetheless related. Each is connected with the notion of betrayal, whether it be self-betrayal, the betrayal of others, or the betrayal of a cause. Together with the notion of compromising one's own principles they constitute a family of uses that have contributed to the pejorative sense of compromise.

COMPROMISE AS PRUDENCE

The term "compromise" is sometimes used simply in connection with limitations on one's freedom imposed by external conditions or circumstances. A stroke, we may say, compromises a person's independence, and various forms of mental impairment may compromise a person's capacity to accept or refuse medical treatment. When we talk in this connection of being betrayed by our bodies (or by our minds), we speak figuratively and not literally. We are limited in what we can do, but assuming that the limitation is a result of unavoidable natural occurrences and that it is not compounded by neglect or substandard social institutions, there is no betrayer and hence nothing ethically untoward in being compromised in this manner.

A related use of compromise involves forced or prudential choice. Consider, for example, an injured athlete who has trained hard to be ready for an important event. If she competes before the injury is fully healed, she runs a high risk of its turning into a lifelong disability. But if she waits for it to heal, she will have to forego this competition. Under such circumstances, prudence seems to require that she scale back, or compromise, her immediate aim of competing and allow her injury to heal. In the same way our efforts to achieve certain ends are often said to be compromised by unforeseeable and unavoidable obstacles such as bad weather, natural disasters, accidents, and so on. Thus our goals will have to be reduced—compromises made—although we cannot be said to have betrayed them.

The distinction between compromise as prudence and compromise as betrayal played a prominent role in Lenin's discussion of an 1874 quarrel between Frederick Engels and the Communard-Blanquists (1920). In their manifesto the Communard-Blanquists urged pursuit of the goals of communism "without stopping at intermediate stations, without any compromises, which only postpone the day of victory and prolong the period of slavery." In response Engels pointed out that the course of historical development occasionally imposes "intermediate stations" and "compromises" on communists and that this poses no danger so long as "they clearly perceive and constantly pursue the final aim, *viz.*, the abolition of classes and the creation of a society in which there will be no private ownership of land or the means of production" (Lenin 1920, p. 49).

In his discussion of this episode, Lenin observes that to "very young and inexperienced revolutionaries," as well as to older petty-bourgeois revolutionaries, "it seems exceedingly 'dangerous,' incomprehensible and incorrect to 'allow compromises.' . . . But," he adds,

proletarians schooled in numerous strikes . . . usually understand quite well the very profound (philosophical, historical, political and psychological) truth expounded by Engels. Every proletarian has been through strikes and has experienced "compromises" with the hated oppressors and exploiters, when the workers had to go back to work either without having achieved anything or consenting to partial satisfaction of their demands. Every proletarian . . . notices the difference between a compromise enforced by objective conditions (such as a lack of strike funds, no outside support, extreme hunger and exhaustion), a compromise which in no way diminishes the revolutionary devotion and readiness for further struggle on the part of the workers who have agreed to such a compromise and a compromise by traitors who try to ascribe to outside causes their own selfishness (strikebreakers also effect "compromises"!), cowardice, desire to toady to the capitalists and readiness to yield to intimidation, sometimes to persuasion, sometimes to sops, and sometimes to flattery on the part of the capitalists (Lenin 1920, p. 50).

The distinction between what Lenin calls a "compromise enforced by objective conditions" and cowardly or self-serving compromises is an important one. But in practice they are not easily distinguished.

How can we tell whether a particular compromise was enforced by objective conditions or was deceptively (and perhaps also self-deceptively) an act of betrayal? In national and international politics, Lenin admits, "very many cases will arise that will be much more difficult than a legitimate 'compromise' during a strike, or the treacherous 'compromise' of a strikebreaker, or of a treacherous leader, etc."

There is no readily applicable criterion. Nor, according to Lenin, is a slogan an acceptable substitute: "It would be absurd to concoct a recipe or general rule ('No Compromise!') to serve all cases. One must have the brains to analyse the situation in each separate case" (1920, p. 51).

Exactly what is involved in case-by-case analyses of compromise in the standard sense will be explored in Chapter 5. For present purposes it is enough to identify the notion of compromise as prudence and to indicate in a rough and ready way its relationship with compromise in the standard sense and compromise as betrayal. What all three senses seem to have in common is the idea of making concessions or scaling back goals or principles. With compromise in the standard sense, such concessions occur in the context of a disagreement between two or more parties, each of whom grants some degree of moral legitimacy to the other side, and the scaling back is more or less mutual.

Compromise as prudence may involve two or more parties; yet it also may not. A single person may compromise her aims on prudential grounds because of external limitations. Moreover, in the case of two-party conflicts, a purely prudential compromise by one party need not concede the moral legitimacy of the other. Lenin, for example, may counsel strikers to compromise in the face of the capitalist's overwhelming power. But this is quite different from the mutual concessions characteristic of compromise in the standard sense. Compromise as betrayal regards any retreat on matters of ethical principle as a deep moral failing. It is interesting to note that though occupying opposite poles on the political spectrum, both Ayn Rand and the Communard-Blanquists would agree on this point. No compromise, they would say, on matters of ethical importance.

MORAL AND NONMORAL CONFLICT

The distinction between compromise in the standard sense (as both process and outcome) and compromise as betrayal suggests a related distinction between two kinds of conflict: conflicts of nonmoral, equally legitimate interests and conflicts of moral principles.[3] A simple conflict of interests arises when, for example, two friends want to do different things on a Sunday in the city. One person has an interest in spending the afternoon in museums and then going to a favorite

Spanish restaurant, whereas the other would prefer to browse through used bookstores and then go to a new Korean restaurant. Suppose, too, that whatever they do, they want to do together. Here the give and take of compromise (in the standard sense) might yield a number of satisfactory, morally unproblematic outcomes: The pair might combine museums with the Korean restaurant; bookstores with the Spanish restaurant; a few hours in museums, a few in bookstores, and flipping a coin for the restaurant; museums and Spanish restaurant today, bookstores and Korean restaurant next week; and so on.

"A conflict of interests," Theodore Benditt points out, "is often a resource-allocation problem, where resources are understood in a wider sense and include anything that is distributable. Money, tangible goods, power and prerogative are distributable and they are also compromisable" (Benditt 1979, p. 30). If, then, the parties to a conflict of interests regard themselves as equals and the conflicting interests are both distributable and equally legitimate from a moral point of view, they may have little difficulty in arriving at a mutually satisfactory compromise. Although ethical considerations are involved in such compromises—for example, as moral equals the parties must not resort to coercion or misrepresentation—the conflict is not, in any interesting sense, an ethical one.

Compromise is more difficult to achieve, however, when the parties to a conflict perceive their respective positions as rooted in moral principles.[4] If one person believes her position is based on an important moral principle, it is unlikely, at least initially, that she will grant moral significance (or the same degree of moral significance) to the opposing position. If, for example, a deeply held moral belief in the sanctity of human life leads me to oppose abortion, I will probably be opposed to compromising with those having more permissive positions because I do not acknowledge the moral legitimacy of their beliefs.

What is at stake for parties to a moral conflict is higher than when the disagreement is perceived in terms of conflicting nonmoral interests. Our interests in going to a museum or a bookstore, or in going to one kind of restaurant rather than another, are not so much a part of us—not so integrally related to our identity, personal ideals, or sense of ourselves—as are our basic moral convictions. To compromise fundamental principles is to compromise not simply a contingent or readily interchangeable interest but rather what one regards as an essential aspect of the self. It is to alter one's fundamental convictions and perhaps to weaken or betray one's wholeness or integrity as a particular self—as a person with a determinate identity who stands for some things rather than for others.

Sociologist George Simmel's notion of "representation" suggests an additional reason why conflicts of nonmoral interests are more open to compromise than conflicts of moral values or principles. In cases of conflict, Simmel points out, the objects of some of our nonmoral interests may be exchanged, or "represented," by others (1955, p. 116); a person may, for example, be persuaded to relinquish nonmoral interests in one thing in return for an adequate substitute, or representation, of it. Thus if each party to a divorce has an equal financial (as opposed to sentimental) interest in retaining their house, an indivisible good, a compromise can sometimes be struck giving one of them the house and the other half its value in cash, or by selling the house and dividing the profit between them. The money in this case represents half or all of the house. Although some nonmoral interests do not appear to be representable (if, for example, the demand for a scarce lifesaving resource like a transplantable human heart exceeds supply, there is no way of adequately representing the resource to those who will die without it but who lose out in a just and efficient method of allocation), most nonmoral interests admit of representation. Basic principles, however, are not so easily represented. As a result, conflicts rooted in them are not so amenable to compromise.

Consider, for example, a disagreement between a terminally ill patient and his physician over whether life-prolonging treatment should be ceased and the patient be allowed to die. Suppose the patient defends his position by invoking his right to self-determination and the principle of autonomy. Deciding such matters for himself, he believes, is more important than life itself. His very identity and the integrity of his life as whole, the patient argues, are at stake. To be kept alive past the point where he would be able to do more than simply lie in a hospital bed, as well as to have to spend his financial resources on himself rather than leaving as much as he can to his grandchildren, he maintains, would be inconsistent with longstanding, deeply held values; it would betray in his waning days much of what he has stood for during the preceding decades.

But the physician, on the other hand, invokes her commitment to the preservation and prolongation of life. The principle of the sanctity of life rather than the principle of autonomy may be fundamental for her—personally, professionally, or both. She may believe, as I have heard one physician say about the profession, "We cease to be physicians when we stop resisting death." If so, then her identity and integrity are also at stake. To give in on this matter, to agree to an earlier rather than a later death, will require the physician to betray her conception of herself and what she stands for.

It is difficult to see how such a disagreement can be resolved by compromise. Not only are the opposing values deeply held, but they seem incommensurable; there appears to be no common scale into which they can be translated, with the difference then (quantitatively) split. Unlike the case of the divorcing couple with equal financial interests in their house, there appears to be no common currency, no way of representing or compensating for what is in dispute in this case—life itself. If the patient "wins," the physician "loses," and vice versa. If one of the parties is to be true to her principles, it seems that the other must betray his. "It is much easier," Robert Paul Wolff observes, "to accept a compromise between competing interests—particularly when they are expressible in terms of a numerical scale like money—than between opposing principles which purport to be objectively valid" (1965, p. 21). Those seeking compromise solutions to conflicts that appear to involve matters of principle often can reach a resolution if they recast such conflicts as conflicts of interests. The appeal of this recommendation to those working to resolve deep, divisive, or potentially violent and destabilizing conflicts is quite understandable. Theirs is a world of pressing practical concerns where resolutions must come sooner rather than later. Politicians, diplomats, mediators, and others on the front lines of social conflict are, as a result, often inclined to construe disagreements that may have originally been formulated in terms of moral values or principles as conflicts of nonmoral interests.

This may partially explain why practical-minded men and women who specialize in resolving conflicts often seem to eschew the vocabulary of ethics. It is not that they summarily reject ethical considerations. Indeed, they frequently seem to have a rather strong commitment to the peaceful resolution of conflicts, an important ethical value. But insofar as they are committed to this end, they may regard the explicit consideration of moral principles as a severe hindrance; the vocabulary of ethics, insofar as it is taken to involve incommensurable and unyielding values and principles, appears to impede the sort of compromises they seek. They are consequently inclined to construe all conflicts, including those initially formulated in terms of competing ethical considerations, as conflicts of nonmoral interests. "The genius of American politics is," as it is sometimes said, "its ability to treat even matters of principle as though they were conflicts of interests" (Wolff 1965, p. 21).

In the legislative domain the result has been what Bruce Jennings calls moral minimalism, a self-conscious effort to restrict ethical considerations to such matters as personal financial disclosure, conflict of interest, and the use of office for personal financial gain. "Behind the argument for moral minimalism," Jennings points out,

> stands a tradition of social theory that grew out of the political turmoil of the sixteenth and seventeenth centuries. According to this tradition, moral discourse is socially polarizing and divisive. When human beings define their often competitive relations in terms of fundamental ethical or religious principles, they lose their capacity to compromise and come to blows. Following the terrible religious warfare that devastated Europe in these centuries, political theorists systematically tried to cordon off ethical discourse in the private realm and redefined politics in terms of material rather than spiritual interests. The argument of moral minimalism shows the legacy of this tradition's wariness about the polarizing effects of ethical discourse in political life (1985, pp. 160ff.).

There is something to be said for this approach to conflict resolution, both within the legislative arena and without. Many disagreements do not, despite an initial appearance to the contrary, turn on conflicts of moral values. Although naively or rhetorically formulated in explicitly ethical language, the opposing interests are not, at bottom, rooted in basic principles. As research in negotiation has revealed, to formulate these disagreements or to allow them to remain formulated as if they are so rooted is to place gratuitous obstacles in the way of arriving at mutually satisfying accommodation (Fisher and Ury, 1981). We should not, however, allow our desire for resolution to obscure the fact that this strategy will not always work. A number of conflicts can only be adequately understood and addressed if we appreciate the extent to which they are grounded in conflicting and incommensurable moral values. The temptation to paper over such conflicts by reformulating them as conflicts of equally legitimate, nonmoral interests should for a number of reasons be resisted.

As the notion of "equally legitimate interests" implies, some interests have no legitimacy at all. Consider the conflict of interests between a rapist and his victim. Here the idea of splitting the difference ("he wants to rape her twice, she does not want to be raped at all; so let's compromise on once") is absurd because the rapist's interests have no standing. They do not, should not, count. Note, however, that we cannot assert or defend this claim without relying, at least implicitly, on the language of moral principles. It is the language of ethical assessment and not simply a utilitarian summing up of interest satisfaction that shows why rape is wrong. Rape would be wrong and morally prohibited even if there were only six people left on earth, five men and a woman, and all of the men were strongly interested in raping the woman. Thus not all conflicts of interests, as this example shows, can be resolved by tabulating interests and then seeing to it that we come as close as we can to maximizing overall satisfaction or satisfying each person's interests equally. Some interests have no legitimate standing, but this cannot be computationally determined; it turns on an explicitly ethical judgment that has little or nothing to do with trying to maximize interest satisfaction or to satisfy each person's interests equally, regardless of their nature from a moral point of view.

If, however, the notion of noncomputational ethical judgment is presupposed by the notion of a "legitimate" interest, why suppose that all legitimate interests, even those grounded in ethical values, are in all circumstances of equal ethical importance? This is indeed what is supposed by those who, for the sake of conflict resolution, urge that we systematically reformulate conflicts of ethical values as conflicts of (more or less equally legitimate) interests. Yet, as the following example reveals, this reformulation will not always work.

Consider a situation in which parents refuse to consent to a series of blood transfusions necessary to save their young child's life. As Jehovah's Witnesses they strongly believe that it is wrong to accept transfusions of blood, either for themselves or for their children. Citing scripture and longstanding, deeply held religious convictions, they steadfastly resist the entreaties of the medical staff to permit the procedure. Suppose, too, that with the blood transfusions it is clear that the child is very likely to lead a normal, healthy life. The medical staff and hospital attorney are, therefore, insisting that the transfusions be administered. This is a moral disagreement that can be characterized in terms of a conflict between the values of freedom of religion and parental autonomy, on the one hand, and the value of (earthly) life, the state's interest in protecting life, and professional responsibility, on the other.

To suggest that this conflict be reformulated in terms of equally legitimate interests and the difference then be split is ludicrous. In the first place, although there are no villains here and although the interests of both parties are legitimate, they are not genuinely in equipoise. Though the matter is not crystal clear, the standard view in cases like this is that the moral claim of the state and the physicians is stronger than that of the parents and should prevail. Moreover, splitting the difference between the contending parties—if, for example, this means giving only half as many pints of blood as the doctors believe necessary to save the child's life—would, in this case, be the worst possible outcome. The child would receive enough blood to violate the parents' religious convictions and parental autonomy but not enough to save her life. Although in subsequent chapters I will argue that there are situations in which conflicts between moral principles can be satisfactorily resolved by compromise, this is clearly not one of them.

Unlike the previous example of conflict between a rapist and his victim, the conflicting interests in the Jehovah's Witnesses case are all legitimate, yet the idea of simply splitting the difference hardly enters our minds. Nevertheless this is what we would be advised to do by those who, in the interests of minimizing conflict, would urge that we replace explicitly moral discourse with the language of nonmoral interests. So unless and until it can be shown that all legitimate interests are from a moral point of view equally legitimate, the resolution of at least some conflicts will have to involve explicitly moral evaluation and judgment. Approaches to conflict resolution cannot, therefore, fully dispense with noncomputational ethical assessment without either trivializing their enterprise (by evading tough and interesting cases) or adopting a quite implausible ethical theory—one that regards all interests (or at least all "legitimate" interests) as equally legitimate from a moral point of view.

In the political arena, the attempt to "homogenize" conflict by ignoring or reformulating conflicts of explicitly moral principles has come under attack from both the right and the left. Theologian Richard John Neuhaus, for example, has argued that efforts to exclude moral assessments, particularly those grounded in religious values, from the public forum endangers American democracy. To exclude historically and communally grounded moral and religious values as such from public debate—to insist on what he calls a naked public square— is to create a kind of moral vacuum that often proves irresistible to partisans of extremist or antidemocratic beliefs (Neuhaus 1984). Political discourse in a pluralistic, democratic society cannot fully exclude reference to the moral and religious values that give shape and meaning to people's lives, Neuhaus argues, without alienating them from public life.

From the other end of the political spectrum, Robert Paul Wolff argues that efforts to exclude explicitly normative considerations from liberal politics "involves ideological distortion in at least three ways" (1965, pp. 40–51). First, in actual application, efforts to mediate conflict by resolution of what are regarded as equally legitimate individual interests favor those belonging to established, influential social groups at the expense of those belonging to equally legitimate but new or minority social groups. The result is a braking effect on social change, which may or may not be desirable but is assuredly not value neutral. Second, in excluding explicitly moral assessment in adjudicating such conflicts we are apt to transform de jure conflicts of interests into de facto conflicts of power. The interests of large, entrenched, and well-organized groups will carry more weight than those of smaller, newer, and less-well-organized groups even if, from a moral point of view, the latter are at least as justifiable as the former. Finally, an emphasis on the interests of particular individuals or groups often leads to a certain blindness with respect to various public or communal goods that cannot be secured without explicitly normative or non-computational consideration of what constitutes a good society. Policies based only on the interests of particular individuals or groups are likely to give short shrift to general or public goods such as natural beauty, historical preservation, cultivation of the arts, and so on.

Despite their good intentions, then, the reach of those who in the interest of peaceful conflict resolution suggest that we routinely reformulate conflicts of moral values or principles as conflicts of non-moral interests greatly exceeds their grasp. A number of ineluctably moral conflicts cannot be expressed as conflicts of commensurable nonmoral interests without either trivializing them or begging important questions. If we are to adjudicate conflicts of this kind through compromise, we must show how the language of compromise is compatible with the language of ethics—how, that is, it is possible to arrive at a compromise (in the standard sense) in cases involving conflicting, noncommensurable ethical values without compromising (or betraying) ourselves or others.

EXTERNAL AND INTERNAL COMPROMISE

Our discussion of compromise in the standard sense has thus far centered on conflicts that arise among two or more separate parties. Whether the parties are individuals or social groups or organizations makes no difference. Compromise in this context we will label as "external" to distinguish it from "internal" compromise, which aims at resolving conflict among competing values, principles, and desires within a single person.[5] To take a simple example, suppose we recognize an apparently deep internal conflict between our career goals and our obligations as spouse or parent or both. We want to satisfy both sides but they conflict, and a choice appears to be necessary. We could pursue one course of action at the expense of another, but few of us are so single-minded. Instead we usually choose to make partial, though not necessarily equal, sacrifices of the competing goals and obligations. Sometimes we do this unconsciously; at other times we engage in what might be called deep or reflective self-evaluation (C. Taylor 1976; Dennett 1976), debating, arguing, negotiating, and bargaining with ourselves just as we do with others. Although we may continue to experience tension and to some extent sacrifice simple consistency, we often prefer an internal compromise of this sort to an all-or-nothing kind of resolution.

The same is true when the competing considerations are both ethical. When, for example, a physician moderates her commitment to the sanctity of life in order to mitigate suffering or distress she compromises between two of her ethical commitments: to preserve and extend life, and to relieve suffering. "It is easy," writes British physician T. B. Brewin, "to denigrate [internal] compromise of this kind. But sometimes the only alternative is to embrace one noble principle and murder another. Which seems even worse. So we compromise; but, we hope, in a civilised and humane manner" (1985, p. 490).

Those who find internal conflict intolerable may seek to order their lives around what Rawls terms a "dominant end," a single most important goal in life to which all other legitimate goals are subordinate or derivative (1971, pp. 552–54). To successfully structure one's life around a single dominant end is to eliminate internal conflict. If, for example, your dominant end is to maximize your own happiness, you will use this as a criterion for determining which values, principles, feelings, intuitions, and so on are to be given serious consideration. Whatever is incompatible with the dominant end can then be disregarded as having no legitimate standing. The same holds true if your dominant end is to maximize overall happiness or to bring about the glory of God or to establish a workers' utopia.

Internal conflict and the indecision frequently accompanying it arise because we seem to have many aims pulling us in different directions and no simple procedure for resolving conflicts. Burdened with inner turmoil and uncertainty, we naturally find the notion of a single dominant end to which all others are subordinate highly appealing. A single dominant end promises to relieve us of internal conflict and indecision. "The procedure for making a rational choice," Rawls writes,

and the conception of such a choice, would then be perfectly clear; deliberation would always concern means to ends, all lesser ends in turn being ordered as means to one single dominant end. The many finite chains of reason eventually converge and meet at the same point. Hence a rational decision is always in principle possible, since only difficulties of computation and lack of information remain (1971, p. 552).

A single dominant end—whether it be one's own happiness, the greatest general happiness, fulfillment of the divine will, or one conception of human perfection or another—provides a basis for mechanically resolving, if not eliminating, internal conflict.

But, as Rawls suggests (and I argue in Chapters 3 and 4), there is no such dominant end, or at least none that is compatible with a full and balanced conception of the self:

The extreme nature of dominant-end views is often concealed by the vagueness and ambiguity of the end proposed. Thus if God is conceived (as surely he must be) as a moral being, then the end of serving him above all else is left unspecified to the extent that the divine intentions are not clear from revelation, or evident from natural reason. Within these limits a theological doctrine of morals is subject to the same problems of balancing principles and determining precedence which trouble other conceptions. Since disputed questions commonly lie here, the solution propounded by the religious ethic is only apparent. And certainly when the dominant end is clearly specified as attaining some objective goal such as political power or material wealth, the underlying fanaticism and inhumanity are manifest. *Human good is heterogeneous because the aims of the self are heterogeneous.* Although to subordinate all our aims to one end does not strictly speaking violate the principles of rational choice (not the counting principles anyway), it still strikes us as irrational, or more likely as mad. The self is disfigured and put in the service of one of its ends for the sake of system (1971, p. 554; my emphasis).

In fact most of us appear to manage quite well without structuring our lives around a single dominant end. We acknowledge a number of different and occasionally competing aims and occasionally compromise between them.

That we are capable of engaging in a certain measure of internal compromise on moral as well as on nonmoral matters while experiencing no deep threat to personal integrity may thus shed some light on our understanding and acceptance of external compromise. For if integrity is not a matter of all or none with regard to internal, or intrapersonal, compromise, it may not have to be a matter of all or none with regard to external, or interpersonal, compromise. As individuals we may be able to engage in a certain amount of external compromise without being compromised. Whether this can be shown will depend in part on whether the appearance of compatibility between internal compromise and individual integrity remains after a more careful examination. Thus in subsequent chapters it will be useful to develop a deeper understanding of internal compromise and integrity and the relationship between them. We may then be able to draw upon this relationship to better understand the relationship between external compromise and individual integrity.

MORAL COMPROMISE

The groundwork for our inquiry is now in place. In the remainder of this book I focus on two-party conflict rooted in opposing ethical convictions and the extent to which they may be mediated by compromise without requiring that either of the parties compromise its integrity. Apart from identifying various senses of compromise so as to better formulate and address the problem of integrity-preserving moral and political compromise in the standard sense, I make no attempt at providing a comprehensive account of compromise in its various meanings. I do not, for example, directly address questions about compromise in contexts of competing nonmoral interests in business, politics, or international relations; nor do I examine how, when confronted with an implacable opponent, we determine when prudential considerations justify compromising our principles and when not. These are important and pressing questions. But the subject of compromise and its relation to integrity in ethics and politics is at this point too vast and unexplored to admit of comprehensive treatment in a single volume. From this point on I shall therefore concentrate on moral compromise, by which I mean compromise in the standard sense as it applies to conflicts rooted in opposing ethical considerations. Such conflicts may simply arise between particular individuals, in which case we characterize them as moral, or between organized groups, in which case they are also political. Now to the first substantive question: Are there any circumstances in which parties to a conflict involving rationally irreconcilable ethical commitments may devise a mutually satisfactory compromise without compromising (or betraying) themselves or others?

2
Moral Compromise

Let not your first thought be your only thought.
Think if there cannot be some other way.
Surely, to think your own the only wisdom,
And yours the only word, the only will,
Betrays a shallow spirit, an empty heart.
—*Sophocles*, Antigone

The aim of this chapter is to show that it is possible to compromise on matters involving conflicting ethical values or principles without compromising (or betraying) oneself or others. It begins with a case study illustrating what I will call the circumstances of compromise.

MORAL CONFLICT
IN THE INTENSIVE CARE UNIT

Ann Chapman is an experienced critical-care staff nurse who enjoys the challenges of the medical intensive care unit in a large medical center.[1] She is regarded by the medical and nursing staffs as thoughtful, sensitive, and exceptionally competent. At the moment, however, she is at odds with most other members of the unit over whether aggressive treatment should be continued for Marsha Hocking, a young single woman who has suffered severe brain damage due to viral encephalitis. Marsha Hocking's parents are so overwhelmed by the situation that they have transferred all decision-making authority to the medical staff. They neither want nor appear to be able to participate in whatever choices have to be made on alternative modes of treatment.

Ann Chapman and the medical and nursing staffs are in general

24

agreement about the medical details of the case—that is, the extent of the patient's brain damage and her (very poor) prognosis. But they disagree on how aggressively she should be treated. Ann Chapman believes there is little hope for recovery and that aggressive treatment should be reduced accordingly. She is the same age as the patient and maintains that it is quite unlikely that Marsha Hocking would want to be kept alive in this condition. She herself, Chapman emphatically adds, certainly would not want to be kept alive if the same thing were to happen to her. Moreover, aggressive treatment for patients like Marsha Hocking represents a terribly inefficient use of resources. The nursing staff, Chapman points out, is already stretched too thin; other patients are likely to benefit significantly from increased attention if the staff were to be relieved of doing so much for Marsha Hocking. Furthermore, Marsha Hocking's care is very expensive. Someone—her insurance company, her parents, the taxpayers, or the hospital—is going to have to pick up the bill. The exceedingly slim chance of significant benefits, Chapman says, hardly outweighs the certainty of continued high costs.

Chapman has asked the other nurses and the physicians to think about her recommendation. Although a few nurses agree with her, most, including the nurse in charge of the case, side with the attending physician, Susan Lehman, in saying that this is not the time to reduce their efforts. In an earlier, fairly heated discussion of the matter, Dr. Lehman pointed to a number of reasons for continuing aggressive treatment. Marsha Hocking's age, the sudden onset of the disease, and her previous excellent condition suggest that if anyone stands a chance of recovery, this patient does. Lehman also struck a responsive chord in many of those listening by mentioning the inherent value of human life and the importance of the continued dedication of medical and nursing professionals to the preservation and prolongation of life.

Things are now at an impasse. Neither Chapman nor Lehman and those strongly favoring the continued aggressive treatment have changed their minds, so aggressive treatment is being continued. But as days pass, a few more nurses have come to agree with Chapman's position; they persuade Dr. Lehman, a fair-minded person who generally does not settle such matters by appeals to authority, rank, or legalisms, to schedule another staff meeting on the matter.

THE CIRCUMSTANCES OF COMPROMISE

The circumstances of compromise are those conditions that provide both the motivation and the grounds for compromise solutions. The exact nature of these circumstances will vary with the context. For example, the circumstances of compromise in a situation involving a conflict of equally legitimate interests will differ somewhat from those involving a conflict of moral principles. Our concern at this point is mainly with the circumstances of compromise for comparatively simple, two-party conflicts involving what the parties (let us say, correctly) regard as important principles. Like many problems in biomedical ethics, the Chapman-Lehman conflict involves factual uncertainty and moral complexity.

Chapman believes that the patient would not want to be kept alive in this condition. But how can she be sure? Perhaps Chapman and all of her acquaintances would not want to be kept alive in this state, but what about the patient? Certainly there are some people who would want to be treated aggressively in these circumstances; Chapman does not know with certainty that Hocking is not one of them. Chapman would be on stronger ground if she knew that before her illness Hocking had considered and expressed a view similar to her own. But she does not know this. Similarly, those arguing for continued aggressive treatment appeal to factors that are roughly related to possible recovery—the patient's age, the sudden onset of the disease, her previous excellent health—but they have little else to go on in predicting her survival. If they knew that she would survive and that her ensuing condition would be good or at least tolerable, their position would be stronger. But they have no such knowledge. Factual uncertainty of this sort is and will remain part of our lives. This is not to say, however, that relevant facts are forever beyond our reach nor that statistical knowledge, though uncertain, is of no value to decision making. But factual information that would significantly strengthen one or the other side in a moral disagreement will often be unavailable or unattainable.

If Marsha Hocking had previously expressed her views through some form of "living will" or through the appointment of a trusted proxy under the appropriate provisions of a durable power-of-attorney statute (President's Commission 1983, pp. 136–53), we would be in a better position to evaluate Chapman's belief that Hocking would not want aggressive treatment under these conditions. And if we knew more about the degree and incidence of recovery from viral encephalitis for similar patients, we would be in a better position to evaluate Lehman's belief. This does not mean, of course, that the missing factual information would be sufficient to settle the matter; the dispute rests on more than this. But if there were agreement on other matters, the resolution of factual uncertainty might be enough to tip the balance one way or the other.

In other situations factual uncertainty may be deeper. For example, the probable effects of such measures as busing and affirmative action legislation to counteract the lingering effects of slavery, the Jim Crow laws, and other forms of racial discrimination in the United States play an important role in contemporary debates over public policy. Yet these effects are notoriously difficult to predict. Factual uncertainty about nuclear war—whether various weapons systems will function as intended, whether a nuclear exchange can remain limited, how leaders of various nations will react in the event of a nuclear attack, the extent and duration of the devastation, psychological aftereffects on possible survivors, and so on—provides a similar limitation on current policy debates. It is important to recognize that the persistence of factual uncertainty in debates over such matters will not be eliminated, or even significantly reduced, by advances of modern science. Indeed, such advances will often create as many unprecedented, factually underdetermined decisions as they will resolve.

Consider in this connection the difficulties in making an accurate prognosis for seriously ill, premature infants in newborn intensive care units. Limitations in predicting the prognosis of low birth-weight infants in neonatal intensive care units greatly complicates decisions on how aggressively they should be treated. Yet as technology advances and viable birth weights go down, empirical knowledge with regard to outcomes invariably trails behind medical capacities. As Albert Jonsen points out, certainty continues to elude us:

> The questions posed to conscientious neonatologists are: to what extent they should try to treat and how extreme the deficiencies in the neonate are. Since these are questions of contingent facts and guesses, there are no rules to answer them. The experiences of other neonatologists to whom one might look for answers are often not well correlated. Further, each year we see improvements in

the science of neonatology, but the disagreements still exist. Assessments of children who were treated five years ago cannot be applied to current neonatology because the technology has changed so dramatically. Thus, the neonatologist's judgment is one of contingent fact and depends little on science. It is a "judgment" call—an informed guess based on one's own experience and on what can be learned from one's colleagues (1982, p. 239).

We cannot, in other words, know how well such infants will do until we have had enough experience with them. And we cannot acquire the relevant experience unless we act without the relevant knowledge. It is thus that advances in science and technology generate new factually underdetermined choices and decisions while helping to resolve others. This and other forms of uncertainty are endemic to the practice of medicine (Katz 1984, pp. 165–206).

In addition, a heightened appreciation of the extent to which certain ostensibly factual disputes (such as whether a human embryo is a living human being protected by a right to life) are largely normative or controversially metaphysical suggests that, in certain contexts, factual uncertainty will always be with us because it cannot be fully separated from moral or metaphysical uncertainty. Bruce Jennings (1986) has examined the role that social scientific inquiry, conceived as interpretative rather than explanatory or (narrowly) scientific, can and should play in ethical reasoning and analysis. The "facts" presumed to be simply and uncontroversially "out there" by more mechanical conceptions of ethics are, Jennings suggests, a will-o'-the-wisp. What we regard as the facts are in part a matter of interpretation, and interpretation is not independent of various ethical (and metaphysical) presuppositions and commitments. Thus in many cases an appeal to the facts cannot settle an ethical disagreement because the parties' reading, or interpretation, of the facts will be inseparable from their respective moral (and metaphysical) convictions. Certainly this is true of the current debate over abortion. At the heart of this controversy are questions about the moral and metaphysical status of the fetus that cannot be resolved by science alone. What one takes to be the salient facts in the abortion debate are, as I argue in Chapters 4 and 6, largely a function of one's particular world view and way of life.

In addition to factual uncertainty, the disagreement between Chapman and Lehman is compounded by moral complexity. Both appeal to morally relevant considerations to support their views. Ann Chapman emphasizes the patient's autonomy and various considerations of utility.[2] She presumably ranks these higher than the sanctity of human life as such. Lehman, on the other hand, appeals to the inherent value of human life and the importance of the continued dedication of the medical and nursing professions to the preservation and prolongation of life. Although Lehman may also value patient autonomy and utility, they do not appear to play as prominent a role in this case as does the sanctity of life. Neither party, then, can be charged with moral indifference. Ethically there is something to be said for each position. At worst each emphasizes certain moral considerations while downplaying or overlooking others that may lead in other directions.

Like factual uncertainty, moral complexity is one of the features of the human condition that contribute to the circumstances of compromise. As Rawls puts it:

> Our individual and associative points of view, intellectual affinities and affective attachments, are too diverse, especially in a free democratic society, to allow of lasting and reasoned agreement [on all moral as well as religious and philosophical matters]. Many conceptions of the world can plausibly be constructed from different standpoints. Diversity naturally arises from our limited powers and distinct perspectives; it is unrealistic to suppose that all our differences are rooted solely in ignorance and perversity, or else in the rivalries that result from scarcity. . . . Deep and unresolvable differences on matters of fundamental significance . . . [must be acknowledged] as a permanent condition of human life (1980, p. 542).

Even if Chapman and Lehman could resolve their moral differences on this particular issue, moral disagreement attributable to moral complexity will still be with us in other contexts.

Aggravating disagreement in situations of moral complexity is our need for integrity. "Truth in philosophy," P. F. Strawson observes, "though not to be despaired of, is so complex and many-sided, so multi-faceted, that any individual philosopher's work, *if it is to have any unity and coherence* [that is, integrity], must at best emphasize some aspects of the truth, to the neglect of others which may strike another philosopher with greater force" (1985, p. viii; my emphasis). And what is true of philosophy in general is, in this regard, true of ethics or moral philosophy in particular. Paraphrasing Strawson we might say that "truth in ethics, though not to be despaired of, is in some cases so complex and many-sided, so multi-faceted, that any individual's position on a particular issue, if it is to have any unity and coherence, must at best emphasize some aspects of the truth to the neglect of others that may strike another party to the case with greater force." To lead an integrated life, as I will argue in Chapters 3 and 4, requires that we place much greater weight on some plausible moral convictions and commitments than on others.

The philosophical difficulties presented by moral complexity are often compounded by practical constraints. As Arthur Kuflik notes (1979, p. 50), limitations of time, energy, and circumstance are often such that individuals become sensitive to and increasingly preoccupied with different aspects of the same reasonably complex moral problem. In the case at hand, both Nurse Chapman and Dr. Lehman are likely to be limited in the amount of time and energy they are able to devote to ethical analysis and discussion. The hectic world of the hospital differs considerably from the more serene and leisurely atmosphere of the seminar room. Thus it would not be surprising if neither of them has been able to give full consideration to the differing point of view and circumstances of the other.

In addition to factual uncertainty and moral complexity, the case under consideration illustrates two more circumstances of compromise: a continuing, cooperative relationship and an impending, nondeferrable decision affecting both parties. As coworkers in the intensive care unit, Nurse Chapman and Dr. Lehman are in some sense stuck with each other. Their work is very complex and neither of them can be fully effective without the other's assistance and cooperation. High technology medicine, like other complex social endeavors, requires the collaborative, closely integrated efforts of a number of different specialists. As a rule the most effective health care teams will be those with the most stable staffing patterns, most congenial relationships among personnel, and highest overall esprit de corps. Anything that increases turnover, breeds resentment or anger, or undermines esprit is likely to limit effectiveness. Thus a resolution to a moral problem that can maximally accommodate differing viewpoints and maintain mutual respect is, from the standpoint of overall team effectiveness, highly desirable.[3] This is also true for other continuing, cooperative relationships even if not so precisely defined. The desirability of preserving continuing, cooperative relationships among members of a family or citizens of a nation—or, for that matter, among nations in a world bristling with nuclear arms—also counts as a circumstance of compromise.

In his important historical study of the value and limitations of informal justice—the resolution of disputes without lawyers—Jerold S. Auerbach emphasizes the bonds of community, both as a motivational factor and as a factor contributing to the justice of various settlements.

> How people dispute is . . . a function of how (and whether) they relate. In relationships that are intimate, caring, and mutual, disputants will behave quite differently from their counterparts who are strangers or competitors. Selfishness and aggression are not merely functions of individual personality; they are socially sanctioned—or discouraged. So is the decision to define a disputant as an adversary, and to struggle until there is a clear winner and loser; or, alternatively to resolve conflict in a way that will preserve, rather than destroy, a relationship (1983, pp. 7–8).

Whereas legal or quasi-legal processes are largely adversarial, emphasizing individual differences and polarization, mediation and arbitration generally express the needs and desires of those who are "mutually bound in continuing cooperative relationships" (Auerbach 1983, p. 34).

A decision on how aggressively to treat Marsha Hocking must be made fairly soon. To postpone the matter while maintaining present efforts is ipso facto to come down on the side of continued aggressive treatment, and this is exactly what is at issue. If there were a way to "freeze" the situation to delay taking action until one side is able to persuade the other that it is correct, compromise would be less appealing. But in a hospital as well as in other practical contexts we cannot always suspend judgment and action. In such circumstances compromise may be better than settling the matter by rank or by force or by simply leaving it unresolved.

The final circumstance of compromise is scarcity of resources. Even if we were not limited by factual uncertainty and moral complexity, compromise might be the best course of action when what is at issue is a distribution of scarce resources. Nurse Chapman's concerns about the nursing staff's being stretched too thin and the cost of Marsha Hocking's care are based on scarcity. If questions of the fair and efficient allocation of nursing resources and the high cost of medical care were not important, her case would be considerably weakened. But limited resources, in this and in other contexts, seems to be a pervasive feature of human life. We often lack the time, money, energy, and other human and natural resources to satisfy everyone's rights or interests, let alone their wants and desires. And when rights or interests conflict because of scarcity, compromise may seem to be both necessary and appropriate.

Factual uncertainty, moral complexity, the need to maintain a continuing cooperative relationship, the need for a more or less immediate decision or action, and a scarcity of resources constitute the circumstances of compromise. If parties to an ethical disagreement in such circumstances are unable to persuade each other of the correctness of their particular positions they would do well to investigate the possibility of compromise. Although, as I will argue in subsequent chapters, there is no pat formula for determining how many of these conditions need to be met before compromise ought to be pursued, an initial case for compromise is likely to be stronger as more of them more fully obtain. The disagreement between Nurse Chapman and Dr. Lehman is characterized by all of these circumstances. Thus we move now to a consideration of how compromise might occur, what the result might be, and the extent to which both process and outcome can preserve integrity.

INTEGRITY-PRESERVING COMPROMISE

At the end of the case presentation a few more nurses were coming to agree with Ann Chapman's position. In response to their concerns, Dr. Susan Lehman had scheduled another meeting on the matter. Suppose that as that meeting begins those present come to appreciate the extent to which their situation embodies the circumstances of compromise. Whether this realization is self-conscious or tacit makes little difference. Suppose, too, that their discussion is marked by mutual respect. Each is prepared to give a fair hearing to opposing viewpoints and to reexamine the reasoning underlying his or her own view; moreover, each is prepared to revise or abandon previously held positions in response to new information, insights, arguments, or understanding. It would not be surprising if, under these conditions, they were to consider compromise. As Kuflik observes, people who "carefully hear each other out and earnestly try to see matters from another's perspective . . . will often find themselves traveling some distance from their original positions and meeting each other partway" (1979, p. 50).

As the discussion proceeds, those on each side of the issue may come to appreciate the possibility that their motivation is mixed, that their positions may be prompted by concern for themselves as well as concern for others. Although Nurse Chapman's concern for the patient's autonomy and the fair and efficient use of limited resources is genuine enough, she may also be frustrated by the difficulties of providing adequate nursing care for patients like Marsha Hocking. Moreover, the problem of juggling nursing resources to provide minimally adequate care for the other patients in the intensive care unit is an additional headache for the nursing staff. Thus Nurse Chapman may have self-interested as well as more high-minded reasons for urging less aggressive treatment. Life would probably be easier for her if she did not have to do so much for Marsha Hocking.

Dr. Lehman's motivation may also be mixed. It would not be surprising, for example, if she were to find sustaining the life of patients like Marsha Hocking a source of great personal satisfaction. Samuel Gorovitz reminds us that:

> Skills that have been acquired at substantial personal cost are skills that people like to use. . . . There is an intrinsic payoff in satisfaction. State-of-the-art medicine is very sophisticated, and people who can do it often find it a very beautiful thing to be doing. We should bear that in mind when we think about the motivation behind a lot of medical care (1982, pp. 89ff.).

In addition, like many other physicians, Dr. Lehman may regard death as an "enemy" with which she daily does battle. Occasionally she may find it difficult to admit defeat, and as a result she may continue to provide aggressive treatment to dying patients in part to satisfy her own psychological needs.

Such mixed motives are, like the circumstances of compromise, not uncommon. Although having mixed motives is not in itself a moral shortcoming, it is important to recognize when one's motives may be mixed. Self-knowledge of this sort is likely to reduce self-right-eousness and generate a greater willingness, in the circumstances of compromise, to acknowledge reasonable differences of opinion and to search for a mutually satisfactory accommodation. The parties may then come to internalize the debate; that is, they may acknowledge that the values and principles underlying the opposing position are not utterly alien to them (Midgley 1985, pp. 452–55). Surely, for example, there is some level at which Nurse Chapman, like Dr. Lehman, agrees that human life is of great value and that it is important that physicians and nurses retain their dedication to preserving and prolonging life. Similarly, there must be a part of Dr. Lehman that, like Nurse Chapman, recognizes the value of patient autonomy and the need to make efficient use of limited personal and technological resources. Indeed, if they are to engage in rational persuasion, they must each suppose that in advancing their positions they are in some sense echoing a voice that is already present or latent in the other (Midgley 1985, p. 453). Their aim is to strengthen or encourage the recognition of this unacknowledged voice in the person taking the opposing position. If both parties are able to internalize the debate and to respond to it with the full, not entirely consistent, self rather than just an aspect, the prospects of an integrity-preserving compromise are greatly enhanced. (The conception of integrity underlying this suggestion is developed and defended in Chapter 3).

Let us suppose, then, that as the meeting progresses the possibility of mixed motivation on both sides is calmly and sympathetically pointed out and acknowledged. As mutually respectful discussion leads both sides to internalize the debate, efforts to find a mutually satisfactory solution intensify and plausible alternatives to both Nurse Chapman's and Dr. Lehman's favored positions are sought.

Suppose, too, that at this point someone at the meeting proposes a compromise, a position that attempts to split the difference between the opposing sides: "Why not agree to continue aggressive treatment for a specified period of time? We can try to agree now about what features of the patient's condition would indicate that her prognosis is better or worse. At the end of this period we will review the matter. If her condition has improved in some of the ways we have specified, treatment will remain aggressive. But if her condition has remained the same or deteriorated, the likelihood of recovery will have lessened considerably. In that case we will place much more weight on the equitable and efficient use of resources and treat her less aggressively." Let us also suppose that after a certain amount of discussion and negotiation about details everyone, including Nurse Chapman and Dr. Lehman, seems to agree with this proposal, and the meeting concludes with a renewed sense of community and mutual respect.

It is now important to ask whether each of the parties to the initial disagreement has replaced her original view with the one proposed above or whether each has retained her original view but has agreed to the proposal in the interest of obtaining a speedy, practical, and mutually respectful resolution. The first of these is not, strictly speaking, a compromise position. Consequently, it raises no special problem of integrity. Although the parties may have engaged in the process of compromise, we do not have compromise in the strict sense unless the outcome itself is also a compromise. And an outcome is not a compromise when each of the parties comes to regard its initial position as mistaken, abandons it, and embraces the same third position, which both now believe to be superior. If this new-found mutually preferred position seems somehow to split the difference between the polar positions, we will characterize it as a synthesis, or middle-of-the-road, position—what we have earlier called compromise in the loose sense—rather than as a compromise in the strict sense.

The circumstances of compromise will have encouraged both parties to rethink the dispute and through the give and take of mutually respectful discussion they will have come to recognize hitherto undetected shortcomings in their own views and perhaps hitherto undetected strengths in the opposing views. After this they will have been able either to combine strengths and eliminate weaknesses in a coherent synthesis or to find an entirely new middle position that each regards as superior to its initial one. There is no problem about being compromised because in autonomously replacing one's initial position with what is now regarded as a superior position, one has changed one's views rather than betrayed them. There have been no concessions, for no differences remain to be split. If ethical values or principles are involved, they would have been rationally modified, qualified, or changed in the light of new evidence or circumstances and not compromised.

A compromise in the standard sense, one that includes compromise (in the strict sense) as outcome as well as process, does raise questions about integrity. For suppose that Nurse Chapman and Dr. Lehman, even after lengthy discussion, remain convinced of the correctness of their initial views but in present circumstances agree to abide by the compromise proposed at the meeting. Here is a genuine question about integrity, about compromising (or betraying) oneself. For each is agreeing to act in accord with a plan that apparently deviates from her basic values. If Nurse Chapman's concern for the patient's autonomy and for the efficient use of resources is undiminished, should she not remain true to herself and hold out for these? And if Dr. Lehman still believes in the inherent value of human life and the importance of the continued dedication of the medical and nursing professions to the preservation and prolongation of life, how can she agree to the possibility of reducing the intensity of life-sustaining measures? Moral wholeness or integrity, it would seem, is incompatible with their each agreeing to such a compromise outcome.

To see how compromises of this sort may be integrity preserving, it is important to distinguish what Nurse Chapman or Dr. Lehman *believes* ought to be done, leaving aside for the moment that they disagree and that the circumstances of compromise obtain from what each *judges* ought to be done when all things, including their disagreement and the circumstances of compromise, are considered. "When an issue is in dispute," Kuflik points out,

> there is more to be considered than the issue itself—for example, the importance of peace, the presumption against settling matters by force, the intrinsic good of participating in a process in which each side must hear the other side out and try to see matters from the other's point of view, the extent to which the matter does admit reasonable differences of opinion, the significance of a settlement in which each party feels assured of the other's respect for its own seriousness and sincerity in the matter (1979, p. 51).

These considerations reflect values and principles that many of us hold dear and that partially determine who we are and what we stand for. If, therefore, we suppose that Nurse Chapman and Dr. Lehman also place a high value on tolerance and mutual respect, it is not so clear that agreeing to the proposed compromise constitutes a threat to their integrity. On the contrary, taking into consideration all of their values and principles plus the fact that they disagree and that they are in circumstances of compromise, the compromise solution may be for them more integrity preserving than any available alternative.

The main point is that, as most of us will on reflection acknowledge, our identity is constituted in part by a complex constellation of occasionally conflicting values and principles. We may, for example, agree with either Nurse Chapman's position or Dr. Lehman's and with values such as respecting others' points of view, not settling matters by rank or force, acknowledging the seriousness and sincerity of opposing positions, and so on. In such cases of internal as well as external conflict we will often, after internalizing the debate, pursue the course of action that seems on balance to follow from the preponderance of our central and most highly cherished and rationally defensible values and principles.

"Where ultimate values are irreconcilable," Isaiah Berlin writes, "clear cut solutions cannot, in principle, be found. To decide rationally in such situations is to decide in the light of general ideals, the over-all pattern of life pursued by a man or a group or a society" (1958, p. 1). If, then, the overall pattern of life favored by most of us is (or should be) one that includes a high degree of trying to see matters from others' points of view, an appreciation of factual uncertainty, moral complexity, and limited resources, a presumption against settling matters by rank and force, and so on, it would not be surprising if a compromise in the case under consideration were to be more integrity preserving than either of the polar alternatives. To choose to preserve as best as possible the overall pattern of one's life cannot be regarded as betraying one's integrity. Indeed, in such circumstances, a compromise may provide the best means to preserving it. It is one thing simply to compromise (or betray) one's principles; quite another to compromise between them.

If they were to acknowledge the uncertainty and moral complexity characterizing their disagreement, neither Nurse Chapman nor Dr. Lehman would be likely to regard her position on the patient's treatment as more central or well grounded than the network of values and principles having to do with mutual respect, the acknowledgment of reasonable differences, not settling matters by force or rank, and so on. Thus if integrity requires that they act in accord with the preponderance of their most basic values and principles, they may in this case agree to the proposed compromise.

This is not, however, to say that the matter is fully settled. Although Nurse Chapman and Dr. Lehman may agree that compromise at this point makes the best of a bad situation, they may try to insure that the same situation does not arise in the future. Thus each may make subsequent efforts to practice in settings where their colleagues are more likely to share their particular views on the treatment of patients like Marsha Hocking; or they may continue to try to convince each other of the correctness of these views. If their coworkers agreed with their respective positions or if the decision were one that they alone were qualified to make, they would not compromise: Nurse Chapman would immediately call a halt to aggressive treatment, whereas Dr. Lehman would see that it continued indefinitely. But as long as they continue to work together on cases like this, and until one of them is able to persuade the other of the correctness of her views, a compromise is most likely to be integrity preserving when they consider all of their important values and principles and not just those that fail to appreciate the full complexity of the nature and circumstances of their disagreement.

FURTHER EXAMPLES

Before considering possible limitations of the foregoing analysis, I want briefly to describe a pair of two-party moral conflicts involving groups and the political arena that appear to have been mediated by integrity-preserving compromises. Consider, first, the report of the Warnock Committee on human fertilization and embryology (Warnock 1985a). Among the questions addressed by this group of British physicians, lawyers, theologians, social scientists, and ordinary citizens, chaired by philosopher Mary Warnock, was the question of the permissibility of research using human embryos. Moral opinion on this matter was at the time (and still is) deeply divided. At the root of the controversy are opposing views of the moral status of the embryo. Those who believe that human life protected by laws against murder begins at conception consider the embryo to have the same status as an adult human being and are thus strongly opposed to any research of this kind. Those who regard the moral status of the human embryo as considerably less than that of an adult are heavily influenced by the undeniable utilitarian advantages of such research with respect to inquiries into infertility, miscarriage, congenital defects, and related matters. The Warnock Committee was charged with making a recommendation at the national policy level on this highly controversial question. Although moral views on this matter were divided, a policy embodied in law would necessarily be singular and binding on all. Moreover, the question could no longer be deferred. Legislation was needed on the matter, and soon.

The most basic recommendation of the majority of the committee's members on the question of research using human embryos—namely, that such research would be permitted, subject to certain restrictions (only up to 14 days from fertilization and unconditionally forbidden thereafter)—seems to have been a compromise between the two polar positions found in British society. As Warnock puts it, "In the end the Inquiry felt bound to argue, *partly* on Utilitarian grounds, that the benefits that had come in the past from research using human embryos were so great (and were likely to be even greater in the future), that such research had to be permitted; but that it should be permitted only at the very earliest stage of the development of the embryo" (1985b, p. 517). Each polar position to the disagreement (that representing an extreme conservative, or prolife, view of the moral standing of the embryo and that representing a considerably more liberal, or utilitarian, view) received part, but not all, of what it was after.

Mary Warnock herself, however, does not quite see it in this way. She notes that the committee's recommendations may be disappointing to ministers of Parliament who, understandably enough, may have been hoping for a "solution to a problem essentially insoluble."

> In the case of our Committee, for example, it was hoped, I now see, that the cool and reasonable voice of philosophy would reconcile the irreconcilable and find a compromise where none can exist. There may even have been a secret belief that there is a right solution which could be proved right, if it were only found. But Ministers, like the rest of humanity, have to realize that in matters of morality this is not possible. Society may value things, genuinely and properly, which are incompatible with each other (Warnock 1985a, p. 99).

Warnock is right to emphasize the limits of philosophy in fully solving the problem. But she is mistaken in identifying an inability to resolve the matter to everyone's complete satisfaction with a failure to compromise. She appears to be using the term "compromise" in the loose sense, not the strict sense. What she means by compromise is similar to a rational resolution or coherent synthesis. It is because, as she correctly points out, neither a rational resolution nor a coherent synthesis of the opposing views on the question of the moral status of the embryo was possible that her committee had to settle for what I have called a compromise in the strict sense.

That the committee's final recommendation on this matter was, indeed, a compromise is reinforced by Thomas H. Murray's observation that no single theory of the moral status of the human embryo can embrace, without contradiction, all of the committee's recommendations (1987, p. 245). But he adds, "the Committee did not need to provide a final authoritative answer to this question. Its task was to find a compromise that would permit important social needs to be fulfilled, without outraging widely and deeply held moral values."

Similar forms of compromise, Murray suggests, are embodied in plausible social policy recommendations addressing other issues in perinatal ethics, including the moral status of the fetus, the moral status of the newborn, the legitimacy of judgments about the quality of life, and the extent to which interests other than those of the newborn ought to be taken into account in making decisions (1987, pp. 245–48). For example, those who argue for more conservative abortion policies on what they regard as a fetal right to life often allow for what appear to be inconsistent exceptions for pregnancy due to rape or incest. Abortion is to be prohibited, they maintain, unless a pregnancy comes about through rape or incest. But, Murray asks, "what makes these reasons more persuasive . . . [from a conservative or prolife point of view] than others? If the fetus is truly an innocent person . . . , then surely the fact that it came into existence as a result of rape or incest is not in any possible way its fault." The exceptions are inconsistent with the prohibitory rationale, but, Murray suggests, they must be included if a more restrictive policy on abortion is to have any chance of becoming public policy in a society as ambivalent about the matter as is ours.

The second case I want to present involves conflicting advice from the American Cancer Society and the American College of Obstetricians and Gynecologists on how often women should undergo the Pap smear test for detecting cervical cancer (Kolata, *New York Times*, 7

January 1988). For many years physicians have recommended that women should have a Pap test annually. In 1980, however, the Cancer Society changed its recommendation to a three-year interval if a woman had had two successive annual Pap tests that were negative. The Cancer Society maintained that few additional lives were saved by annual Pap tests and that given annually, it was an unnecessary burden and expense for most women. In 1980 the society evaluated the costs and benefits of various screening intervals and concluded that the benefits of annual screening were negligible when compared with screening every three years. This conclusion was corroborated by a panel of the National Institutes of Health that had subsequently and independently considered the evidence. The obstetricians and gynecologists, on the other hand, continued to hold out for an annual test for all women, regardless of past test results. The physicians' organization maintained that if women were advised to be tested once every three years, they would do it even less often. Moreover, the physicians were concerned about laboratory errors on annual Pap tests that they regarded as too common.

This situation involved all of the circumstances of compromise. First, the facts were uncertain. For example, how many lives would be saved by an annual test? Would women, in fact, be able to adhere to a once-every-three-years schedule less well than an annual one? Second, the moral dimensions were complex. The Cancer Society emphasized overall social costs when compared to benefits, patient inconvenience, and informed patient decision making, whereas the physicians emphasized maximally saving lives, regardless of cost, convenience, or patient autonomy. Third, the parties were involved in a continuing cooperative relationship. They worked closely together and had an overlapping membership. Fourth, they faced an impending, nondeferrable decision. Continued disagreement on this matter was understandably confusing and disconcerting to women, probably undermining their confidence in both groups. It was becoming increasingly important that the two groups speak with one voice on this matter. And fifth, the situation involved scarcity: We can no longer remain oblivious to the spiraling costs of health care. One estimate of the difference in total costs between annual and triannual Pap smears would be $4 billion per year.

The compromise outcome, as reported in the *New York Times*, combined aspects of both the society's and the college's views (Kolata

1988). Women are advised to have three annual Pap smears starting when they reach the age of eighteen or become sexually active. If all three tests are negative then "at the discretion of their physicians," the women can have the test less frequently. The Cancer Society seems to have made two significant concessions: The precondition for going from annual to triannual Pap smears is now three annual negative tests rather than two, and a woman should make the change only at the discretion of her physician. The physicians' concession was in explicitly acknowledging the appropriateness, under certain conditions, of the triannual Pap smear. Yet, as the newspaper report indicates, this is not a final resolution or simple synthesis of the opposing positions; they still have not reached closure. It is instead a clear case of a compromise in the strict sense.

"It was clear in interviews with medical specialists," the *Times* reported, "that the new guidelines would not bring to an end the long-standing disagreement among medical specialists about whether most women need annual Pap smears." For example, Dr. Harold Kaminetzky, director of practice activities for the American College of Obstetricians and Gynecologists, is quoted as saying: "We would like all women to have annual Pap smears, but we yielded because we think it is important that all organizations involved speak in the same voice. . . . Our message was clearer before, but if we did not change it we would have literally had to continue a war with the American Cancer Society" (Kolata 1988). Assuming, then, that the process involved a certain amount of mutual respect, give-and-take discussion, and so on, we have a clear example of a compromise in the standard sense. The matter is not closed, and neither party is entirely satisfied. Still, there is agreement on a single course of action. And if the analysis of the foregoing section can be upheld, it may have been achieved with neither of the parties compromising (or betraying) its integrity.

FURTHER QUESTIONS

Underlying this account of integrity-preserving compromise are two controversial assumptions. The first is that a person can retain moral integrity even when morally ambivalent or divided about a certain course of action. The second, related assumption is that intrapersonally as well as interpersonally at least some of our values and principles are, and are likely to remain, irreducibly plural or rationally irreconcilable. When asked how he and his colleagues felt about compromising on the frequency of Pap smear tests, Dr. Kaminetzky responded, "Not as good as we used to feel." If, as I suggest, Dr. Kaminetzky and his colleagues can retain their integrity while compromising on this matter, they will not do so in any simple sense. Kierkegaard, for example, characterized integrity as "purity of heart" or being utterly undivided. "Purity of heart," he maintained, "is to will one thing" (Kierkegaard 1847). Yet compromise in the strict sense presupposes that the parties will at least two things. How, then, can compromise in this sense be integrity preserving? The self is still somewhat divided—as Dr. Kaminetzky reports, he does not feel quite so good as he would feel if his polar position had prevailed. In exactly what fully developed sense of integrity can we say that compromise may preserve integrity? Certainly not in Kierkegaard's sense. An adequate response to Kierkegaard and others who share his conception of integrity will require an alternative account of integrity and its relationships to compromise and personal identity. This I provide in the next chapter.

The second controversial assumption is that there will always be at least some values and principles that are rationally irreconcilable. What reason is there to think that this is or will remain the case? Certainly there are many among us who believe that their own (often religiously grounded) moral outlook is consistent, comprehensive, and, moreover, true (even if they do not or cannot always act in accord with it). If everyone were to acknowledge the validity of this particular moral framework and were to act in accord with it, moral conflict and the need for compromise would, in their view, become a thing of the past.

A more sophisticated version of the same objection might be made by certain ethical theorists. To assume that rationally irreconcilable moral conflict will always be with us, they might argue, reveals a certain faintheartedness or failure of nerve. How can one be sure that we will never develop a consistent, comprehensive theory that recommends itself to all rational beings and that will resolve all moral conflicts and disagreements without remainder? An ethical theory of this sort would, once widely propagated and accepted, make compromise unnecessary.

In response to this objection I will, in Chapter 4, identify and defend a particular conception of moral knowledge and principles. Is compromise on ethical matters at best a temporary expedient—something with which we must make do until the discovery or development of the single true morality—or is compromise likely to be a more permanent feature of human interaction? In addressing these and related questions I will suggest that the most plausible conception of ethics is not only compatible with but also requires a certain amount of internal as well as external compromise.

We will then be prepared to address a number of further questions raised by the notion of integrity-preserving compromise. First, how can we know when we should seek compromise and when not? To what extent can theory or principles provide us with a set of necessary and sufficient conditions that will more or less dictate when to devise and maintain a compromise and when, like Sir Thomas More, to dig in our heels and firmly say no? In Chapter 5, I argue that from the standpoint of abstract theory, we can provide at best only rough guidelines for answering this question. Further determinations in particular cases will depend on the exercise of moral judgment that is highly context dependent.

Once we determine that compromise in the case of two-party moral conflict may be desirable, what can we do to actually achieve it? I will also address this and related questions in Chapter 5. Devising a well-grounded, mutually satisfactory compromise will often, for example, require a considerable amount of imagination. One cannot always, or perhaps even often, mechanically "split the difference" between two opposing positions. We must also concern ourselves with what might be called ethics in compromise as opposed to the ethics of compromise. What constraints ought we to observe in engaging in the process of compromise on ethical matters? May we, for example, as in other forms of bargaining, overstate our demands in order to negotiate a settlement that is more favorable to our position than to that of our "opponent"? Or must we always state our position exactly as it is?

Finally, I turn in Chapter 6 to democratic politics and the question of when, if ever, politicians should seek or endorse moral compromise. To take a familiar example, may a Catholic legislator who strongly believes that human life begins at conception and that abortion is, as a rule, tantamount to murder propose a political compromise on the question of abortion while maintaining overall integrity as a person?

Whether someone can actually do this on a wide range of issues as a matter of vocation is the question of whether a politician can at the same time be both politically effective and personally whole.

3
Integrity

We must therefore examine whether we should act in this way or not, as not only now but at all times I am the kind of man who listens only to the argument that on reflection seems best to me. I cannot, now that this fate has come upon me, discard the arguments I used; they seem to me the same. I value and respect the same principles as before, and if we have no better arguments to bring up at this moment, be sure that I shall not agree with you, not even if the power of the majority were to frighten us with more bogeys, as if we were children, with threats of incarcerations and executions and confiscations of property.

—*Plato*, Crito

This chapter develops an account of individual integrity that is at once determinate enough to provide for a unified self and flexible enough to respond to new circumstances and the requirements of social as well as individual existence. I begin by identifying the elements of integrity and then turn to its importance and various limits and complexities. The principal subject of integrity, I conclude, is an entire life; an optimally integrated life will, as a rule, require a certain amount of moral compromise.

ELEMENTS OF INTEGRITY

We often use spatial metaphors in characterizing integrity. Gabriele Taylor, for example, says that we think "of the person possessing integrity as being the person who 'keeps his inmost self intact,' whose life is 'of a piece,' whose self is whole and integrated" (1981, p. 143). The person who lacks integrity, she adds, "is corrupt in the sense that his self is disintegrated." Similarly, Raimond Gaita characterizes individuals markedly deficient in integrity as having "no centre, everything is soft and scattered . . . there is no core below the surface"

46

(1981, p. 166). But when we try to go beyond these pictures of having a "core" or being "of a piece," it is not so easy to explain what we mean when we attribute integrity to persons.

Everyday usage centers on lapses or deficiencies in integrity. This or that sort of conduct, we say, shows a lack of integrity; there are certain identifiable character types we usually regard as deficient in integrity (G. Taylor, 1981). A more positive and literal understanding of integrity as it applies to persons may, therefore, emerge from an examination of ways individuals are customarily said to fall short of integrity. Like the darker parts of a black and white photograph, the network of negative characterizations may, by contrast, throw into relief a more positive picture of individual integrity, and hence a more positive and literal understanding of what we mean by it.

Consider, first, the *moral chameleon* (Chapter 1, p. 8). Anxious to accommodate others and temperamentally indisposed to moral controversy and disagreement, the moral chameleon is quick to modify or abandon previously avowed principles in order to placate others. Apart from a commitment to accommodation, the moral chameleon has little in the way of a central or core set of values that determines who she is and what she stands for. She has little sense of moral identity and even those whose colors she assumes cannot turn their backs on her for too long. The moral chameleon bears careful watching. If placed in a situation where retaining her principles requires resisting social pressure, she is likely to betray others as she betrays herself.

The *opportunist* is similar to the moral chameleon in that his values and principles are quite fluid. What he does and aspires to, together with his various loyalties, will often change with his circumstances. But whereas the moral chameleon places overriding value on avoiding alienation from those nearest to her by trying to reduce conflict and disagreement, the opportunist places overriding value on his own short-run interests. The moral chameleon will "change her colors" for the sake of fitting in, whereas the opportunist will alter his beliefs and behavior whenever he thinks it will lead to personal gain or advancement. As we have characterized them, both the moral chameleon and the opportunist have little in the way of substantive commitments. Apart from accommodation and agreement, the moral chameleon has no overriding values or principles, and the opportunist is committed more strongly to personal success or advancement in themselves than to success or advancement in any particular field or endeavor. The moral chameleon's ruling principle comes to little more than "Above all, get along," whereas the opportunist's is roughly "Above all, get ahead."

The *hypocrite* has a more determinate center or core than either the moral chameleon or the opportunist. "The hypocrite," writes Gabriele Taylor, "pretends to live by certain standards when in fact he does not. In the clearest case he consciously and calculatingly exploits for his own ends the fact that certain types of behaviour are seen by others as constituting or implying certain commitments and that therefore he will be seen by others to be acting as he does because he is so committed" (1981, pp. 144ff.). Admittedly insincere, the hypocrite has one set of principles for public consumption and another, more authentic set that actually guides conduct whenever she believes it unnecessary to make a certain kind of (false) impression. Although a close, continual observer would detect apparent inconsistencies between the hypocrite's words and deeds, a deeper understanding of her rather calculating and manipulative values and principles would reveal a coherent internal rationale. Underlying the hypocrite's apparent external inconsistencies, then, is a deceitful internal unity. Hypocrites may be "rotten to the core," but they are not wholly without a center.

Those who are characteristically *weak-willed* have a reasonably coherent set of principles, but they lack the courage of their convictions or fail to make conscientious efforts to act in accord with them. Their words or deeds will deviate from these principles in the face of external, but not irresistible, pressures or constraints. Socrates appears to have the courage of his convictions when he says to Crito, "If we have no better arguments to bring up at this moment, be sure that I shall not agree with you, not even if the power of the majority were to frighten us with more bogeys, as if we were children, with threats of incarcerations and executions and confiscations of property."

Victor Navasky's account of the responses of various Hollywood actors, writers, and directors to the investigations of the House Un-American Activities Committee (HUAC) in the 1950s conveys differing degrees of moral courage and cowardice. Many, when threatened with being blacklisted and losing their opportunity to work, agreed to inform on those who may at one time have been members of the Communist party. Those who named names were accused of betrayal. In doing what they did, Navasky argues, most of them were for various reasons afraid to voice their distaste for HUAC's witch hunt:

"They knew better than to condone Stalinism but they also knew better than to cooperate with McCarthyism" (1980, p. 313). There is no general rule as to how far one must go before we attribute a loss of integrity to weakness of will as opposed to external coercion or external circumstance. In many cases, these will be difficult to distinguish; in others, they will be readily identifiable. Our judgment will turn on the magnitude of what is given up and the extent to which we believe a person is responsible for the strength of her will and her courage (C. Taylor 1976).

Self-deceivers are often motivated by a discrepancy between the values and principles that they like to think of themselves as acting upon and conduct that is motivated by quite different, incompatible interests and desires. To resolve this tension and, at the same time, to preserve the idealized self-conception while indulging the incompatible interests and desires, they deceive themselves about what they are in fact doing. In this way, a self-deceiver is able to retain the internal appearance of integrity (or wholeness) even though the discrepancy between his avowed values and principles and the conduct motivated by the (unavowed but unsuppressed) incompatible interests and desires may be obvious to others (Fingarette 1969). Consider, for example, a man who, while conceiving of himself as a faithful husband, nonetheless indulges a strong desire to have an affair with a particular woman. Reluctant to relinquish his conception of himself as a faithful husband and unwilling to forego the satisfaction of desire, he engages in the affair while deceiving himself about it. He deliberately refrains from spelling out, or "avowing," this particular way of engaging the world (Fingarette 1969), or he purposely or intentionally evades fully acknowledging to himself what he is doing (Martin 1986). Perhaps he refuses to admit to himself that he is even having an affair or, more plausibly, he tells himself it is of no lasting significance to his relationship with his wife. His motivation is to preserve his conception of himself as essentially faithful to her. Oddly enough, however, his efforts to preserve the (internal) appearance of integrity require him to radically compartmentalize different aspects of the self, the result of which is a further corruption of wholeness or intactness. Self-deception of this type, though motivated by a desire to preserve integrity, preserves only the (internal) appearance of it and at a high cost in psychic energy (Camus 1956).

The moral chameleon, the hypocrite, the weak-willed person, and the self-deceiver can all be said to betray their integrity. The loss is in a sense self-imposed or attributable to themselves. In some cases, however, a loss of integrity is attributable not to weakness or corruption from within but rather to pressures from without. Consider, for example, a person who is *coerced* into acting, and perhaps also talking, in ways that are at odds with her most deeply held and cherished convictions. She is in some respects the converse of the hypocrite. Although hypocrites have a certain rather duplicitous internal unity, what they say and do will often be systematically discrepant. One who is coerced into acting in accordance with an alien, externally imposed set of values and principles displays a superficial or external unity while from her point of view—the internal point of view—she may be on the verge of total disintegration. Her life is not of a piece. Her inmost self is not intact; her words and deeds, though perhaps integrated by an alien set of values and principles, do not express values and principles with which she deeply and authentically identifies.

Consider in this connection a battered housewife who, for self-protection and the protection of her children, assumes the demeaning role forced on her by her overbearing and physically abusive husband while hating him (and perhaps also herself) and nursing hopes of someday leading a life more in accord with her own, bitterly suppressed values and principles. Although there is a sense in which she acts honorably under these desperate and coercive circumstances, her life is not adequately integrated insofar as her outward behavior does not reflect her own values and principles. The hypocrite lacks external integrity while preserving internal integrity. One who is coercively alienated from her authentic values and principles—such as the oppressed and battered housewife—displays external integrity while lacking internal integrity. Each lacks integrity overall.

These sketches of the moral chameleon, the opportunist, the hypocrite, the weak-willed person, the self-deceiver, and the alienated victim of external coercion are, of course, very rough and border on caricature. In actual life those who embody these characteristics do so in ways much more subtle, varied, and complex (Martin 1986; Fingarette 1969; Bok 1982). Moreover, the characteristics appear in varying combinations and degrees. A person may, for example, be mildly hypocritical and quite cowardly even though she uses self-deception to maintain the internal illusion of a fearless champion of unpopular causes.

Our sketches are, however, sufficient for piecing together a more literal, comprehensive, and positive understanding of individual integrity. What emerges is a conception of the person as an integrated triad consisting of: (1) a reasonably coherent and relatively stable set of highly cherished values and principles; (2) verbal behavior expressing these values and principles; and (3) conduct embodying one's values and principles and consistent with what one says. These are the elements of integrity. Taken together they constitute the formal structure of one's identity as a person.

From this perspective, the problem with both the moral chameleon and the opportunist is that (for different reasons) each lacks a stable and substantive set of highly cherished values and principles. The hypocrite's principles, though perhaps stable, coherent, and highly cherished, are duplicitous, entailing in certain circumstances significant discrepancies between words, on the one hand, and principles and conduct, on the other. From the external point of view the hypocrite is not "all of a piece." The person whose will is characteristically weak, we have supposed, has a coherent set of values and principles that she wants to embody in both word and deed, but a lack of courage will prevent her from doing so in the face of external, but not overwhelming, pressures or constraints. The self-deceiver also wants his conduct to reflect a coherent set of principles that will occasionally conflict with certain desires. Unwilling either to revise his idealized principles to accommodate these conflicting desires or to refrain from acting in accord with these incompatible desires to reaffirm the principles, he seeks the internal appearance of integrity by screening out, or refusing to avow as his own, words and deeds motivated by these desires. The self-deceiver preserves the internal appearance of integrity but at a high price. And from the external point of view, his integrity is not intact. The person who is coerced into speaking and acting in accord with a coherent and stable yet alien set of values and principles is not "all of a piece" from the internal point of view. She is, in some ways, the converse of the hypocrite, who is integrated from the internal but not the external point of view. Despite appearances, her words and deeds do not express her most deeply cherished values and principles. These, for the sake of self-protection or the protection of others, she must bitterly suppress.

Individual integrity, then, requires that one's words and deeds generally be true to a substantive, coherent, and relatively stable set of values and principles to which one is genuinely and freely committed. Integrity can be viewed internally, from the point of view of the agent, and externally, from the point of view of others. One's life is "of a piece" only if it is integrated from both points of view. Neither the hypocrite, who possesses internal but not external integrity, nor the alienated victim of coercion, who possesses external but not internal integrity, leads a genuinely integrated life.

THE IMPORTANCE OF INTEGRITY

Corresponding to its internal and external dimensions, integrity has both internal and external importance. Internally, it provides the structure for a unified, whole, and unalienated life. Those who through good fortune and personal effort are able to lead reasonably integrated lives generally enjoy a strong sense of personal identity. They know who they are and what they stand for; they will experience the satisfaction and self-respect that comes with living in accord with their deepest and most highly cherished values. An entire life that has been integrated in this way is, in many ways, an enviable achievement. Perhaps nothing attests so strongly to its internal importance as our understanding and admiration of those who, like Socrates and Sir Thomas More, when forced to choose between the length of their lives and leading lives of integrity, opt for the latter.

Viewed from the outside, individual integrity provides the basis for reliance, trust, friendship, and love. Social relationships and institutions would be impossible without a certain amount of integrity among the individuals who compose them. Integrity, as Peter Winch expresses it,

is to human institutions generally what truthfulness is to the institution of language. There are important formal analogies between language and other social institutions; for to act in the context of a social institution is always to commit oneself in some way for the future: a notion for which the notion of being committed by what one *says* provides an important parallel. But the concept of integrity is inseparable from that of commitment. To lack integrity is to act with the appearance of fulfilling a certain role but without the intention of shouldering the responsibilities to which the role commits one. If that, *per absurdum*, were to become the rule, the whole concept of a social role would thereby collapse (1972, p. 70).

Integrity is especially important in social organizations involving a great deal of interdependence and requiring a high degree of coordination among those who compose them. The military, for example, places a premium on the integrity (reliability) of its members. Shortly after the revelation of falsified reports solicited and subsequently forwarded by high ranking officers in Vietnam, General John D. Ryan, air force chief of staff, issued a statement to his commanders that emphasized the preeminence of integrity among military virtues:

> Integrity—which includes full and accurate disclosure—is the keystone of military service. . . . In any crisis, decisions and risks taken by the highest national authorities depend, in large part, on reported military capabilities and achievements. In the same way, every commander depends on accurate reporting from his forces. Unless he is positive of the integrity of his people, a commander cannot have confidence in his forces. Without integrity, the commander in chief cannot have confidence in us. Therefore, we cannot compromise our integrity—our truthfulness. . . . False reporting is a clear example of a failure of integrity. Any order to compromise integrity is not a lawful order (Ryan 1972, p. 180).

What is true of the relationship between individual integrity and the overall integrity of a complex social organization like the air force is true of similar organizations such as, for example, a hospital (Mitchell 1982).

We can, therefore, appreciate the concerns of those who appeal to integrity to justify their opposition to compromise, especially on matters of ethical significance. Much would be lost, socially as well as for individuals, if for the sake of resolving conflict we always placed a higher value on compromise than on integrity.

LIMITS AND COMPLEXITY OF INTEGRITY

Nonetheless, integrity is not sufficient for morality, nor does it always provide clear and straightforward direction. A person may display a high degree of integrity and in many respects be morally contempt-ible. Moreover, tensions between integrity's internal and external as-pects as well as between the dimensions of wholeness and consistency limit its role as a constraint on compromise.

Consider, first, that integrity is largely a formal notion. It regulates the connections among values, words, and deeds, but it does not fully specify them. Truthfulness, sincerity, lucidity, authenticity, and commitment—the virtues usually associated with integrity—are per-haps necessary, but not sufficient, for moral goodness. The limitation of these virtues is, as John Rawls points out, that "their definition al-lows for most any content" (1971, p. 519). We can readily recall or at least imagine powerful oppressors who are quite truthful, sincere, lu-cid, and authentically committed to oppressive acts, plans, and poli-cies. Their superior power makes it unnecessary for them to deceive or dissemble in any way. That such oppressors display a high degree of integrity renders them no less reprehensible. Being "virtues of form," the virtues of integrity are, Rawls reminds us, "in a sense secondary." Indeed, in some cases the fact that certain courses of action are under-taken with integrity makes them worse rather than better. "The con-centration [camp] commandant towards the end of Irwin Shaw's *The Young Lions*," writes Winch, "exhibited integrity of a particularly re-volting sort from the point of view of Western liberal morality. He was morally revolting because of the unspeakable role he was playing; to say he was playing it with integrity is, for most of us, an additional count against him, not a point in his favor" (1972, p. 71). That moral compromise may compromise aspects of a person's integrity is, there-fore, not a decisive consideration against it. We must also assess the worth or significance of what would be compromised. Integrity is im-portant, but it is not all important; nor is it a matter of black and white, all or none.

We must also acknowledge tensions between the internal and exter-nal aspects of integrity. Perfect integrity requires that one's conduct be integrated from an inner perspective emphasizing authentic and highly cherished values and principles and from an outer perspective emphasizing social roles and expectations. This may be achievable within a rather closed, homogeneous, and stable society or subculture. Where the rules and roles of individual and social existence are highly integrated and unchanging, there may be little tension between inter-nal and external integrity. In more modern, rapidly changing, pluralistic societies, however, the tensions between internal and external integrity are more pronounced. Conduct required by one's authentic, deeply cherished values and principles may be at odds with the not unreasonable expectations of one's society, as, for example, when an absolute pacifist is conscripted to participate in a "just war" (Walzer 1977) or a vehement opponent of abortion is required to pay taxes used to fund abortions for the very poor. If absolute pacifists or vehement opponents of abortion resort to deception or subterfuge to preserve internal integrity, they compromise external integrity; if they fulfill the requirements or expectations of their society, they sacrifice internal integrity. To urge that individuals always opt for internal integrity at the expense of external is to deny the demands and restrictions of social life. To invariably favor external integrity is to embrace a form of collectivism that denies the integrity (and hence the existence) of the self.

Further difficulties arise when we acknowledge the tension between consistency and wholeness. If by integrity we mean only consistency among our genuine values and principles, our words, and our deeds, we could perhaps maximize integrity by sharply restricting our values and principles. A person of strong will whose words and deeds flow from a deliberately restricted, comparatively small set of closely related and coherent values and principles may have little difficulty in maintaining overall consistency. But as such single-mindedness shades into fanaticism or distorts the self by systematically disregarding important aspects of it, we may question the person's humanity or the extent to which he or she is like the rest of us (Rawls 1971, p. 554). For integrity involves wholeness as well as consistency. If a preoccupation with consistency requires that we deny or repress a number of authentic feelings, attachments, commitments, values, and principles that are not in themselves ethically untoward and that occasionally incline us in contrary directions, we will have sacrificed wholeness. A fixation on one dimension of integrity will result in neglect of another.

At one point in his trenchant criticism of utilitarianism, Bernard Williams suggests that many of its defenders are simple-minded. "Simple-mindedness," he says, is "having too few thoughts and feelings to match the world as it really is" (1973, p. 149). Those who identify integrity with simple consistency may also be charged with simple-mindedness. That the notion of integrity is more complex— that its value is social as well as individual, that it involves wholeness as well as consistency, and that its social and individual aspects as well as wholeness and consistency are frequently at odds—should become apparent to anyone who attempts to understand and respond to the world "as it really is."

Internal conflict, as variously portrayed and explored by dramatists, poets, biographers, autobiographers, and novelists, is a feature of human life. Great drama and literature continue to appeal because the various conflicts recounted and explored by, say, Sophocles and Shakespeare, Tolstoy and Dostoevsky, and Arthur Miller and Iris Murdoch are conflicts that trouble us, the audience and the reader. In representing the world "as it really is," great literary artists illuminate and help us to understand our own conflicts. Conceptions of integrity that take little note of various forms of internal conflict or that try to paper them over by emphasizing consistency at the expense of wholeness therefore lack credibility. Walt Whitman (1855, sec. 51, p. 88) sings of us as well as of himself when he writes:

> Do I contradict myself?
> Very well then I contradict myself,
> (I am large, I contain multitudes.)

The types of internal conflict are many. Consider conflicts between our moral principles, on the one hand, and contrary inclinations, on the other. Let us for convenience (and at the risk of oversimplification) label the former "duties" and the latter "desires." Conflicts between duty and desire arise when, for example, one's faithfulness as a spouse is tested by strong sexual attraction to someone else. In a number of cases we will be able to eliminate, or at least reduce, conflict by bringing our desires in line with what we regard as our duties, or at least to render them ineffective. Indeed, the capacity and inclination to do so may be what distinguishes us as persons and gives us our special worth (Frankfurt 1971; C. Taylor 1976). But few, if any, of us are entirely successful. Although the gap between duty and desire may be narrowed, it is unlikely ever to be fully closed. There is a sense in which each of us is still all of the "persons" we have ever been: ourselves as infants, children, adolescents, young adults, and so on. Psychological development is more a matter of accretion than it is of wholesale replacement. We add or accumulate values and inclinations without fully extinguishing those that preceded them and that, for the sake of integrity, we may now consciously disavow. Inclinations emanating from the depths of our unconscious, where the wishes, fears, and anxieties of childhood and adolescence never fully disappear (Fiedler 1984, p. 42), will occasionally reach the surface and contend with more mature and reflective inclinations. Other biologically or psychologically rooted desires that are closer to the surface are also likely to be the cause of considerable conflict as when, for example, sexual attraction or desires for wealth, pleasure, or fame contend with duties rooted in various moral values or principles. Eliminate conflicts like these from human life and future readers of Shakespeare, Dostoevsky, and Arthur Miller will find the likes of Hamlet, Ivan Karamazov, and Willy Loman nearly unintelligible, so radically different will they be from themselves.

Even if we were able to bring our inclinations fully in line with our most basic values and principles, we would not enjoy "perfect integrity" unless these values and principles were themselves complete and fully integrated. But there are two obstacles to an individual's developing a complete and fully integrated set of values and principles. First, there is little consensus on what counts as a justifiable, consistent, and complete set of moral values and principles. And second, we frequently encounter conflicts between two kinds of values: the explicitly moral and the nonmoral.

A growing number of philosophers are raising doubts about the possibility of a complete and wholly integrated set of moral values and principles—even for one person (Nagel 1979; Hampshire 1983; Williams 1985). I examine their concerns in the following chapter and show them to be justified. A complete and fully integrated set of moral values and principles is, I will argue, unattainable. At this point, however, it is sufficient to suggest that intrapersonal ethical conflict may be nearly as common as interpersonal conflict. Indeed, as Williams points out, these two types of conflict are probably related:

Some one-person conflicts of values are expressions of a complex inheritance of values, from different social sources, and what we experience in ourselves as a conflict is something which could have been, and perhaps was, expressed as a conflict between two societies, or between two historical states of one society. The same point comes out the opposite way round, so to speak: a characteristic dispute about values in society, such as some issue of equality against freedom, is not one most typically enacted by a body of single-minded egalitarians confronting a body of single-minded libertarians, but is rather a conflict in which one person, equipped with a more generous range of human values, could find enacted within himself (1979, pp. 22ff.).

It should not, then, be surprising that among and within societies marked by external (or two-party) disagreement grounded in conflicting values and principles, the very same conflicts will to some extent be mirrored or internalized in a large number of people.

The second obstacle to a person's developing and maintaining a complete and fully integrated set of values and principles has to do with conflicts between what are usually regarded as moral values and principles, on the one hand, and various personal (nonmoral but not in themselves immoral) values, on the other. Conventional wisdom says that in cases of conflict one's moral values and principles are of overriding importance. This, however, may be profoundly alienating and destructive of overall integrity. Williams (1976) forcefully argues that moral values and principles may, if always given overriding importance, alienate us from those "fundamental ground projects" that shape and give considerable meaning to our lives. The claims of morality, if omnipresent, unremitting, and overriding, may force us to relinquish commitments to develop certain morally unobjectionable skills or talents or to complete certain similarly unobjectionable undertakings and, in some instances, our reason for living.

This sound warning against relinquishing nonmoral commitments (such as creating works of art or cultivating one's skills as a woodworker) for the sake of any moral value or principle whatsoever goes too far, however, if it does not acknowledge that in some circumstances moral requirements will indeed be overriding. It is one thing to say that an amateur artist need not send all of her discretionary income to Oxfam rather than buying paints, and quite another to say that she may spend as much as she wants on paints and give no consideration whatsoever to famine relief or other moral concerns such as the more basic needs of her friends, relatives, and so on.

A further complication arises when we note that overall integrity, like personal identity, has diachronic as well as synchronic dimensions. It requires that our values and principles, words, and conduct cohere not only at a particular time but also over time. Thus it is difficult to see how they can remain perfectly consistent without being hidebound and unresponsive to new situations and knowledge. Indeed it might seem that we have only two alternatives here, neither of them attractive: Either we lead perfectly consistent but rigid and perhaps fanatical moral lives or we respond to new circumstances and understanding at the expense of integrity and our identity as persons.

Thus it is one thing to say that integrity requires that one's words and deeds reflect a coherent and relatively stable set of values and principles to which one is authentically committed and quite another to flesh this out given: (1) human complexity as it is portrayed and explored in the work of great dramatists, poets, historians, biographers, autobiographers, and novelists, together with an honest examination of our own lives; (2) the demands of social as well as individual existence; (3) conflicts among what appear to be equally plausible and important moral values and principles; (4) conflicts between moral and nonmoral values; and (5) the vicissitudes of modern life. These limitations and tensions should make us wary of people whose categorical opposition to moral compromise is rooted in ritualized incantations of individual integrity. Underlying their high-minded opposition is a simple-minded conception of integrity and of what it means for one's integrity to be compromised. If, as I have indicated, integrity has social as well as individual importance and involves wholeness as well as consistency, an optimally integrated life (as opposed to the fantasy of a perfectly integrated life) will in the modern world require a certain amount of both internal and external compromise.

AN INTEGRATED LIFE

When Socrates says to Crito, *"Not only now but at all times* I am *the kind of man* who listens only to the argument that on reflection seems best to me" (emphasis added), he is referring to diachronic integrity or the notion of an integrated life. One's life as a whole—conceived temporally as having a beginning, middle, and end—is the principal subject of integrity as it applies to persons. The identity-conferring values and principles that integrity helps to secure should therefore be understood first and foremost as shaping the pattern of an entire life. Thus an adequate account of integrity in the modern world must show how it is possible to lead a reasonably well-integrated life while acknowledging the complexities identified in the previous section.

The ideal of an integrated life is, as Alasdair MacIntyre puts it, that of "a unitary life, a life that can be conceived and evaluated as a whole" (1981, p. 191). Subjects of such lives, he suggests, should regard themselves as authors of a narrative. The unity of the self "resides in the unity of a narrative which links birth to life to death as narrative beginning to middle to end." With an eye to one's biography or obituary, the individual as both agent and narrator asks, "Given the constraints of biology, society, and fortune, what will my life as a whole look like when it is nearly over? What will it have stood for, what values or principles will it have represented, and will it, when all is said and done, be regarded by myself and others as a good, worthwhile, or meaningful life or not?"

Tolstoy's cautionary tale of *The Death of Ivan Ilych* shows the importance of these questions and how denying our mortality may keep us from asking them until it is too late. It is not until he is near death that Ivan Ilych, reluctantly and with considerable effort, acknowledges that his life has been largely meaningless. Overemphasizing the expectations of middle-class society he had, as a young man, progressively alienated himself from spontaneous feeling and genuine attachment to others. His principal values were instead those of a cold and distant bureaucrat obsessed by professional ambition and personal vanity. As a public prosecutor he did what he could "to exclude everything fresh and vital, which always disturbs the regular course of official business, and to admit only official relations with people, and then only on official grounds" (Tolstoy 1886, p. 117). Largely the same in his personal life, he eschewed close personal relationships with family members and acquaintances. His greatest pleasure was playing "a clever and serious game of bridge" with "good players, not noisy partners, . . . and then to have supper and drink a glass of wine" (Tolstoy 1886, p. 119).

On his deathbed, deserted by "friends" and family members who ignore his intensely personal needs for pity, understanding, and human touch as he has always ignored theirs, Ivan Ilych can no longer deceive himself about his life. His ability to do so in the past was aided by refusing to acknowledge his mortality. If we think we are going to live forever, there is little need to worry about the shape and meaning of our lives as a whole. A succession of pleasant experiences is enough.

But once we acknowledge our finitude, Tolstoy suggests, life becomes meaningless unless it assumes a particular shape or direction and in so doing becomes part of something we regard as worthwhile and larger and more enduring than our singular and all too mortal self.

Ivan Ilych comes to this realization shortly before he dies. He had, it is true, largely squandered his life. But perhaps it was not too late to make amends, to "rectify" matters. How then, he asks, should he have lived his life? What values and principles can give shape and meaning to a life in the face of finitude and impending death? Taking as his mentor his faithful servant, Gerasim, Ivan finally identifies the larger good with God and with God's plan for how we should live, that is, connected to and with compassion for other human beings whose predicament we share. Thus shortly before he dies Ivan acknowledges the sorrow and despair of his son and his wife, who are standing by his bedside, and "feels" sorry for them. He finally acts to spare them further hurt: "With a look at his wife he indicated his son and said: 'Take him away . . . sorry for him . . . sorry for you too. . . .' He tried to add, 'forgive me,' but said 'forgo' and waved his hand, knowing that He whose understanding mattered would understand"(Tolstoy 1886, p. 155). Thus despite Ivan Ilych's lack of integrity during most of his life—the discrepancy between repressed inner feelings and outward behavior—and despite his largely trivial preoccupations, his finally getting it right at the end was, for Tolstoy, sufficient to rectify matters and to bring his life to a satisfactory conclusion: "He [God] whose understanding mattered would understand."

One may, of course, reject both Tolstoy's religious metaphysics and the apparent ease with which one may, on his account, rectify at the last moment a near lifetime of egoistic indifference grounded on self-deception. If, however, we hesitate to accept Tolstoy's solution, we cannot reject the question he poses: How, in the face of mortality, can our lives acquire significance or value that in some sense outlives the self? There is nothing we can do to prevent death, though we may frequently hope to postpone it. Yet it is one thing to acknowledge that we will one day die and quite another to admit that our lives invariably come to a "dead end" (Kotre 1984, p. 116). For our lives to be other than dead ends they must somehow be identified with or become part of one or more worthwhile projects or endeavors that are larger than and outlive the self. And to do this they must "be of a piece" or attain a certain unity; our lives must, in other words, acquire a particular shape, direction, or pattern that allows us to identify with one or more of these larger, longer-lived projects or endeavors, be they ultimately transcendental, like God or God's plan, or more naturalistic, like raising or teaching children to perpetuate a world view or way of life or to further certain values like justice, world peace, various forms of human perfection, and so on (Baier 1980).

Underlying the notion of an integrated human life is a conception of ourselves as temporal (or historical) beings. A human life is something that endures through time and can only be understood in terms of past, present, and future. Toward the beginning of a life, the prospects for the future may play a larger role in the subject's thinking than constraints of the past; toward the end, remaining true to one's past may be more important than prospects for the future. At all times, however, the closely related notions of "leading a life" and an "integrated life" presuppose that a person's life is conceived as having a beginning, a middle, and an end and that in attempting to integrate or connect values and principles with words and deeds, she also attempts to integrate or connect the past with the present and the future.

The relationships between past, present, and future in a single human life are complex. An essential component, as Richard Wollheim (1980) points out, is mental connectedness. "Mental connectedness is . . . a dyadic relation holding between mental events" belonging to the same person that satisfies "the two following conditions. One: the earlier of the two mental events that it relates causes the later of the two events. And two: the later event is caused by the earlier mental event in such a way that it—the later event, that is—then passes on to the whole person the causal influence of the earlier mental event" (Wollheim 1980, p. 304). Mental connectedness is, Wollheim maintains, "creative" of personal identity

> because, on each occasion of its instantiation, it brings the person somewhat under the influence of the past: A mental event is assigned to a person because of its relation with some earlier event in his life; and, when this happens, the relation ensures that the later event is a carrier of the influence of this earlier event, an influence that then pervades the person *so that his biography is bound together even as it unfolds.* The present is tied to the past, a new past is thus constructed under whose influence the future

may then be brought, and so the diachronic expansion of the person, his life, gets its unity (1980, p. 305, my emphasis).

Most important for our purposes is the relationship between mental connectedness and the way in which people manage to integrate their lives or give them a distinctive pattern or sense of what Wollheim calls overallness (1980, p. 299).

A person's life, which is stitched together by mental connectedness, is, Wollheim adds, "of a piece just insofar as at successive moments he is under the due influence of the past. His life exhibits pattern or wholeness to the degree to which the influence of the past, as it bundles up his life through the instrumentality of mental connectedness, is neither excessive nor insufficient" (1980, p. 312). The influence of the past is excessive when certain people's obsessions with it lead us to characterize them as living in the past and having little or no regard for their present or future condition. The past's influence is insufficient when severe mental illness or self-deception obstructs access to it.

As an example of the latter, consider Oliver Sacks's moving account of Jimmie G., "The Lost Mariner," a victim of Korsakov's syndrome who in 1975 at the age of forty-nine still thought of himself as nineteen and the year as 1945 (1985). Korsakov's syndrome is an acute disturbance of recent memory as a result of the destruction of neurons in a certain part of the brain brought on by alcohol. Although his intellectual and perceptual powers were quite acute, Jimmie G. had little short-term memory (two minutes after having a conversation with Sacks he could not recall having met or seen him before) and had no recollection at all of the years 1945 to 1975. In his notes, Sacks thinks about Jimmie and wonders "how one might establish some continuity, some roots, for he was a man without roots, or rooted only in the remote past" (1985, p. 28). Other cases of rootlessness are, of course, less extreme. Still, the lives of those who deny or otherwise compartmentalize or refuse to own up to their past are also deficient in overall integrity. Being under due influence of the past is not something that simply befalls a person, although luck or fortune will often play a significant role in determining the extent to which one's efforts are successful. How does one attempt to order or connect parts of one's life into a more or less coherent whole?

Central to the process of shaping a morally integrated life is the notion of an enacted personal narrative. "Narrative," MacIntyre observes, "is not the work of poets, dramatists and novelists reflecting upon events which had no narrative order before one was imposed by the singer or the writer; narrative form is neither disguise nor decoration" (1981, p. 197). Rather, most human conduct is intelligible only in the context of a narrative. To identify and understand what someone else is doing is always to

> move toward placing a particular episode in the context of a set of narrative histories, histories both of the individuals concerned and of the settings in which they act and suffer. . . . It is because we all live out narratives in our lives and because we understand our own lives in terms of the narratives that we live out that the form of narrative is appropriate for understanding the actions of others. Stories are lived before they are told—except in the case of fiction (MacIntyre 1981, p. 197).

As tellers and creators of our own stories we strive to preserve coherence and intelligibility. Changes in direction are embedded in a narrative that attempts to connect or integrate what came before with what follows. Thus an account of the reasons for adopting a change in our values, principles, world view, or way of life aims at showing the reasonableness of the alteration from the standpoint of our prior views given certain changes in knowledge or circumstance. In this way the intelligibility and coherence of our life as a whole is preserved. And to the extent that the relevant changes and reasons are made public, our subsequent conduct may also seem to others to be integrated with our prior conduct. So long as the changes are not too many or too rapid to be incorporated into the projects and commitments of others, our integrity is preserved from the external as well as from the internal perspective.

A conflict that erupted between consumer advocates Ralph Nader and Joan Claybrook in 1977 provides a useful illustration. Nader's life has been characterized by an uncompromising commitment to the cause of consumer rights, particularly with regard to auto safety. His efforts as an outsider or gadfly to protect the individual consumer against what he regards as the powerful and often opposing interests of large corporations have met with remarkable success. Claybrook had been his organization's chief lobbyist until, in 1977, she joined the federal government as the first head of the newly formed National Highway Transportation Safety Agency (NHTSA). In making this change she hoped to further the cause of consumer protection from the inside as she had done earlier from the outside as a member of the Nader organization.

Eight months later, however, Nader wrote an open letter in which he attacked his former colleague for failing the public and leaving "a trail of averted or broken promises" (*Newsweek*, 12 Dec. 1977). "What soured Nader," according to *Newsweek*, "was a recent decision by Transportation Secretary Brock Adams to let automakers delay phasing in air bags and other passive safety features—a decision that Claybrook had opposed in private, but supported publicly once it had been made. 'If you are determined to keep your job at any cost,' Nader wrote in his open letter, 'you can make the public pay any price.' Her only course now was 'resignation accompanied with full explanation and revelation.' " Claybrook's failing, Nader added, "is more than a failure of leadership; it is a failure of nerve" (*Consumer Reports*, April 1978). These strong words indicate that Nader believed that Claybrook had compromised her integrity and betrayed those who had trusted her to further a cause with which she had long been identified.

Nonetheless, it is possible to argue in Claybrook's defense that she had in fact retained her integrity and that in accepting an insider's role the values and principles to which she had been and still was committed required conduct different from that of an outsider committed to the same values and principles. Those who defended her at the time maintained that the matter of mandatory passive restraints was a political as well as a safety problem and that the political dimensions had to be respected. *Consumer Reports*, a strong supporter of greater auto safety, noted that Claybrook's superior, Brock Adams

had promised a final decision on the issue by July 1. Once he had ruled in favor of passive restraints it fell to Claybrook to pacify Congress, since the law gave Congress 60 days to veto any such decision (Congress had insisted on this unusual veto power following a storm of complaint from constituents over a 1974 safety regulation—the seatbelt-ignition interlock). . . . "The Congressional veto possibility had to be taken very seriously," says one House staff member involved with the issue. "That was the overwhelming reality of 1977." Claybrook's negotiating skill and the compromises embodied in the Adams proposal are widely credited with persuading Congress not to override the decision (April 1978).

Viewed in this light Claybrook's narrative account of her conduct might be quite coherent and intelligible. Her principles with regard to passenger safety, she might plausibly argue, remained the same. What had changed were her circumstances and role. From external critic she had now become internal advocate and negotiator in a highly politicized system with painful memories of an earlier, unsuccessful attempt at similar legislation. One's responsibilities and commitments as an insider in a political system are different from those of an external critic of that same system. Given her overarching commitment to the cause of auto safety, a less insistent, more conciliatory posture was required if she were to further the values and principles to which she remained committed in this new context. The narrative she would tell, then, might reveal that her integrity as a moral person was still intact. If there was any shortcoming it was either a failure on her part to make clear the implications of her new role to others—so they would not expect the letter of her conduct as insider to be the same as that of an outsider—or a failure or high degree of naiveté on the part of Ralph Nader to recognize that those furthering a particular cause from within highly politicized power structures are subject to constraints that do not affect those advocating the same cause from without.

In Chapter 6 I develop a more detailed and comprehensive account of the relationship between individual integrity and political compromise. The present aim is simply to show how personal narrative can account for a certain amount of change in a morally integrated life. Joan Claybrook's altered conduct was largely based on a change in role and circumstance. This change and a change in the facts or of our perception of them probably account for most integrity-preserving changes in our patterns of conduct. But it is also possible that a change in one's values or principles can be incorporated into an integrity-preserving narrative. Consider in this connection the journalist Rambert in Camus's *The Plague* (1947), who gradually replaces his self-centered efforts to escape plague-stricken Oran with solidarity with his fellow exiles and joint resistance to their shared fate.

Of course, not all personal narratives will be both coherent and true.

Some, if true, will reveal arbitrary changes, "failures of nerve," or other forms of sharp discontinuity. Others, if coherent, will be rationalizations or self-deceptions, departing in crucial respects from the facts. Here we draw on the external dimensions of a morally integrated life. Opportunism, hypocrisy, weakness of will, and self-deception can often be detected by a careful observer as can the sincere but shallow pattern of commitments of the moral chameleon. Because moral integrity requires that one's words and deeds generally be true to a relatively coherent and stable set of substantive values and principles to which one is authentically committed, we will usually have access to public criteria for evaluating the truthfulness of personal narratives. Indeed, public and personal accounts will serve the interests of truth as mutual correctives as do biography and autobiography. It is possible, then, at least in principle, to determine whether Joan Claybrook's account of her conduct at NHTSA is coherent, true, and therefore sufficient to rebut Ralph Nader's charge that her decision with regard to air bags represented a "failure of nerve" and thus a loss of integrity.

An interesting case in this connection and one that may provide an illuminating contrast with that of Joan Claybrook is that of Harvard President Derek Bok (Noble 1988). As a professor of law and a labor arbitrator, Bok had strongly endorsed the value and role of labor unions in the work place. "Unions are the most potent organized body," he wrote in 1970, "to represent the political interests of workers and to a lesser extent of the poor and disadvantaged." Yet eighteen years later, as a university president, he strongly opposed efforts of the university's office, service, and technical employees to organize a union. After writing a letter in which he set out arguments against unionization at Harvard, questions naturally emerged about his integrity:

> But for all the force of Mr. Bok's arguments in the letter to employees, what was most striking to labor leaders, some students and faculty members, was that here was a man who had made his academic reputation defending the right of collective bargaining, warning in the harshest terms of the threat unionization posed to the university. . . . "Derek Bok makes me feel sad," said Kristine Rondeau, a 35-year-old former Harvard medical technician who is directing the Harvard organizing drive. "He spends his entire life on one side of the fence, and now that he is the head of a corporation, he's forced to wear a different hat. . . . Derek Bok has one

foot in one world, and one foot in another world, and he's being torn apart by it" (Noble 1988, p. 8).

Whether President Bok is able to provide a true and coherent narrative account in which he is able to integrate his conduct as university president with the values and ideals set forth in his role as author and professor is an open question, one that is beyond the scope of the present inquiry.

There is, of course, more to be said about the complex social dynamics of adaptation to change while preserving one's integrity. A particularly illuminating account can be found in sociologist Peter Marris's *Loss and Change* (1975). Marris begins by identifying "the conservative impulse," the fundamental and universal desire and need to "defend the predictability of life" by assimilating our experiences in terms of familiar categories and structures of meaning. Underlying the conservative impulse is a deep-seated need for continuity or diachronic integrity. He then shows how the conservative impulse can accommodate loss, growth, and change by summarizing and reinterpreting his previous research on bereavement among widows.

Those whose lives have been "intimately involved with the dead are faced by a radical disruption in the pattern of their relationships" (Marris 1975, p. 26). The bereaved not only lose the person who has died but also that part of the present and future self whose existence depended on that person. "When the dead person has been, as it were, the keystone of a life, the whole structure of meaning in that life collapses when the keystone falls" (Marris 1975, p. 36). Overwhelmed by "feelings of disintegration," the bereaved widow is confronted with the task of restructuring the self to meet the future in ways that do not betray the significance of the past. She

has to give up her husband without giving up all that he meant to her, and this task of extricating the essential meaning of the past and reinterpreting it to fit a very different future seems to proceed by tentative approximations, momentarily comforting but at first unstable. For a while she may not be able to conceive any meanings in her life except those which are backward-looking and memorial, too tragic to sustain any future. In time, if all goes well, she will begin to formulate a sense of her widowhood *which nei-*

ther rejects nor mummifies the past, but continues the same fundamental purposes (Marris 1975, p. 38, my emphasis).

Extrapolating from this, Marris goes on to develop a more general account of what might be called identity- or integrity-preserving loss and change in the face of various types of social and personal dislocation.

Thrust into a circumstance that appears to be radically discontinuous with one's past and therefore threatening to overall integrity,

> a conflict arises between the yearning to return to the reassuring predictability of the past, and a contradictory impulse to become the creature of circumstance, abandoning the past as if it belonged to another, now repudiated being. Both impulses are self-destructive in themselves, but their interplay generates a process of reformulation by which the thread of continuity is retrieved. This reformulation of the essential meaning of one's experience of life is a unique reassertion of identity which takes time to work out. In this it resembles grief: for though the circumstances are not tragic, and the gains may outweigh the losses, the threat of disintegration is similar (Marris 1975, pp. 88ff.).

Related to this is the notion of a second (or third) chance. Recall Ivan Ilych's efforts to rectify his life on his deathbed. Although we may hesitate at the suggestion that one can fully atone (that is, become *at one*) or make amends (that is, to *mend*) in one's last hours for a largely alienated life characterized by self-centeredness, callousness, vanity, ambition, and self-deception, an adequate account of integrity must allow for acknowledging false starts and mistakes and, in some sense, making a new beginning (Kotre 1984, pp. 85-91).

Consider a *New York Times* editorial comparing the response of Kurt Waldheim, president of Austria and former secretary general of the United Nations, to his Nazi past with that of Richard von Weizsäcker, president of West Germany. For years Waldheim had repeatedly lied about his proximity to and knowledge of Nazi violations of human rights. As a commission of historians charged by the Austrian government to look into Waldheim's wartime record concluded, "In many points, Waldheim's presentation of his military past is not in harmony with the results of the work of the commission. He tried to let his military past pass into oblivion and as soon as this was no longer possible, to make it harmless" (*New York Times*, 10 February 1988).

The newspaper noted that von Weizsäcker, on the other hand, has forthrightly owned up to the dark side of his and his nation's past, emphasizing the danger of forgetting and distorting it. "All of us," the editorial reports him saying, "whether guilty or not, whether young or old, must accept the past. We are all affected by the consequences and liable for it. . . . We Germans must look truth straight in the eye—without embellishment and without distortion. . . . There can be no reconciliation without remembrance." The editorial then goes on to say that

> for 40 years Mr. Waldheim concealed the truth of his military service. He wrote in his memoirs that he was in Austria studying law while in fact he was in the Balkans. When he could no longer deny his presence there, he said he knew nothing of the notorious deportation of Greek Jews to death camps, the mass deportation of Austrian Jews. And now that his knowledge of these activities is also established, he falls back to a third defense; the report, he exults, charges no legal guilt.
>
> Such poverty of character is lamentable. It is particularly so in this case, because Austria's self-perception as "Hitler's first victim" has long kept its own confrontation with the past at bay. Where some, like Mr. von Weizsäcker, can see reconciliation after honest confrontation with the truth, Mr. Waldheim can see only blame. So he squirms and runs. His cowardice is Austria's loss (*New York Times*, 12 February 1988).

In terms of Wollheim's notion of mental connectedness (1980), we might say that von Weizsäcker's life is integrated or of a piece because he appears, in his public life at least, to be "under the due influence of his past." Waldheim's mental life appears, however, to be disconnected; the influence of the past on the present is insufficient for his life's being integrated or of a piece. And if in fact his mental life is not disconnected—if he is a hypocrite rather than a self-deceiver—it is the discrepancy between word and deed that undermines his integrity.

The fate of Socrates notwithstanding, it was probably easier, or at least simpler, to lead an integrated life in his day than in our own.

Comparatively closed, homogeneous societies not characterized by rapid social, scientific, and technological change are more conducive to leading integrated lives than the more open, heterogeneous, and rapidly changing societies of the modern world. The fluidity of many contemporary social roles and the emphasis placed on social and geographical mobility provide a range of tempting choices not found in the ancient world or in more traditional societies. Nor are we as certain in our more cosmopolitan, pluralistic culture as to what values or conception of the good ought to unify or be at the center of our lives. Here, too, the range of choices is extensive and the knockdown arguments are few. And all of this is compounded by the extent and rapidity of social, scientific, and technological change that is questioning old assumptions and providing new choices at a dizzying rate. Consider, for example, the confusion and dislocation brought about by the new reproductive technologies: in vitro fertilization and embryo transfer, surrogate motherhood, genetic testing and screening, fetal therapy and surgery, court-ordered Caesarean deliveries, and so on (Warnock 1985a; Singer and Wells 1985; Weil and Benjamin 1987).

Critical reflection on one's life as a whole and the corresponding exercise of freedom or autonomy (Frankfurt 1971; C. Taylor 1976) provides the connecting thread and the basis for an integrated life in the modern world. Again we pay homage to Socrates: The integrated life, especially in the modern world, must be the examined life—the life that, though rooted in and never fully transcending our biologically, culturally, and historically determined starting points, is characterized in part by listening "only to the arguments that on reflection seem best" to us and refusing to discard our earlier arguments unless there are good reasons for so doing. In acknowledging internal conflict and then finding good reasons for making what alterations in values and principles one makes and in making these alterations and reasons public, one is able to maintain continuity while incorporating change—one leads a morally integrated life without denying complexity or ambivalence or remaining hidebound or unresponsive to changing situations and circumstances.

The ideal of an integrated life in the open, heterogeneous, and rapidly changing societies of the modern world is rooted in the biological, cultural, and historical circumstances within which one is born and raised. Nonetheless, a certain amount of alteration and accommodation to changing circumstances and the opposing outlooks of others is possible if one's outlook places a sufficiently high value on critical reflection and the Socratic virtues of giving a fair hearing to opposing viewpoints, reexamining one's own reasoning, and being prepared to revise or abandon certain elements of one's plans or projects in response to new information, insights, or understanding (Vlastos 1971, pp. 10–12). The thread of continuity through such changes is personal autonomy and responsibility for a true and coherent narrative account of one's life as a whole. In articulating good reasons—reasons that are considered good against the background of one's previous values and principles together with new circumstances, information, or understanding—for making particular alterations and in making both alterations and reasons public, one may lead an integrated, but nonetheless flexible, life. "I value and respect the same principles as before," Socrates says to Crito, "and *if we have no better arguments to bring up at this moment*, be sure that I shall not agree with you" (my emphasis). Like Socrates, then, we "respect the same principles as before" unless we meet with "better arguments" to the contrary. To alter our course under these circumstances is, so long as we give adequate notification to others, not to betray our integrity but rather, to the extent that we are rational, to preserve it.

INTEGRITY AND COMPROMISE

Among the factors that may call for an alteration in one's values and principles are the conflicting values and principles of others. "What the agent is able to do and say intelligibly as an actor," MacIntyre writes, "is deeply affected by the fact that we are never more (and sometimes less) than the co-authors of our own narratives. Only in fantasy do we live what story we please." Carrying this image further he adds,

> We enter upon a stage which we did not design and we find ourselves part of an action that was not of our making. Each of us being a main character in his own drama plays subordinate parts in the dramas of others, and each drama constrains the others. In my drama, perhaps, I am Hamlet or Iago or at least the swineherd who may yet become a prince, but to you I am only a Gentleman or at best Second Murderer, while you are my Polonius or my

Gravedigger, but your own hero. Each of our dramas exerts constraints on each other's, making the whole different from the
parts, but still dramatic (1981, p. 199).

To acknowledge this feature of the human condition is to make room
in one's outlook for a certain amount of mutual accommodation. If
only in our fantasies "do we live what story we please," then only
in our fantasies may we live without a certain amount of moral
compromise.

Those who categorically reject all such compromise with high-
minded appeals to integrity often fail to appreciate the limitations and
complexities of integrity. As a largely formal notion, integrity is compatible with base as well as with lofty values and principles. That the
integrity of a questionable life structured around questionable values
and principles would be weakened by one or another compromise
should not be counted against the compromise and may even be a reason in its favor. In addition, tensions between internal and external
integrity and between integrity as wholeness and integrity as consistency, as well as the elusiveness of a fully unified and complete set of
moral values and principles, require that most of us make a number of
internal compromises and that we regard our integrity as a matter of
degree and not all or none. The notion of pure or perfect integrity is at
best a utopian ideal and at worst a recipe for fanaticism.

In its place we must substitute a more complex conception of
integrity, one that provides the basis for personal identity while acknowledging limitations, complexity, and the need for mutual accommodation. To arrive at such a conception we must first abandon the
image of integrity as the perfectly interlocking pieces of a completed
puzzle. The principal subject of integrity is not static or synchronic as
this image suggests. Rather, the subject of integrity is an entire personal (as opposed to simply biological) life—a life that begins with the
gradual development of the powers of moral reflection and choice and
that ends with their total decline or demise. Although composed of a
sequence of synchronic states requiring coherence among cherished
values and principles, words, and deeds, individual integrity is primarily diachronic or longitudinal. Our concern is for the long run and our
aim is to lead and to have lived a good and optimally integrated life in
conjunction with others whom we regard as in some sense equals and

whose commitments, values, and principles will not always be the same as ours.

As we proceed, the best means to this end will occasionally require accommodation to conduct and practices and to values and principles that conflict with our own. In order to remain true to the complex set of values and principles most central to our overall identity and integrity, we will refrain, at least temporarily, from acting in accord with certain values and principles that are more peripheral. The resulting agreement, peace, and good will, we hope, will ultimately be more conducive to preserving the overall pattern of our lives than continued conflict and acrimony. Compromise in such circumstances, when incorporated into a true and coherent narrative and (where possible) announced and justified in advance, does not threaten integrity but rather preserves it. Given a sufficiently complex characterization of the larger network of our values and principles, then, integrity—understood as wholeness as well as simple consistency and set in the context of an entire life—will occasionally require moral compromise.

4
Compromise and Ethical Theory

Archangels, at the end of their critical thinking, will all say the same thing on all occasions on which moral argument is possible; and so shall we to the extent that we manage to think like archangels.
—R. M. Hare, Moral Thinking

When a philosopher "solves" an ethical problem for one, one feels as if one had asked for a subway token and been given a passenger ticket valid for the first interplanetary passenger-carrying spaceship instead.
—Hilary Putnam, "How Not to Solve Moral Problems"

As shown in Chapter 2, moral compromise grows out of particular disagreements involving factual uncertainty, moral complexity, continuing personal (or professional, political, and so on) relationships, and an impending, consequential, nondeferrable decision. The opposing positions appear to be incommensurable and postponement is usually out of the question; to refrain from making a decision in these circumstances is tacitly to endorse or reject at least one of the contending positions. Because this kind of situation seems to be a frequent and abiding feature of our lives, one would think that ethical theory would explicitly address moral compromise. Why is this not so?

Ethical theorists have traditionally been drawn to the more abstract and general rather than to the more practical and immediate concerns of morality. They have sought a fully consistent, comprehensive set of values and principles that, when embraced by all, would—at least in principle—eliminate rationally irresolvable (or incommensurable) moral conflict. Discovery or development of the single true ethical theory that commends itself to all insofar as they are rational would enable us to resolve all disagreements without remainder. Those who aspire to this ideal will naturally regard compromise as at best a stopgap; useful, perhaps, for the time being but eventually rendered unnecessary by advances in ethical knowledge and understanding.

I argue that the quest for theories of this sort is unlikely to be successful. Deep and rationally irreconcilable conflicts of values and principles will remain part of our lives regardless of advances in ethical knowledge and understanding. A theory—like Hare's (1981), for example—that claims in principle to be able to resolve all conflicts without remainder will, as the passage from Putnam (1983) suggests, require a degree of idealization and abstraction that limits its usefulness for many of the practical concerns that give morality its point. Prominent among these concerns is devising sound and mutually satisfactory outcomes to rationally irreconcilable conflict.

After showing that our values and principles are, and are likely to remain, irreducibly plural, I trace the implications for ethical theory. The result is a broadly pragmatic conception of ethical knowledge and reasoning tempered by an emphasis on moral integrity, critical reflection, and comparatively firm but limited principles of overall welfare and equal respect. I also identify certain psychological and metaphysical concomitants of this conception, particularly the capacity of human beings to view the world and themselves from multiple perspectives. What makes compromise necessary is that many of our values and principles are rooted in diverse and occasionally conflicting cultural and historical standpoints; what makes compromise possible is that we are capable of approximating standpoints other than our own, including comparatively external or detached ones.

THE PLATONIC QUEST

The day before he is to be tried for the murder of his father, Dmitri Karamazov is visited by his brother Alyosha. Full of emotion and with tears rolling down his cheeks, Dmitri expresses his latest torment:

> It's God that's worrying me. That's the only thing that's worrying me. What if he doesn't exist? What if Rakitin's right—that it's an idea made up by men? Then, if He doesn't exist, man is the chief of the earth, of the universe. Magnificent! Only how is he to be good without God? That's the question. I always come back to that. . . . [A]fter all, what is goodness? Answer me that Alexey. Goodness is one thing with me, another with a Chinaman, so it's a relative thing. Or isn't it? Is it not relative? A treacherous ques-

tion! You won't laugh if I tell you it's kept me awake two nights. I only wonder how people can live and think nothing about it (Dostoevsky 1880, p. 721).

Many ethical theorists share Dmitri's worry (though not, perhaps, to the point of staying awake two nights in a row). Morality, they believe, must be grounded on something other than whether one happens to be Russian or Chinese, a member of this or that culture, living in this or that historical period, wedded to one world view and way of life or another, and so on. Although they may try to steer clear of religion, they agree with Dmitri that the touchstone for ethics must, like God, be "out there," wholly independent of various personal, cultural, and historical contingencies. Without an "objective" foundation for ethics, we are in their view doomed to interminable conflict and chaos.

The desire for externally grounded ethical standards is quite understandable. Human conflict, especially that rooted in ethical conviction, has been the cause of great misery. In extreme cases it erupts into violence and war, resulting in large-scale death and destruction. Even when less extreme, the apparently endless debates engendered by moral disagreement are often bitter, alienating, and deeply divisive. The desire to put an end to this sort of conflict motivates the philosophical quest for a single (set of) ethical standard(s) capable, in principle, of fully resolving all moral disagreement.

The quest for such a universal, comprehensive ethical standard is part of a larger philosophical project that aspires to conceptions of knowledge, reality, and ethics whose claims to validity are entirely independent of particular social, cultural, historical, and linguistic practices. Philosophy, in this view, is the discipline that transcends the merely contingent in order to identify foundations of knowledge, reality, and moral value that are independent of any particular social, cultural, historical, or linguistic point of view. This project has, with some notable exceptions, dominated Western philosophy from Plato to the present. To the extent that ethical theory is part of this endeavor (with or without Platonic metaphysics) it will, of course, pay little attention to questions of compromise. It will aim instead at the discovery of universal, rationally justifiable values and principles that will ultimately make compromise unnecessary.

Yet the overall project, of which the quest for transcultural and ahistorical values and principles is a part, has not been without its critics.

In recent years Richard Rorty has skillfully marshalled a sustained and comprehensive critique of the entire Platonic tradition (1979, 1982). Weaving together themes, insights, and arguments from Wittgenstein, Dewey, and Heidegger, as well as from more contemporary philosophers, Rorty's aim is to shake our faith in a conception of philosophy—including moral philosophy—as somehow foundational, independent of particularities of culture, language, and history, and as having access to timeless and immutable conceptions of the Real, the True, and the Good.

Motivating the Platonic tradition, in whose footsteps Rorty situates Descartes, Locke, and Kant, among others, is a desire for more or less mechanical procedures that will finally put our philosophical doubts and questions to rest: "It is the search for a way in which one can avoid the need for conversation and deliberation and simply tick off the way things are. The idea is to acquire beliefs about interesting and important matters in a way as much like visual perception as possible—by confronting an object and responding to it as programmed" (1980, p. 164). Those embarking on this quest long to be constrained not simply by our conventional categories but rather

> by the ahistorical and nonhuman nature of reality itself. This impulse takes two forms—the original Platonic strategy of postulating novel *objects* for treasured propositions to correspond to, and the Kantian strategy of finding *principles* which are definatory of the essence of knowledge, or representation, or morality, or rationality. But this difference is unimportant compared to the common urge to escape the vocabulary and practices of one's own time and find something ahistorical and necessary to cling to (Rorty 1980, p.165).

The aim is to "touch bottom," to get in touch with and be constrained by the Moral Law, Reality, and Truth in a manner that is wholly free of the merely contingent constraints of language, history, and culture.

In opposing this view, Rorty argues that we are unable to "step out of our own skins—the traditions, linguistic and other, within which we do our thinking and self-criticism—and compare ourselves with something absolute" (1982, p. xix). The price we pay for yielding to the "Platonic urge to escape from the finitude of one's time and place, the 'merely conventional' and contingent aspects of one's life," is a degree of generality and abstraction that leaves many of our most difficult and pressing moral problems largely untouched.

We may ask, first, about the success of the Platonic Quest in ethics. After more than two thousand years to what extent have many of the greatest philosophical minds been able to approximate the ideal of a true, transcultural, ahistorical standard (or ordered set of such standards) capable of resolving all our moral problems without remainder? Although the fact that no individual or school of thought has discovered such a standard does not show it to be unrealizable or misconceived, it does raise serious doubts about it, especially when we find ourselves continually faced with pressing moral conflicts.

Impeding the Platonic project, in ethics no less than in epistemology or metaphysics, is the "ubiquity of language" (Rorty 1982, p. xx). No one has ever been able to get outside of language and compare what we say about whether something is good, true, or real with what is actually—and independently of language, culture, and history—Good, True, or Real. Knowledge, construed as justified true belief, is essentially linguistic because justification is essentially linguistic. We justify our beliefs by indicating linguistically how they cohere with (and hence are supported by) other beliefs. Both the beliefs to which we appeal and the act of appealing to them are ineluctably linguistic; the language we use is a product of particular cultural and historical contingencies.

To say this, however, is not to say that the world is the creation of our beliefs. The world, as common sense would have it, is for the most part independent of our beliefs about it. But the truth about the world is not. Truth is a feature not of the world itself but rather of certain sentences or descriptions of the world. And sentences are elements of human languages and human languages are human creations, rooted in various human activities (Rorty 1986, p. 3). If, then, we conceive of knowledge as justified true belief, it cannot be separated from the languages and activities of human beings.

Ethical theorists working within the Platonic tradition have been preoccupied with discovering basic principles, the truth or validity of which is independent of linguistic, cultural, or historical contingencies and can thus serve as a permanent, neutral standard for evaluating and deriving our more particular actions and judgments. The effect of this endeavor, unfortunately, has been to marginalize ethical theory and to remove philosophical ethics from the world of genuine, as opposed to merely academic, moral conflict and disagreement.

Rorty, in this connection, distinguishes between "a specifically philosophical use of 'good,' a use which would not be what it is unless Plato, Plotinus, Augustine, and others had helped construct a specifically Platonic theory of the absolute difference between the eternal and the spatio-temporal," and a more "homely and shopworn sense," the sense in which in everyday life we say that this or that act, object, desire, argument, and so on is good (1979, p. 307). The latter sense is, of course, heavily context dependent and resistant to sweeping theories and principles because the contexts are so diverse. It is only by abstracting the word from the settings in which it does its work, when it really matters to us whether something is good or bad, that the philosopher in the Platonic tradition has the remotest chance to say something sweeping—sweeping, perhaps, but also without much practical significance. For this reason the pronouncements of most moral philosophers within this tradition have little to contribute to men and women who must cope with the most difficult and pressing ethical issues of the day.

What motivates the Platonic Quest? The answer is probably quite complex, but one important factor is the fear of relativism. Although they might reject the comparison, many whose conception of philosophy is dominated by the Platonic Quest are looking for a secular equivalent of the God whose existence is worrying Dmitri Karamazov. There is a deep desire to have our beliefs about goodness, truth, and reality compelled and constrained by something external, entirely independent of historically, culturally, and linguistically conditioned beliefs. Even the positivists, Rorty suggests, who claimed to eschew metaphysics for the hard-headed reality of empirical science, went only halfway in doing without God: "For positivism preserved a god in its notion of Science (and its notion of 'scientific philosophy'), the notion of a portion of a culture where we touched something not ourselves, where we found Truth [with a capital 'T'] naked, relative to no description" (1982, p. xliii). Though we might think them strange bedfellows, positivists and Platonists are quite alike in this regard:

> The Platonists would like to see a culture guided by something eternal. The positivists would like to see one guided by something temporal—the brute impact of the way the world is. But both want it to be *guided*, constrained, not left to its own devices. For both, decadence is a matter of unwillingness to submit oneself to something "out there"—to recognize that beyond the languages of

men and women there is something to which these languages, and these men and women, must try to be adequate (Rorty 1982, p. xxxix).

In both instances the flight from relativism goes too far and is tantamount to a flight from the conditions of human life.

Following Sartre, Rorty regards the Platonic Quest as partly a failure of nerve, a reluctance to cope with the complexity and uncertainty of the world as it is. If, as the Platonists wish, "we could convert knowledge from something discursive, something attained by continued adjustments of ideas or words, into something as ineluctable as being shoved about, or being transfixed by a sight which leaves us speechless, then we should no longer have the responsibility for choice among competing ideas and words, theories and vocabularies" (Rorty 1979, pp. 375–77). Although Rorty is opposed to the more vulgar and pernicious forms of epistemological and moral relativism, he suggests that they can be resisted well short of embarking on one or another form of Platonic Quest (Rorty 1980).

Even if these criticisms of the Platonic project are largely correct, as I believe they are, it is still possible perhaps that one set of values and principles will emerge from our various discussions and debates as consistent, comprehensive, and capable in principle of rationally resolving without remainder all moral conflict. One might, that is, reject the Platonic conception of a complete and coherent ethical theory as a matter of discovery while retaining the aspiration of inventing or devising such a theory (Walzer 1987, pp. 3–32). To abandon the Platonic Quest is not to rule out the possibility of eventually harmonizing our ethical values and principles, the realization of which would significantly reduce the need for compromise. This undertaking is, however, also misconceived. A significant number of values and principles, intrapersonal as well as interpersonal, are and are likely to remain irreducibly plural, diverse, and resistant to efforts to fully harmonize them.

THE DOCTRINE OF MORAL HARMONY

Many believe that all good things must somehow ultimately be compatible. They are encouraged in this conviction by situations in which ethical inquiry has—by identifying inconsistencies, drawing distinctions, unmasking raw prejudice, clarifying concepts, acquiring additional information, refining principles, and so on—contributed to resolving or ameliorating conflicts and rendering our prereflective choices and judgments more coherent and systematic. Extrapolating from these achievements, they maintain that additional knowledge and further reflection will ultimately allow us to devise a consistent and comprehensive theory that will be capable, at least in principle, of resolving all moral conflicts without remainder.

Underlying this rationalistic outlook, Isaiah Berlin points out, are a number of assumptions: (1) that our only true purpose is rational self-direction; (2) that all of our rational ends must ultimately fit into a single, universal, harmonious pattern; (3) "that all conflict, and consequently all tragedy, is due solely to the clash of reason with the irrational or the insufficiently rational—the immature and undeveloped elements in life—whether individual or communal, and that such clashes are, in principle, avoidable, and for wholly rational beings impossible"; and (4) that insofar as we are rational, we will all obey the same moral rules and principles that emanate from our rational nature (1958, p. 154). Yet, Berlin argues, these assumptions and thus "the conviction that all the positive values in which men have believed must, in the end, be compatible, and perhaps even entail one another" cannot survive scrutiny. "It is a commonplace," Berlin points out,

> that neither political equality nor efficient organization nor social justice is compatible with more than a modicum of individual liberty, and certainly not with unrestricted *laissez-faire;* that justice and generosity, public and private loyalties, the demands of genius and the claims of society, can conflict violently with each other. And it is no great way from that to the generalization that not all good things are compatible, still less all the ideals of mankind (1958, p. 167).

Thus, he concludes,

> that the belief that some single formula can in principle be found whereby all the diverse ends of men can be harmoniously realized is demonstrably false. If, as I believe, the ends of men are many, and not all of them are in principle compatible with each other,

then the possibility of conflict—and of tragedy—can never wholly be eliminated from human life, either personal or social. The necessity of choosing between absolute claims is an inescapable characteristic of the human condition (1958, p. 169).

Our efforts at systematization and unification will, on this view, never be complete. Although we should do what we can to reduce or mitigate moral conflict, it is fantasy—and dangerous fantasy at that—to think it is possible, even in principle, to fully eliminate it. Throughout history too much blood has been spilled and too many lives lost or ruined for the sake of one or another conception of ultimate moral harmony. Whatever efforts at systematization and unification that we undertake should, therefore, be retail rather than wholesale, piecemeal rather than all at once. Only then can we avoid the Procrustean oversimplifications that—when harnessed to political power and the means of oppression—have contributed with such depressing regularity to the world's ills.

In recent years a number of philosophers have developed variations on this general theme. Bernard Williams, for example, observes that philosophical writing "has typically tended to regard value-conflict, except perhaps in the most contingent and superficial connections, as a pathology of social and moral thought, and as something to be overcome—whether by theorising, as in the tradition of analytical philosophy and its ancestors, or by a historical process, as in Hegelian and Marxian interpretations" (1978, p. 72). He then adds, "It is my view, as it is Berlin's, that value-conflict is not necessarily pathological at all, but something necessarily involved in human values, and to be taken as central by any adequate understanding of them." Indeed, taking Williams's point a step further we might add that it is not value conflict in itself that is pathological but rather the obsession with wholly eliminating it, especially when this obsession leads to systematic denials of the nature and complexity of human life.

Stuart Hampshire's account of the persistence of moral conflict is especially instructive. Hampshire identifies Hume, Kant, the utilitarians (particularly Mill and Moore), the deontologists (for example, Ross and Prichard), and ideal social contract theorists (such as Rawls) with "the doctrine of moral harmony" (1983, pp. 143–44).[1] Whatever the well-known differences among them, Hampshire maintains, these moral philosophers are united and in agreement in one respect: their theories of moral judgment agree with Aristotle, first, in stating or implying that moral judgments are ultimately to be justified by reference to some feature of human beings which is common throughout the species; secondly, they agree with Aristotle in stating or implying that a morally competent and clear-headed person has in principle the means to resolve all moral problems as they present themselves, and that he need not encounter irresoluble problems (1983, p. 144).

But, Hampshire argues, Aristotle and those who follow him in this respect are largely mistaken: Many moral judgments are (and can only be) ultimately justified by considerations that are not common throughout the species. And, because these considerations are often conflicting and incommensurable, a number of moral problems are not, in the desired sense, rationally resolvable. Abstract or universal reason of the sort favored by philosophers is, though indispensable to ethics, insufficient to resolve all (or perhaps even most) of our moral disagreements.

If "moral judgments are ultimately to be justified by reference to some feature of human beings which is common throughout the species," exactly what is this feature? Two main candidates are: a conception of the good rooted in one or more universal features of human nature; and the equal capacity among human beings for reason. Both are usually identified with Aristotle, though in recent times it is Kant's version of the second that has received the most attention. Yet neither version is able to bear the justificatory burden placed upon it by the Doctrine of Moral Harmony.

Consider, first, the possibility of a conception of the good that is rooted in our common human nature. If we can indisputably ground a complete conception of the good in human nature, we may then with increasingly improved knowledge and powers of prediction be able, at least in principle, to harmonize differences and resolve or eliminate internal and external conflicts by reference to what contributes to and what detracts from the common human good. Everything would then come down to maximizing the good, either collectively or individually. (Let us disregard for the moment possible conflicts between collective and individual good.) Aristotle's conception of the good was rooted in his conception of our common biology.

Now it is certainly true that our common biology places constraints on our conceptions of morality. Common vulnerabilities relating to (physical) pain and death are, for example, sufficient to ground widespread prohibitions against murder or causing gratuitous pain. With this there can be no argument. Moreover, "the dependence of very young children on adult nurture, the onset of sexual maturity, the instinctual desires associated with motherhood, the comparative helplessness of the old, are all biological features of a standard outline of human life, which may be appealed to as imposing some limits on moral requirements at all times and in all places" (Hampshire 1983, p. 142). But as an elementary understanding of history and anthropology clearly reveals, these limits will take different (and occasionally conflicting) forms at different times and in different places. To point out that young children are universally dependent and in need of nurture is one thing; to maintain that there is one, and only one, form that the provision of nurture is to take is quite another. With regard to the common sexual and reproductive needs of the species, Hampshire points out, "history and anthropology together show that the natural constraints still leave a wide area for diversity: diversity in sexual customs, in family and kinship structures, in admired virtues appropriate to different ages and to the two sexes, in relations between social classes, also in the relation between the sexes, and in attitudes to youth and old age" (1983, p. 141). Indeed, taking a less reductionist conception of human nature (one with no hidden philosophical agenda and that does not, as a result, attempt to reduce everything to, say, biology), one might say that human nature as revealed by literature, history, psychology, anthropology, and sociology as well as biology reveals diversity itself to be "a primary, perhaps the primary, feature of human nature, species wide" (Hampshire 1983, p. 141). Thus Hampshire concludes, "human nature, conceived in terms of common human needs and capacities, always underdetermines a way of life and underdetermines the moral prohibitions and injunctions that support a way of life" (1983, p. 155).

It is, of course, open to those hoping to ground a common, more determinate conception of the good in human nature to resort to more metaphysical conceptions. Aristotle's biological grounding of morality was embedded in a metaphysical conception that no longer seems plausible (MacIntyre 1981, p. 152; Williams 1985, pp. 43–53). Yet enriching our scientific understanding of universal human biology with a more up-to-date metaphysics has two defects as a strategy for grounding a comprehensive and consistent moral theory. First, as Williams has suggested, far from grounding an ethical theory, such a biological-cum-metaphysical theory of human nature is likely to already be (or at least presuppose) an ethical theory itself (Williams 1985, p. 52). Hence the enterprise will be circular. Second, in attempting to avoid charges of circularity, proponents of this view may be tempted to embark on one or another variation of the Platonic Quest, which is to exchange the perils of the frying pan for those of the fire.

Let us turn from biology to the equal capacity for reason as a possible ground for the Doctrine of Moral Harmony. Does it fare any better? I think not. Hampshire illuminatingly compares efforts to resolve all ethical conflict by appeal to abstract impersonal reason with the project of Esperanto, the attempt to devise a comprehensive universal language. The project of Esperanto does not succeed, Hampshire points out, because it cannot account for the local and particular circumstances and history that give shape and meaning to our lives: "A language distinguishes a particular people with a particular shared history and with a particular set of shared associations and with largely unconscious memories, preserved in the metaphors that are imbedded in the vocabulary" (1983, p. 135). The same is true of some parts of morality, especially those that govern sexual and family relationships and matters of life and death. To restrict the resolution of conflicts involving these aspects of morality to abstract, impersonal reason is to be as remote and detached from what actually matters to (particular) people as is the project of Esperanto—or, to echo Putnam, as is the development of an interplanetary passenger-carrying space ship (1983, p. 3). Conflicts about the structure and nature of the family (which, for example, underlie controversies over the use of new reproductive technologies, the legitimacy of homosexual marriage, child raising, and adoption, and the authority of parents to accept or refuse medical treatment for seriously ill newborns [Benjamin and Weil 1987, pp. 3–29]) turn on values and principles that are historically conditioned, contingent, and not fully determined by abstract, impersonal reason.

Contrary to what many ethical theorists would like to believe, the values governing our convictions on such matters are more closely related to sentiment and personal circumstance than to abstract, impersonal reason (Warnock 1985b). They are bound up with particular conceptions of ourselves and the world that are themselves rooted in divergent personal, cultural, and historical ways of living. As such, they will often conflict. For example, the world view and way of life of a housewife and mother of five with strong fundamentalist convictions is likely to differ considerably from that of a single, female executive who wants to become a mother through artificial insemination but who has little or no inclination to be married. We can reasonably assume, for example, that they would have differing ethical views on the use of new reproductive technologies or abortion (Luker 1984a; Strong and Schinfeld 1984).

In emphasizing the limits of abstract, impersonal reason we need not deny that general principles of, say, justice or utility are at some level applicable to everyone. But like our understanding of human biology, which is also applicable at some level to everyone, such principles underdetermine many of our ethical choices and judgments. General principles of justice and utility can as a rule be used to show murder, rape, slavery, racism, and so on to be clearly wrong. But many actual conflicts cannot be resolved by considerations of justice or utility alone. These general principles fail to determine the whole of morality; they do not, to adapt a phrase from Williams, "go all the way down" (1985, p. 108). They do not, for example, go all the way down to the level of particular disputes about surrogate motherhood or the moral status of the embryo. Such disputes are rooted in opposing world views (including opposing religious and metaphysical beliefs) and ways of life that do not clearly violate general principles of justice or utility.

Attempts to resolve these matters in terms of one or another abstract, general principle will be either controversial or vacuous. Close examination of the frequently labored attempts to "deduce" a concrete, more or less purely utilitarian or Kantian solution to these issues invariably reveals a number of question-begging factual and metaphysical assumptions. The reasoning will incorporate an unacknowledged bias toward one or another world view and way of life (Warnock 1985a, 1985b). The practical conclusions will, as a result, be unacceptable to those who do not share the relevant world view and way of life. It is not, as the proponents of such arguments often suggest, that those who disagree with them are "irrational" or "illogical" but rather that what is at stake involves more than the sort of abstract, impersonal reason to which academic philosophers are by temperament and training generally drawn. Ethical arguments that studiously avoid commitment to one or another particular world view and way of life may avoid such biases, but they pay a heavy price for their neutrality; on many questions they will be so abstract and theoretical as to have no practical bearing whatever.

WORLD VIEWS AND WAYS OF LIFE

A *world view* is a complex, often unarticulated (and perhaps not fully articulable) set of deeply held and highly cherished beliefs about the nature and organization of the universe and one's place in it. Normative as well as descriptive—comprising interlocking general beliefs about knowledge, reality, and values—a world view so pervades and conditions our thinking that it is largely unnoticed. The components of a world view are, as Luker points out, usually, "so deep and so dear to us that we find it hard to imagine that we even have a 'world view'—to us it is just reality—or that anyone else could not share it. By definition, those areas covered by a 'world view' are those parts of life we take for granted, never imagine questioning, and cannot envision decent, moral people not sharing" (1984a, p. 158). Among the elements of world view are one's deepest convictions about (1) God—that is, whether there is a God and, if so, what God is like; (2) the nature and purpose (if any) of the universe and human life; (3) the nature, justification, and extent of human knowledge and our capacity to acquire further knowledge; (4) the basic nature of human beings (including, for example, their capacities for free will, goodness, compassion, selfishness, and, in certain world views, "sin" and "redemption"); (5) the best way to structure human relationships (including sexual and familial relationships, friendships, political institutions, and obligations to strangers); (6) the demands of morality, especially injunctions and principles having to do with the taking of life, the nature of equality, respect for liberty, and so on; and (7) the moral standing of nonhuman animals and the intrinsic value of the natural environment. A world view may, as this list suggests, be religious or entirely naturalistic or secular.

Closely related to a particular world view is a corresponding *way of life*. "Ways of life are," Hampshire writes, "coherent totalities of customs, attitudes, beliefs, institutions, which are interconnected and mutually dependent in patterns that are sometimes evident and sometimes subtle and concealed" (1983, p. 6). "Alongside repeated patterns of behaviour," he adds, "a way of life includes admired ideal types of men and women, standards of taste, family relationships, styles of education and upbringing, religious practices and other dominant concerns" (1983, p. 5). A particularly distinctive and easily recognizable way of life is that of the Amish.

Originating in Europe as followers of Jakob Ammann, a seventeenth-century Mennonite elder, the Amish began migrating into North America around 1720. Although the Amish differ little in formal theological doctrine from other Mennonites, they have adopted a distinctive way of life, in large part to preserve the integrity of their world view. The men wear broadbrimmed black hats, beards, and homemade plain clothes fastened with hooks and eyes instead of buttons. The women wear bonnets, long, full dresses with capes over the shoulders, shawls, and black shoes and stockings. They do not wear jewelry. Their patterns of dress have more to do with maintaining group identity (their clothing is largely the same as that worn by the rural populace in seventeenth-century Europe) than with biblical restrictions. In addition, they reject telephones and electric lights and prefer horses and buggies to automobiles. Although regarded as excellent farmers, they are inclined to reject modern farm machinery. Their self-conscious distinctiveness and their reluctance to send their children to public schools are largely motivated by their desire to preserve and perpetuate their world view and way of life. The demands of individual and group integrity, they believe, require that they remain a people apart.

The majority of world views and ways of life in modern pluralistic societies are more difficult to identify and delineate. A complex amalgam of a wide variety of beliefs, attitudes, ideals, and practices, a typical modern world view and way of life will often be highly personalized. Understanding and articulating a person's world view and way of life becomes the task of the sensitive biographer, requiring a thorough grounding in a particular historical and cultural setting as well as a detailed understanding of the individual's personal and familial history. Even then we may reasonably entertain doubts as to whether we have fully and accurately identified the core of a person's outlook and practices, whether that of ourselves or of others. But this is not to say that these more individualized world views and ways of life are less significant to those who identify with them than are the world view and the way of life articulated by Jakob Ammann to the Amish.

World views and corresponding ways of life may be placed on a spectrum ranging from more to less readily identifiable. At the right end will be those of the Amish, Hassidic Jews, and Christian and Muslim fundamentalists. At the other end will be world views and ways of life of iconoclasts like Thoreau, Margaret Sanger, and Bertrand Russell. In between, reading from right to left, will be those of Conservative Jews and practicing Catholics, Reformed Jews and nonpracticing Catholics, and various atheists and agnostics. Although world views and ways of life toward the left end of the spectrum may be more flexible and difficult to delineate than those at the other end, their wide and overlapping variety and occasional fluidity should not prevent us from acknowledging the important role they play in determining an individual's identity and integrity.

A person's world view and way of life are dynamically interrelated. A world view helps to govern a way of life; a way of life presupposes and embodies a world view. Deep changes in one are likely to occasion related changes in the other. Those who, like Ivan Karamazov or his half-brother Smerdyakov, believe that "if there is no God then everything is permitted" will live quite differently depending on whether God remains part of their world view. And children brought up within a particularly restrictive, religious way of life may alter their world view if, for example, a secular state enjoins their parents to place them in a public school where they will come into sustained contact with and be encouraged or tempted to participate in a significantly less restrictive way of life. Consider the reluctance of the Amish to send their children to public high schools or the efforts of other religious groups to have organized prayer become a part of public schooling and to replace or supplement instruction in the theory of evolution with instruction in "creation science."

These groups have some ground for complaint when they charge the state with imposing the alien "religion of secular humanism" on their children, although they are mistaken in identifying what they call secular humanism with religion. A religious outlook involves more than a set of deep, fundamental beliefs about the cause, purpose, and nature of the universe; it must also include some reference to supernatural agency either as the cause of the universe or as somehow overseeing and governing it, or both. To construe religious belief simply as a person's deepest convictions about the universe is to trivialize it. Because everyone has some beliefs that are deeper or more fundamental than the others, we all become religious believers by definition. But characterizing someone as religious is not empty or tautologous. Not everyone believes in a God either as the cause of the universe or as somehow providing guidance in how we should live. Those characterized as secular humanists, for example, differ from religious believers in embracing world views and ways of life that have little or nothing to do with the supernatural, including the notion of a Supreme Being. When, therefore, the courts uphold, in the name of the separation of church and state, laws prohibiting organized prayer and the teaching of creation science in state-supported schools they are not promoting one religion, the "religion" of secular humanism, over others. They are, however, endorsing an outlook that acknowledges the equal legitimacy of a number of different world views and ways of life. And it is this (broadly) liberal or pluralistic outlook that is incompatible with the world views and ways of life of the Christian fundamentalists who make the complaint. In attending public schools, the children of Christian fundamentalists will be exposed to books, materials, world views, and ways of life that are to their lights "Godless" and contrary to their beliefs in the literal and uncompromising truth of the Bible. They are mistaken in claiming that this amounts to the imposition of an alien religion. But they are quite correct about its constituting a significantly different world view and way of life, one that, given their singular and totalizing outlook, may somehow be threatening to the maintenance of their own.

Many bitterly divisive moral and political conflicts are grounded in conflicting world views and ways of life. For example, Luker, in her revealing study of prolife and prochoice activists (1984a), shows that for members of these groups what is at stake in the abortion debate is more than a moral position on one discrete issue.[2] "In the course of our interviews," Luker writes, "it became apparent that each side of the abortion debate has an internally coherent and mutually shared view of the world that is tacit, never fully articulated, and, most importantly, completely at odds with the world view held by their opponents" (1984a, p. 159). Underlying their opposing positions on abortion are different interrelated beliefs about the roles of the sexes, the meaning of motherhood, the extent to which there is goodness or order in the universe, and the extent to which one ought to accept or attempt to alter nature.[3] Luker's account of the prochoice activists, whose world view is for the most part more secular than that of the prolife activists, shows, too, that just as "you don't have to be Jewish to enjoy Levy's rye bread" (a memorable caption on an advertisement picturing an American Indian biting into a sandwich) one does not have to be Amish, Hassidic, or a devout Mormon or Catholic to have a particular world view and corresponding way of life. That one person's view of the world is centered around a conception of the universe as largely indifferent to human striving and aspiration, together with a way of life emphasizing scientific reason, planning, and autonomous decision, is as much a matter of historical, cultural, and personal circumstances as is another's world view that is centered on a conception of the universe as a divine creation—basically benign and having a certain order and purpose (even though its exact nature may elude our finite understanding)—and a corresponding way of life. An appeal to nothing more than reason and science to determine which of these two world views is "more accurate" is no more neutral than an appeal to God or religious authority.[4]

Not all strongly held positions on the question of abortion are, however, identified with stereotypical world views and ways of life. Mary Meehan and Sidney Callahan, for example, combine strong opposition to abortion with what they regard as equally strong commitments to feminism and opposition to violence. As a member of Feminists for Life and the peace-prolife group Prolifers for Survival, Meehan does not fit the profile of prolife activists sketched by Luker (Meehan 1984b). Callahan's eloquent portrayal and defense of a particularly attractive and coherent prolife world view and way of life is equally idiosyncratic. In tracing her southern Protestant origins, her going north to college and embracing "Quakerlike" liberal politics, and her conversion to Roman Catholicism, she says, "I have always lived between worlds, constantly moving back and forth. I have to carve out my own territory in my own way and stand by it." She characterizes her world view and way of life as, among other things, "feminist, pacifist, and prolife" (Callahan 1984, p. 286).

A person's commitment to a particular world view and way of life is, as Callahan's words and the example of the Amish suggest, identity conferring. This is why we are often reluctant to give up a world view and way of life or even to modify them. A particular world view and way of life determines who we are and what we stand for. At stake in a disagreement rooted in conflicting world views and ways of life, therefore, are the identity and integrity of each of the contending parties. To be forcibly and irreversibly deprived of one's world view and way of life occasions grief and mourning for the loss of a particular self.[5]

World views and ways of life come into conflict because they acquire their shape and direction from local and particular, rather than more general and universal, aspects of human life. They embody perspectives, values, and principles that are historically conditioned, contingent, and sometimes fiercely personal and parochial. Loyalties to particular institutions, practices, projects, and persons are regarded as essential to one's way of life; they largely constitute one's identity and set one off from others as a particular person or type of person. To celebrate these loyalties is to celebrate what is distinctive about oneself or one's group and not what is common to all. To relinquish them or to be stripped of them is often to surrender or to be deprived of one's integrity and identity as a particular person.

As suggested by our rejection of the Platonic Quest and the Doctrine of Moral Harmony, there is no single world view and way of life that can claim to be uniquely supported by reason or "the facts." Certainly abstract, impersonal reason and a widely shared, publicly accessible understanding of the facts can rule out certain world views and ways of life—for example, those presupposing morally significant differences between blacks and whites or Jews and Aryans. But after this essentially negative, or winnowing, process is completed, there will still be a variety of different and occasionally conflicting world views and ways of life, each of which seems compatible with abstract, impersonal reason and a widely shared, publicly accessible understanding of the facts.

It is therefore a perfectly adequate initial justification of a course of action to show that it flows from a decent or legitimate world view and way of life, one that does not appear to violate well-grounded principles of justice and utility and that is not in conflict with a widely shared, publicly accessible conception of the facts. Appeals to our identity and integrity, historically rooted and contingent though they may be, are in this view no less important for ethics than impersonal appeals to justice and benevolence. "I know he's guilty, but I've got to help him, he's my son," is a perfectly coherent and sometimes decisive justification for a person's undertaking a particular course of action as is "I'm a Catholic, so I've got to do what I can to help bring about a change in the law on abortion."

So long as one's commitment to a reasonably coherent, particular world view and way of life does not cause evident and avoidable suffering or is not clearly unfair or unjust, it needs no additional justification. The following are all, as Hampshire puts it, "justifications in a moral context . . . which appeal to the agent's sense of his own identity and character as a person and of his history, which partially determines his sense of identity":

> "This is the approved practice of the people to whom I belong, and to whom I am committed, and *I find nothing harmful in it*": "This is an essential part of the way of life to which I am committed and *it is not an evil way of life*": "This has always been our practice, and, *properly understood, it is not unfair*, and it is important in our way of life": "This is how I feel, and how I have always felt: to change now would be to repudiate my past, and *I find nothing unjust or harmful in the practice*; . . . "This is my ground and I must stand on it. I do not claim that everyone everywhere must do what I do: but this is my character, and because it is, I must act in this way." Such justifications are sometimes spoken of as appeals to integrity, a distinctive virtue to be ranked with justice and benevolence (1983, p. 8; my emphasis).

As the emphasized passages indicate, appeals to the integrity of one's world view and way of life are not beyond criticism. Widely shared, publicly accessible, and rationally justifiable considerations dealing with harm, evil, justice, or unfairness constrain appeals to integrity. Integrity is not the only or most important value. A life can be fully integrated and wholly reprehensible if it clearly and systematically violates principles of justice and utility. Thus Nazis, professional murderers, racists, sexists, thieves, and other unsavory characters cannot justify their conduct simply by invoking the integrity of their world views and ways of life.

It might at this point be argued that conflicts rooted in opposing world views and ways of life will soon be eliminated. Advances in knowledge and understanding will, for example, reduce differences among people and thus contribute to a convergence or merging of various world views and ways of life. But this argument overlooks the fact that new knowledge also brings new possibilities—possibilities that create or aggravate as many conflicts as they eliminate or reduce. At the same time that scientific understanding reduces differences based on ignorance and superstition, new modes of intervention multiply possibilities and new ways of differing from one another. Consider how advances in our understanding of reproduction and various new reproductive technologies have provided new and conflicting conceptions of motherhood and family life (Benjamin and Weil 1987, pp. 4–9). And technological advances in contraception and abortion together with various social and cultural changes have, as Luker points out, sharpened the conflict between the two very different world views and ways of life that are at stake for activists on both sides of the abortion debate. Like many other conflicts between "traditional" and "modern" values and ways of life, this debate is a product of new knowledge and technology, not simply a problem to be solved by it.

Thus new knowledge, although eliminating or reducing conflicts based on ignorance, also creates new possibilities, which in turn may become the cornerstone of new or radically different ways of life for men and women who, for various reasons, are strongly dissatisfied with those into which they were born (Marris 1975, pp. 111–56). Perhaps they find their received ways of life obsolete and unresponsive to new circumstances and possibilities; or they find them stifling, allowing insufficient outlet for their imaginative and creative energies. With others of like mind they will adapt or develop different and more satisfying ways of life that set them apart and at the same time sow the seeds for new conflict with those in whom what Marris calls the conservative impulse is stronger. This has repeatedly happened in the past and there is little reason to believe the future will be different.

PERSONAL AND IMPERSONAL PERSPECTIVES

Related to the notions of a world view and a way of life is the fact that most human beings view the world from two not always reconcilable perspectives. The first is the personal, subjective, or internal viewpoint. Closely connected with personal agency, it is the standpoint of the participant rather than the spectator and involves commitment to a particular world view and corresponding way of life. The second perspective views the world from an external standpoint. This more impersonal or objective perspective is closer to that of the detached observer than to that of the fully engaged agent. Although the external point of view may provide grounds for modifying or correcting the world view and way of life embraced from the internal perspective, it cannot by itself generate or maintain a way of life; it approximates what Thomas Nagel (1986) calls "the view from nowhere" and, if fully realized, would be the view of no one in particular.

Normal human beings, Nagel emphasizes, have the impulse and capacity to view the world from both perspectives. In ethics we cannot escape, if we do not want to relinquish our identities as particular persons, the internal or subjective viewpoint. It is largely from this viewpoint that we understand and express our identity-conferring commitments and our particular world view and way of life. To be a particular person is to see the world in a particular way, from a particular point in space and time, and to have certain commitments and connections to persons, places, ideas, and institutions that are not those of everyone else. It is, indeed, the multiplicity of world views and ways of life emanating from this viewpoint that gives rise to the myriad of conflicts that historically have driven human beings first to fighting, then to war, and more recently to ethics and politics. Yet what makes ethics and politics possible—and what distinguishes us from our distant ancestors and most, if not all, nonhuman animals and seriously mentally handicapped or mentally ill human beings—is our additional capacity to more or less transcend our particular world view and way of life and to view ourselves and the world as a whole from a more detached or external standpoint. From this viewpoint we can appreciate the contingency of our different and occasionally conflicting particular world views and ways of life and the extent to which they are the products of particular circumstances of history, culture, biology, and psychology that are, to a large extent, beyond our control.

The distinction between the two standpoints is, as Nagel points out, "really a matter of degree, and it covers a wide spectrum" (Nagel 1986, p. 5). During the normal course of psychological development, for example, a person gradually develops the capacity for an increasingly objective viewpoint. Moreover, Nagel adds, "a standpoint that is objective by comparison with the personal view of one individual may be subjective by comparison with a theoretical standpoint still farther out. The standpoint of morality is more objective than that of private life, but less objective than the standpoint of physics."

Both viewpoints are necessary for civilized life. Yet they often generate internal conflict; despite the heroic attempts of philosophers to do so, there appears to be no way to unify them or to reduce one to the other to entirely eliminate the tension (Beardsley 1960; Strawson 1962; Nagel 1986). As a married person, for example, one generally takes the personal perspective toward one's spouse. One regards him or her as an agent and responds accordingly, expressing gratitude and affection for some things and anger and disappointment at others. As a psychotherapist, on the other hand, one takes a more impersonal or detached attitude toward one's patients. The aim is to view their conduct and problems from an external, largely deterministic perspective and to employ one's knowledge and therapeutic skills to ameliorate what is troubling them. Problems arise, however, when one assumes both of these perspectives toward the same person. "The conflict between the therapeutic attitude," writes Lawrence Stern, "and that of normal personal relations is epitomized by Fitzgerald's hero in *Tender is the Night*, Dick Diver, who is psychiatrist and husband to the same woman. It is the conflict between the spontaneous enjoyment of a relationship and its calculated management" (Stern 1974, pp. 77–78). It is perhaps for this reason that physicians generally and psychotherapists in particular do not usually treat members of their own families and why some of us are always a bit uneasy about close personal friendships with members of the psychotherapeutic profession.[6]

People who become locked into one perspective or the other are in a number of senses unbalanced. Those who find it difficult to assume the more detached or impersonal viewpoint will overpersonalize their inevitable losses and frustrations and thereby find it difficult to contend with the vicissitudes of life. Consider how in consoling the bereaved we often remind them that we are all mortal and that if death had not come now to the person for whom we are mourning it would have come eventually. We may point out, too, that time is a great healer and that they will not always feel as empty and sad as they now feel. In so doing we encourage those who have suffered a great loss to balance (but not replace) their painful personal perspective with a more impersonal perspective. Attempts at this sort of balancing are common enough in certain situations to be embodied in some of our clichés, as, for example, when we remind a rejected and despondent lover or suitor that "there are other fish in the sea."

We can also become locked into the objective or impersonal perspective and here the balancing must go the other way. Those who find themselves incapable of forming close personal attachments and relationships as well as uncommitted to any particular projects are usually as unhappy and as in need of our support as the bereaved. In some cases, their loneliness and emptiness may be all the more desperate, leaving them seriously depressed or suicidal. Their need is to embrace a less-detached world view and way of life, one that will allow them to participate in the joy and risks of human relationships and to commit themselves to projects giving shape and meaning to their lives.

The metaphor or image suggested by these examples is that of tacking. In sailing into a wind we cannot set a direct course. Instead we proceed indirectly, heading first toward one side of our eventual destination, then toward the other side, then back to the first side, and so on. We sail back and forth along these opposing, counterbalancing tacks until we reach our destination. In life, too, we often find ourselves "heading into the wind" and we must judiciously tack between the personal and impersonal perspectives. Although there are situations in which we largely commit ourselves to one tack rather than another—for example, in (initially) falling in love or in conducting a particular scientific investigation—most of us cannot do so permanently nor should we so desire. Successful navigation in life, as on the sea, requires knowing when and how to tack between viewpoints. Those who remain utterly blind to a more objective or detached perspective of their lovers are ill-advised to make longstanding personal commitments to them; psychotherapists who cannot resist analyzing the actions, motives, and choices of everyone they meet are not yet ready for friendship or love.

The capacity to view the world from these two standpoints is what underlies our capacity for critical self-reflection, freedom of the will, and self-direction. Each perspective provides a standpoint for critically examining and constraining the other, providing the possibility for intelligently adapting to new circumstances and assuming some degree of control and responsibility for our lives. This capacity also allows us to understand and enjoy the works of Sophocles, Aristophanes, Shakespeare, Ingmar Bergman, and Woody Allen. Comedy, no less than tragedy, depends on the capacity to view the world (and ourselves) from different and often incongruous perspectives.

Can we, however, retain the personal or internal standpoint (and our identities as particular persons) if we acknowledge the truth of various descriptions of the world—including ourselves and our behavior— from the impersonal or external standpoint? Bernard Williams suggests that there is a sense in which the growth of reflective consciousness, based largely on viewing our conduct from outside, may "destroy ethical knowledge" if it undermines our confidence in the validity or applicability of the ethical concepts and categories associated with our particular world views and ways of life (1985, pp. 148, 167–69). If, for example, I come to understand my world view and way of life as determined by a particular set of historical, cultural, and psychological circumstances and that under different circumstances my values and principles would therefore have been correspondingly different, I may no longer be able to remain committed to them. It is thus that some religious fundamentalists and conservative nationalists worry about an approach to public schooling that emphasizes ecumenicism or, worse yet, secularism and internationalism. Either prayer, the Ten Commandments, and patriotism play a central role in the classroom or, they say, they will send their children to a different school or remove them from school entirely. What troubles them is that an approach to education based almost entirely on an external perspective—one that views our particular world views and ways of life as a product of various historical, cultural, and psychological contingencies—will significantly weaken the students' commitments to the world view and way of life of their parents.

This concern is not restricted to religious and political conservatives. Parents endorsing a particular world view and way of life may be troubled by their children being taught that it is just one among many and that in different historical and cultural circumstances it could have been otherwise. Will not this approach, as Yeats suggests in "The Second Coming," destroy all conviction and leave them vulnerable to the "passionate intensity" of those whose aggrandizing belief in one or another world view and way of life has been untempered by the external standpoint?

In most cases, however, our identity-conferring convictions—those grounded in particular world views and ways of life—are not as tenuous as this worry suggests. First, the impersonal viewpoint is not alien. It is, after all, our viewpoint (Nagel 1986). When I try to take a more objective, detached, or external view of myself or the world it is *I* who am trying to do so. I do not become someone else; nor do I cease, as an individual, to be anyone at all. The capacity to assume a more impersonal viewpoint is one of the things that characterizes me as a person (though not as a particular person). Thus to deny or repress the external perspective on the world and ourselves is to deny or repress an important aspect of the self as a person. Second, consider the way the internal perspective as manifested in participation in competitive games or athletics is able to survive external understanding. In the midst of playing a competitive game or participating in a competitive athletic event nothing may seem as important to one as winning. Yet later on, viewed externally, winning does not seem so important after all. It was "only a game"; whether one happens to have won or lost usually makes little difference to the world or one's life as a whole. But this does not mean that the next time one is engaged in the game or event one is not going to participate with the same level of intensity and place the same amount of importance on winning. The same is true of the resilience of the internal perspective in life generally. Viewing ourselves from outside may induce us to modify or alter, sometimes quite radically, our internally held world view and way of life. But to modify or alter a particular world view or way of life is still to have one.

Indeed, retaining a personal perspective and thus a particular world view and corresponding way of life may be entirely "natural" for us in the sense of being practically inescapable (Strawson 1985, pp. 31–50). It seems to be a brute fact about human beings that, whatever the external perspective reveals about the genesis of our world views and ways of life, we simply cannot help having a particular world view and way of life emanating from an internal perspective. If we are to remain sane we must regard ourselves as particular people—we must have a particular identity. And this we cannot do unless we have certain identity-conferring commitments that distinguish us from others. Thus we can no more be reasoned out of our proneness to the internal perspective and committing ourselves to a world view and way of life than we can be reasoned out of our belief in the existence of material objects (Strawson 1985, p. 32). World views, ways of life, and our understanding of material objects may as a result of scientific investigation and objective understanding be significantly altered. But they cannot be categorically abandoned. The internal perspective is deeply rooted in our nature as agents and as social beings. It can be modified and deeply transmuted by observations from the more impersonal and detached perspective, but it cannot be wholly transcended. Adopting an external perspective, then, will not in itself cause us to "lose all conviction." It may induce us to modify or revise our particular internal or personal perspective, but it cannot replace it. Dogmatically refusing to take an external perspective is, however, likely to leave us full of "passionate intensity" and unable to consider the possibility of compromise.

What makes compromise necessary is a multiplicity of conflicting, rationally irreconcilable world views and ways of life rooted in the personal perspective. What makes compromise possible is that we are also capable of adopting a more external perspective, one that allows us to acknowledge the contingency of our world views and ways of life and the equal legitimacy of others with which ours is, on at least some occasions, bound to conflict. The external perspective provides both the idea of the circumstances of compromise and our capacity to recognize them.

What do we do, however, when those with whom we are in conflict do not appear to acknowledge the external perspective? They do not appear to have the concept of a world view; theirs, they believe with more or less passionate intensity, is not a world view (that is, one among many more or less equally legitimate world views), it is rather the (only correct) view of the world. Is it possible, without begging the question, to show them why they should in some circumstances acknowledge the legitimacy and value of compromise? Are we, in other words, assuming the superiority of our own particular view of the world—a more or less liberal view that emphasizes pluralism and tolerance—when we urge others who may be inclined to view us as infidels to consider the virtues of compromise? I address this difficult and important question in Chapter 6.

RETHINKING ETHICAL THEORY

To abandon the Platonic Quest and the Doctrine of Moral Harmony is to relinquish the conception of an ethical theory as a complete, consistent, and comprehensive set of principles and rules, the less general derived from the more general, that commends itself to all insofar as they are rational and that provides, at least in principle, a decision procedure for resolving all moral conflicts and disagreements without remainder. This is not, however, to consign the principle of utility or Kant's categorical imperative to the dustbin of history; nor is it to embrace ethical skepticism or the more vulgar forms of ethical relativism. Much can be said for general principles, and they will be part of any adequate conception of ethics. They will not, however, be able to resolve all or perhaps even most of our moral problems.

Consider, for example, the principle of utility (that we ought to maximize the overall good, construed variously as pleasure, happiness, preference satisfaction, and so on) and the second formulation of Kant's categorical imperative (that persons ought to be respected, equally, as ends in themselves). These impersonal principles are connected to important and widely shared features of human life: sentience and the capacity for (rational) self-direction. A moral view or outlook that is indifferent to or contemptuous of either of these principles must be rejected. The principles of utility and respect for persons, regardless of certain difficulties and limitations, show that certain acts in certain circumstances are morally right while others are morally wrong. Other things being equal, it is morally right to do what we can to prevent, ameliorate, and cure painful and debilitating diseases. And it is morally wrong to coerce or manipulate another human being to serve as an object of one's sexual pleasure. These uncontroversial applications of the principle of utility and the principle of respect for persons, respectively, are sufficient to refute wholesale ethical skepticism and relativism. It is simply false that general, rationally justifiable principles have no role to play in regulating our moral judgments and choices and that morality is, at bottom, nothing more than a matter of personal preference or cultural mores. No ethical outlook making a claim to rational justification can wholly disregard the principle of utility or the Kantian principle of (equal) respect for persons. They are grounded in common characteristics of human life and there are, as the preceding examples show, situations in which their application is clear and decisive.

In addition to providing direct guidance in certain circumstances, these principles place significant limits on our world views and ways of life. World views and ways of life that, for example, systematically cause or permit avoidable pain and suffering or that fail to respect persons as ends in themselves must be rejected (or at least constrained) regardless of their historical roots or the threat to the integrity of those holding them. It is thus that world views and ways of life endorsing what clearly amounts to wanton cruelty, torture, human sacrifice, and slavery have over the course of history become fewer and those that remain are widely condemned. Campaigns against more subtle violations of the principles of utility and respect for persons are now being undertaken. Some—for example, those that have added "racism" and "sexism" to our vocabulary and thus identified moral wrongs that were not generally regarded as serious moral wrongs before—have already achieved significant success. Others—for example, those calling attention to the moral standing of nonhuman animals and prejudice against homosexuals—still have a long way to go.[7] But the general point remains. World views and ways of life that clearly and systematically violate these well-grounded principles must be restricted. Yet important as they are, the principles of utility and respect for persons fall short of serving as complete action guides. Taken by themselves, each underdetermines the full range of moral choice and judgment; taken together, they occasionally point in different directions.

Utilitarianism (the doctrine that the principle of utility is the only or most basic moral principle) founders when we disagree on what counts as the good to be maximized. When sharing the same world view and way of life or when, on certain issues, the requirements of different world views and ways of life coincide, we may well agree on what it is that we should maximize. It is thus that the Amish qua Amish, for example, can readily formulate the principle of utility in terms of a particularly Amish conception of the good and then use it to make decisions internal to their community; or that both the Amish and the non-Amish can agree on utilitarian grounds that the ravages of a preventable disease would be a bad thing and then join forces to combat it. There is no agreement, however, on a complete or comprehensive conception of the good apart from a particular world view and way of life; these are bound to differ and occasionally conflict. Thus we cannot appeal to the principle of utility to resolve conflicts rooted in opposing world views and ways of life without either begging the question (that is, favoring one conception or the other) or resorting to empty platitudes ("We should do whatever produces the most good").

Kantianism as a complete moral theory also presupposes agreement

in or overlapping of world view and way of life. One of the most heat-
edly contested moral controversies in the United States has to do with
the moral status of the embryo, the fetus, and the newborn (Weil and
Benjamin 1987). Should, for example, the fetus count as a full moral
person with an equal right to life or not? This question, which lies at
the heart of the abortion controversy, also underlies a number of other
controversies in biomedical ethics, including embryo research, the
treatment of seriously ill newborns, the use of anencephalic infants as
sources of transplantable organs, the "definition" of death, and treatment of persons who have suffered a permanent loss of consciousness
and who are in what has come to be known as a persistent vegetative
state (Cranford 1988; Wikler 1988). We cannot employ the principle of
respect for persons to resolve these problems because what is at issue
is precisely whether this principle is applicable to such entities. And
whether one regards the principle applicable to one or another class of
beings is largely a function of one's world view and way of life (Luker
1984a).[8]

Moreover, even if the principles of utility and equal respect were
able to provide more direct and complete guidance than in fact they
do, we would still be confronted with well-known difficulties where
the guidance that they give is conflicting when taken jointly. Consider, for example, the utilitarian's enthusiasm for biomedical research
on human subjects based on the good of the expected consequences as
opposed to the Kantian's scruples about respecting the experimental
subject's autonomy. If the results of the study promise to bring about
great good and if sound scientific design will not permit fully informing the subjects of its nature or risks, the doctrinaire utilitarian will
nonetheless be inclined to proceed. The Kantian, however, places
greater importance on individual self-determination than on overall
social good and is likely to oppose such a study. Similar conflicts involving the principle of utility and the Kantian principle of equal respect pervade the literature of normative ethics.

In cases—and there will be many—in which widely shared, rationally justifiable general principles, such as the principle of utility and
the principle of equal respect, do not provide clear direction either because they are indeterminate or because they conflict, we must acknowledge the legitimacy, as a moral justification, of appealing to
one's integrity and the important identity-conferring commitments
that it preserves. In such circumstances, it is a sufficient initial justifi-

cation of one's action or point of view to show that it is part and parcel of a world view and a way of life that do not clearly violate widely shared, rationally justified principles and that largely determine one's identity and give shape and meaning to one's life.[9]

An adequate initial justification of a particular ethical position on, say, the treatment of a seriously ill newborn will therefore acknowledge that it is rooted in a certain world view that gives shape and meaning to a certain way of life and that this is a legitimate, perhaps superior, way of life that does not violate more general principles of utility or equal respect. In giving such a justification one would be trying to persuade others of the validity of this world view and this way of life and urging—through words, witness, or example—that they either adopt these themselves or modify their own views to approximate them more closely. But as for oneself, one thinks at the outset there is no choice. To abandon one's position on this issue would be to do wrong and compromise one's identity and integrity as a particular person.

Ethical theorists who dismiss this type of justification out of hand—who disregard the importance of culturally and historically conditioned sentiment and the importance of identity, integrity, and a person's world view and way of life—overestimate the power of abstract general principles and underestimate the extent to which many of the things that really matter to us are grounded in what is local and particular rather than universal and general. How, then, should we address conflicts rooted in opposing world views and ways of life when general principles of utility and equal respect provide no clear direction or only question begging or conflicting direction? If we cannot resolve these conflicts, how can we ameliorate them? What help or guidance can ethical theorists provide?

Contemporary philosophers who criticize the ambitions of ethical theory have disappointingly little to say in response to these questions.[10] Only Putnam (1983, pp. 4–6) and Berlin (1988, pp. 17–18) endorse the notion of compromise, and only Berlin can actually bring himself to use the word:

> If the old perennial belief in the possibility of realizing ultimate harmony is a fallacy, . . . if we allow [that] Great Goods can collide; that some of them cannot live together, even though others can—in short, that one cannot have everything, in principle as well as in practice—and if human creativity may depend upon a

variety of mutually exclusive choices: then, as Chernyshevsky and Lenin once asked, "What is to be done?" How do we choose between possibilities? What and how much must we sacrifice to what? There is, it seems to me, no clear reply. But the collisions, even if they cannot be avoided, can be softened. Claims can be balanced, *compromises can be reached*: in concrete situations not every claim is of equal force—so much liberty and so much equality; so much for sharp moral condemnation, and so much for understanding a given human situation; so much for the full force of the law, and so much for the prerogative of mercy; for feeding the hungry, clothing the naked, healing the sick, sheltering the homeless (my emphasis).

This is good so far as it goes. But it does not go far enough. We need also, for example, to understand how compromise can be integrity preserving. One thing that keeps even moral philosophers who explicitly reject the Platonic Quest and the Doctrine of Moral Harmony from talking about compromise is the understandably high regard they have for integrity. The notions of compromise and integrity do not easily fit together. It is therefore one of the tasks of philosophical reflection to indicate insofar as possible under what circumstances and for what reasons compromise on a matter of ethics can be integrity preserving (Benjamin 1987).

More must also be said about when we should seek or maintain a compromise and when not, and about what we may do to facilitate the search for compromise and assure its stability. It is here that the principles of utility and equal respect play important roles. The principle of utility will often serve to motivate the search for compromise. And the principle of equal respect will help us to determine when to seek compromise and, in seeking compromise, what we may do to advance our favored position.

Thus the role of abstract or impersonal reason in ethics, although more limited than presupposed by the Platonic Quest or the Doctrine of Moral Harmony, is more extensive than suggested by most contemporary critics of these outlooks. In addition to placing restrictions on world views and ways of life, the principles of utility and respect for persons play important roles in determining when and how to devise well-grounded, integrity-preserving compromises.

5
Judgment and the
Art of Compromise

> Moral judgments are judgments, not deductions; they are not themselves deduced; they can be supported, defended, argued for or against, justified or established, but not deduced.
> —*Marcus George Singer*, "The Ideal of a Rational Morality"

> Judging is in important respects the mark of our humanity; it contributes to the humanizing of our world as no other human faculty does. To attempt to reflect on this human capacity is thus to meditate on what is distinctive of our humanity, on what it is to be human or to constitute a human world.
> —*Ronald Beiner*, Political Judgment

Some two-party moral conflicts are rationally irreconcilable—the most we can hope for in the way of peaceful accommodation is an integrity-preserving compromise. But how do we know when to seek compromise and when not? And if we wish to compromise, how do we identify those that are both well grounded and integrity preserving? Is there a method that will yield determinate answers to these and related questions? The demand for such a method is, I believe, misconceived. Deciding to seek, accept, or maintain a moral compromise is a matter of judgment.

MORAL JUDGMENTS ARE JUDGMENTS

Influenced by impressive achievements in the mathematical and empirical sciences, philosophers often aspire to a model of ethical reasoning that leaves little or no room for the exercise of judgment. Their aim is an algorithmic decision procedure for resolving moral problems. Dubbed by Arthur Caplan the engineering model of applied ethics, this approach requires first that we acquire knowledge of ethical theories and then that we "apply" them by: "a) *deducing* conclusions from theories in light of relevant empirical facts and descriptions of circumstances and b) analyzing the process of the deduction" (1983, p. 314; my emphasis). Once one has determined the correct or appropriate theory, ascertained the facts, and checked the validity of the deduction, there is little room for the exercise of judgment. The truth of the premises, as in valid deductive reasoning generally, forces or guarantees the truth of the conclusion.

I have, in the preceding chapter, rejected the quest for the sort of comprehensive, widely acceptable ethical theories required by the engineering model. Yet even those who can be persuaded to abandon the Platonic Quest and the Doctrine of Moral Harmony and to acknowledge the (occasional) need for compromise are likely to ask us to specify a set of conditions that will tell us when and how to compromise. But this is not possible; to insist that we specify such conditions is to embrace a mistaken conception of ethical reasoning, one that denies Marcus G. Singer's important reminder that "moral judgments are judgments."

Underlying the request for a decision procedure or set of necessary and sufficient conditions for moral compromise is an idealization of method. "Methodism," as Sheldon Wolin calls it, is the doctrinaire demand that all rational thought and decision be modeled on the impersonality, precision, and quantifiability of mathematical or (certain forms of) scientific reasoning (Wolin 1972). The aim is to devise a uniform procedure or set of rules that if correctly applied to a certain question will yield the same determinate conclusions for all—a moral algorithm. Once formulated, the method can be employed more or less mechanically by anyone capable of learning the rules.

This "rationalistic conception of rationality," as Bernard Williams suggests, is closely allied to contemporary "administrative ideas of rationality" or "modern bureaucratic" conceptions (Williams 1985, pp. 18, 197, 206). Its aim is to replace the essentially social or dialogical nature of reflective judgment, as well as its variability, uncertainty, and unpredictability, with a set of impersonal rules that can and should be followed to the very same end by anyone capable of understanding them.

Whatever the value and success of methodism in other areas and disciplines—and they are considerable—it plays a more limited role in ethics and politics, especially in connection with moral compromise. Compromise in ethics is more a matter of practical rather than technical reasoning, and more the outcome of reflective judgment rather than of a rationalistic decision procedure. We cannot reduce what is often called the art of compromise to an impersonal algorithmic method or science. Even if it were possible to do so, it would in certain respects be undesirable. It would relieve us not only of the burdens of judgment but also of our freedom and, as Beiner suggests, our humanity (1983, p. 166). Those who aspire to replace the discretionary aspects of moral judgment with a more determinate method or decision procedure often point to the sciences as a model of what they seek. But their conception of scientific rationality bears only partial resemblance to actual scientific practice. A historical understanding of the nature of scientific reasoning, as Kuhn maintains in *The Structure of Scientific Revolutions* (1970), reveals a different picture.

Although there are aspects of scientific practice (what Kuhn calls normal science) that involve the application of a fairly determinate method, the more foundational questions and decisions in science— those involving choices between competing comprehensive theories or "paradigms"—do not. Conflicts between competing overarching theories or paradigms cannot be resolved by a more or less mechanical application of determinate, theory-neutral criteria. No such criteria were available to those who had to choose, for example, between Ptolemy's astronomical theory and that of Copernicus, between the oxygen theory of combustion and the phlogiston theory, or between Newtonian mechanics and the quantum theory. When a group of scientists disagree about such matters, Kuhn points out, "there is no neutral algorithm for theory choice, no systematic decision procedure which, properly applied, must lead each individual in the group to the same decision" (1970, pp. 199–200).

This is not to say (as Kuhn's dramatic overstatements occasionally imply and his critics uncharitably infer) that rationality has no role in deciding between competing comprehensive theories. This would be so only if technical rationality were the sole form of rationality; only if, in other words, a choice could not be regarded as rational unless it were the deductive outcome of applying a standardized set of fully determinate, wholly consistent, theory-neutral rules or criteria. But a priori exclusive commitment to this highly idealized conception of scientific reasoning reduces to absurdity. The actual practice of good science provides our best model of scientific rationality (Kuhn 1970, p. 144). And this practice, when carefully examined, reveals that choices among competing comprehensive theories are not the product of mechanically applying a set of theory-neutral rules or criteria. If a philosophical account of rational decision making in certain areas of science is not embodied in the practice of good scientists doing good science, it is the philosophical understanding that must give way, not scientific practice.

How, then, do scientists choose between competing comprehensive theories? If they do not and cannot appeal to an algorithmic decision procedure to fully resolve their differences and yet are said to choose rationally, how do they reason? Kuhn acknowledges standard criteria for evaluating the comparative adequacy of competing comprehensive theories. Accuracy, consistency, scope, simplicity, and fruitfulness, he agrees, all "play a vital role when scientists must choose between an established theory and an upstart competitor" (1977, p. 322). But two difficulties arise when we assume that these useful and important criteria provide a mechanical procedure for choosing between competing theories. First, taken separately they are *imprecise*: "Individuals may legitimately differ about their applications to concrete cases." Of two competing theories, for example, one might be more accurate in one respect and the other more accurate in another respect. Second, when taken together these criteria "repeatedly prove to *conflict* with one another; accuracy may, for example, dictate the choice of one theory, scope the choice of its competitor" (Kuhn 1977, p. 322; my emphasis). Thus

> when scientists must choose between competing theories, two men fully committed to the same list of criteria for choice may nevertheless reach different conclusions. Perhaps they interpret simplicity differently or have different convictions about the range of fields within which the consistency criterion must be met. Or perhaps they agree about these matters but differ about the relative weights to be accorded to these or to other criteria when several are deployed together. With respect to divergences of this sort, no set of choice criteria yet proposed is of any use (Kuhn 1977, p. 324).

Instead of construing accuracy, consistency, scope, simplicity, and fruitfulness as rules that fully determine choice, Kuhn proposes that we regard them as values that influence it. As a set of rules, accuracy, scope, and so on underdetermine theory choice, but as values they frame the arguments and debates and help to shape and support the judgments that scientists make that one theory is, on balance, better than another.

The exercise of human judgment in choosing between competing, comprehensive scientific theories is, according to Kuhn, inescapable. But judgment, he hastens to add, is not to be confused with arbitrary preference. Judgments, as opposed to mere expressions of individual taste, are "eminently discussable" and need to be backed up by reasons even if these reasons (for example, greater accuracy, more consistent, wider scope, and so on) do not deductively or methodically function as determinate rules or criteria and thereby "dictate" choice. Judgment falls somewhere between algorithmic decision procedures, on the one hand, and expressions of mere preference or taste, on the other. It is rational without being narrowly (or mechanically) rationalistic. Within the parameters established by uniform, impersonal rules or criteria, different people's judgments will reflect their differing experiences as scientists, differing wider cultural commitments, and differing attitudes toward, say, the value of comprehensive, unified theories as opposed to "precise and detailed problem solutions of apparently narrower scope" (Kuhn 1977, p. 325). Fully understanding an individual scientist's particular judgment of the superiority of one comprehensive theory over another requires acquaintance not only with shared, general criteria, but also with "idiosyncratic factors dependent on individual biography and personality" (Kuhn 1977, p. 329). The criteria significantly guide and limit the scientist's choice, but they do not in themselves deductively entail or "dictate" it.

A judgment may be rationally supportable—we can provide what John Stuart Mill calls "considerations . . . capable of determining the intellect either to give or withhold its assent" (1861, p. 7)—without satisfying the orthodox methodist's demand for deductive certainty. Judgment differs, in this respect, from both matters of (mere) taste and matters of (conclusive) proof. Making a judgment requires more in the way of rational dialogue than either expressing a preference or deducing a conclusion. There is, as the saying goes, no disputing matters of taste (such as one's preference among flavors of ice cream). Similarly, there is no disputing matters of algorithmic rationality (such as finding the greatest common divisor of a pair of numbers). It is, however, always possible to question even the best judgment about which of two competing theories or paradigms is best—though to be taken seriously one must provide reasons for one's doubts and be prepared to engage in dialectical discussion of the matter (Kuhn 1977, p. 336–37). Scientific judgment is in this respect similar to moral judgment, as one can see by replacing "moral" with "scientific" in the following: "Moral judgments are judgments, not deductions; they are not themselves deduced; they can be supported, defended, argued for or against, justified or established, but not deduced" (M. G. Singer 1986, p. 26).

To carry the comparison further we might add that within a particular world view and way of life, as within a particular scientific theory or paradigm, one may come very close to "deducing" conclusions from the values and principles that help structure that world view and way of life (Gewirth 1960)—though even here there are important limits to pure deduction (Williams 1985, pp. 126ff.). But when conflicts are rooted in conflicting (and incommensurable) world views and ways of life, we cannot without begging the question resolve a conflict by appealing to criteria justified by only one of them. If more or less neutral, commonly held principles of utility or equal respect do not straightforwardly settle the matter we must, in deciding what to do, exercise our judgment. The result may with luck be either a plausible synthesis position that combines the strengths of each initial position and is rooted equally in both world views and ways of life or a well-grounded, integrity-preserving compromise. Judgment would be involved not only in deciding to seek a synthesis or compromise but also in attempting to craft or devise one and, having done this, deciding whether to accept it. If we decide not to seek a mutually acceptable synthesis or compromise or if our efforts to devise one or the other are unsuccessful, we shall have to make other judgments about what we should do about the conflict.

JUDGMENT AND PRACTICAL KNOWLEDGE

So long as we must make decisions in unprecedented or unpredictable situations and circumstances, we will have to rely on judgment. Consider in this connection the difference between evaluating the performance of speed skaters and the performance of figure skaters. The aspiration of methodism is to model all evaluation on the evaluation of speed skating. Certainly there is a clear decision procedure for determining that one skater is faster than another. Indeed, properly designed and programmed machines can probably do a better job at evaluating and comparing speed skaters than humans can. Machines cannot, however, take over the evaluation of competitive figure skating. "In a world of triple axels, double toe loops, death spirals and sit spins," Michael Janofsky writes, "clocks and yardsticks have no place. Figure skaters can be measured only for their height, weight and boot size" (1988, pp. 27ff.).

Olympic figure skating is evaluated by a panel of as many as nine judges from different countries. But their judgments are not purely arbitrary or simply a matter of taste. Judgment, in this context as in most others, falls between simply expressing an opinion and deducing a conclusion. Becoming a qualified judge requires training and experience. One employs criteria—analogous in many respects to the values Kuhn identifies as regulating judgments among competing scientific theories or paradigms—in determining that one skater's performance is better than another's. Nonetheless, qualified judges will occasionally disagree. Sometimes this is attributable to conscious or unconscious bias or to mistake, but not always. The judges may later give reasons for their decisions and discuss and debate them. But when both the skaters and the judges are very good, there is no external court of appeal that is anything more than yet another human judgment. We cannot, as we might if we were to disagree about which of two skaters is faster, appeal to an accurate clock.[1]

Among the aspects of figure skating that systematically resist methodist modes of assessment are "the artistry of the performance, with consideration given to a mix of athleticism and esthetics" (Janofsky 1988). One cannot antecedently specify determinate criteria for evaluating this component of a figure skater's performance without denying his or her artistic creativity. To presume to do so is to imply that the skater will be unable to come up with anything of artistic merit that the judges have not already conceived.

This should remind us of an important aspect of human judgment. Contexts calling for its exercise are not antecedently closed; we cannot presume to know everything there is to know about them. As David Wiggins points out in an interpretative reconstruction of Aristotle's account of deliberation and practical reason, "The unfinished or indeterminate character of our ideals and value structure is constitutive both of human freedom and, for finite creatures who face an indefinite or infinite range of contingencies with only finite powers of prediction and imagination (*Nicomachean Ethics* 1137b), of practical rationality itself" (1980, p. 234). In the limited but instructive case of figure skating, the point is that the open-ended nature of creative activity does not permit us to mechanically apply antecedently determined criteria for evaluating the artistic aspects of a performance. More generally, finite beings like ourselves, in acknowledging the indefinite or infinite range of (occasionally unprecedented) contingencies in which we are called upon to act, cannot replace the exercise of judgment with the methodical application of antecedently determined rules or criteria. To do so would, pace methodism, be irrational.

The law provides an especially good illustration of this point. Perhaps nothing comes as close to a determinate, comprehensive, widely acceptable system for the regulation of conduct in certain areas of life as the law. Yet the legal system employs judges, and judges, as Annette Baier observes, are required to judge:

> The judge is an expert on the law, but the law does not make his decisions for him. A judge, making up his mind on a case, has, to guide him, a stable background of valid statute, accepted precedent, agreement about the spirit as well as the letter of the law; but these give him room for judgment. A judge in a court of appeal may reverse that original decision, change the Law's mind on a case, but not by rejecting that background" (1979, p. 63).

Even the best legal system, then, must remain unfinished or not fully determinate if it is to respond rationally and with integrity to unprecedented or hitherto unrecognized circumstances and conditions. What is true of legal judgment is also true of moral judgment. Moral judgment requires "a sense of the moral requirements and possibilities of the situation which goes beyond what the rules by themselves can tell us" (Larmore 1981, p. 279).

Yet the ideological power of orthodox methodism is a force to be reckoned with. Its manifestation in constitutional law is the dubious doctrine of original intention. But this notion that constitutional questions can be resolved by straightforwardly consulting the original intentions of the framers is beset with intractable difficulty. Not only must we rely on interpretation and judgment in determining the framers' intentions as they drafted the Constitution, but we must also do so in seeking constitutional direction about issues unforeseen two centuries ago. The original intentions of the framers, supposing they can be determined, will not, for example, tell us whether a wiretap is the sort of "search" for which the police must obtain a warrant.

Elsewhere what might be called the mania for method or the flight from judgment runs rampant in philosophy and the social sciences, at least in the United States (Wolin 1972; C. Taylor 1971; Rorty 1979). It is particularly acute in bureaucratically or administratively driven education where so-called objective or standardized tests foster the illusion that (mere) human judgment has been transcended. But reliance on multiple-choice testing and mechanical scoring does not eliminate the exercise of judgment; it simply relocates it, keeping it out of view of the corrective power of critical assessment. Determining what to teach and what to test is a matter of judgment as is the belief that answering the teacher's multiple-choice or true-false questions is the best indication of knowledge or mastery of the particular subject matter. Moreover, an emphasis on "objective" or short-answer testing implies that practically everything worth knowing or learning about a particular area is already known by the teacher or the authors of the textbook. This, however, is no more plausible when applied to education—especially higher education—than it is when applied to figure skating. In writing a critical or creative essay or paper, a student can display not only factual understanding (analogous to the compulsories in figure skating competition) but also creative performance in raising new questions, making new criticisms, seeing new connections, putting things together in new ways, and so on. The "scoring" or evaluation of such endeavors can no more be left to a machine than can the evaluation of a figure skater's performance. It requires that the teacher, like the scientist comparing rival theories or the judge evaluating a figure skater, exercise reflective judgment.

Judgments of this kind are inescapable; we make or tacitly endorse them all of the time. That one skater is faster than another or that one student does better than another on a true-false test is determined by a mechanical decision procedure; but that speed skating is an important or worthwhile activity or that true-false tests are a valid, educationally sound measure of student ability or progress is not. Plausible answers to questions about why we should compare the speed of various skaters or measure the number of correct answers students give to a true-false test cannot come to an end in the outcome of yet another decision procedure; for the locus of inquiry will then shift to the value or importance of this higher-order decision procedure, and so on *ad infinitum*. Yet chains of deductive justification do come to an end, and where they do one will find that they rest on judgment, which in turn rests on practical reasoning and practical knowledge. They come to an end where we judge (reflectively or pre-reflectively, rightly or wrongly) in this circumstance that continued "why" questions will have little or no bearing on our actions or that the (practical) costs of further questioning outweigh the benefits of acting on the basis of the current level of justification (Wittgenstein 1953, secs. 217, 485). It is thus that even deductive justification rests ultimately on (practical) judgment.

What, then, is involved in judgment, particularly moral judgment? What makes one moral judgment better than another? How does one learn to make good moral judgments? How, when one is a party or witness to what appears to be a rationally irreconcilable moral conflict, does one judge, first, that a compromise may be in order; second, that of the alternatives, one compromise position is more plausible than the others; and third, that, all things considered, the parties to the disagreement should either accept the compromise or reject it? We cannot provide very full answers to these questions. In some respects, this is because a fixation on methodism has until comparatively recently kept psychologists from undertaking the relevant lines of research. In other respects, the very nature of judgment places limits on what can be said in books or articles in response to questions of this kind.

It is useful at the outset to distinguish "technical" knowledge from "practical" knowledge. Technical knowledge can be abstractly acquired from books and lectures and then employed in step-by-step fashion. The method of truth tables for assessing validity in propositional logic is a good example. Practical knowledge, by contrast, "exists only in practice, and the only way to acquire it is by apprenticeship to a master—not because the master can teach it (he cannot), but because it can be acquired only by continuous contact with one who is perpetually practicing it" (Oakeshott 1962, pp. 10–11). Insofar as judgment is more a matter of practical than technical knowledge, it cannot be fully acquired by reading theoretical or how-to books or by attending a series of lectures.

This is especially true of moral judgment. "There is very little positive we can say about the nature of moral judgment itself," Larmore rightly observes. "We find ourselves providing what are really negative descriptions: the activity of moral judgment goes beyond what is given in the content of moral rules, characteristic sentiments, and tradition and training. We appear able to say only what judgment is *not*, and not what it *is*" (1981, p. 293). This is not, however, because judgment is an utterly mysterious, almost mystical faculty that should be replaced by more explicitly discursive or rational decision procedures. The limitation is not with judgment but rather with the sort of technical reason for which books, articles, and lectures provide such a useful medium of communication. It is a prejudice of methodism, and one that most of us brought up in a relentlessly methodist culture must constantly resist, that anything worth knowing or acquiring must be able to be articulated and conveyed as technical knowledge.

Situations calling for the exercise of judgment are moving targets whose existence and trajectory cannot be antecedently determined, at least not fully. Because we cannot adequately predict the circumstances calling for judgments of various kinds, we cannot provide a determinate or deductive decision procedure for making them. This is a logical point. Judgments so determined are no longer, strictly speaking, judgments. Just as we cannot logically predict the course of radical conceptual innovation in science, we cannot provide a conclusive decision procedure for making judgments.[2] If we have a complete decision procedure, there is no room for the exercise of judgment; the exercise of judgment implies a gap between whatever deductive procedures may be instrumental in our decision making and our final decision (Williams 1985, pp. 126–27). It is in filling this gap that our minds, as Annette Baier puts it, find "room to operate":

> Neither the adoption of necessary means to one's ends nor the observance of categorical imperatives (of morals or manners or mathematics) gives one's mind any room to operate. Where matters are cut and dried, where there is not choice of what to do, we can "use our brains," exhibit intelligence, even conscientiousness, but not wisdom or even prudence. These show only in matters where there is room for difference of opinion, where no problem-solver gives *the* correct answer, where thoughts tend to be followed by second thoughts (1979, p. 63).

Psychological understanding of the development and nature of practical knowledge is comparatively primitive. As one might expect in a culture dominated by methodist assumptions, psychologists have for the most part been preoccupied with the capacity for and development of technical knowledge. Some, however, have recently turned their attention to forms of intelligence or understanding involved in practical knowledge or judgment (Neisser 1979; Gardner 1983; Sternberg and Wagner 1986). Acknowledging the limitations of technical knowledge in making sound judgments in social or practical contexts, these theorists are attempting to identify what additional factors are involved. Once the factors have been identified, we may be able to trace their development and draw some conclusions as to how they may best be cultivated or fostered.

Frederiksen, for example, has found that standard tests of aptitude or intelligence administered by schools measure, at best, skills that are taught in school or that predict success in school. This is academic intelligence.

> "Practical" intelligence, on the other hand, may be thought of as what is reflected in one's cognitive responses to almost everything outside the school—the problem situations that arise naturally as one goes about his daily life. Such problems are often ill structured: they do not provide all the information needed to solve the problem, there are no definite criteria for determining when the problem is solved, they are often complex . . . . The settings and the tasks generally do not resemble those encountered in school, and the problems rarely appear in multiple-choice form. Responses are not necessarily motivated by a need to get the right answer, and performance can be described in terms of many dimensions other than the number of correct answers. In view of such contrasts, it is not surprising that aptitude and intelligence tests often fail to predict very successfully evaluations of success in anything except educational accomplishment (Frederiksen 1986, p.84).

Improved understanding of practical intelligence requires not only studies of complex behavior in a variety of natural settings (including, for example, how scientists solve actual scientific problems and how politicians solve actual political problems) but also more adequate conceptions of human intelligence, conceptions that acknowledge its practical and experiential dimensions, its context dependence, and its reliance on judgment.

In an intriguing study, Ceci and Liker (1986) identify fourteen racetrack handicappers who were able to predict the top finisher in ten harness races 93 percent of the time and the top three horses in their correct order of finish in these races 53 percent of the time. The probabilities of these outcomes attributable to chance alone were 12 percent and .00025 percent, respectively. These fourteen men, dubbed experts by Ceci and Liker, made their predictions on the basis of their extensive past experience and study of a publication detailing the past performance of competing horses and drivers. This publication, the *Early Form*, is published one day prior to race day and "contains all of the relevant past performance statistics for the next day's racing card but does not contain official assessments of probable favorites, post-time odds, or any other evaluative information" (Ceci and Liker 1986, p. 124). Ceci and Liker administered standard IQ tests to these fourteen men and discovered no correlation between their IQ scores and their ability either to predict the top finisher in a race or to predict the top three finishers in correct order. The investigators then attempted to show that the experts' handicapping skill involved quite high-level reasoning processes and that the judgments involved were enormously complex. "We doubt," they say, "that any profession—be it scientists, lawyers, or bankers—engages in a more intellectually demanding form of decision making than these expert handicappers" (Ceci and Liker 1986, p. 132). Among other things, this study casts doubt on the prevailing conception of intelligence as a "single underlying intellectual force" that can be adequately measured and then simply applied irrespective of practical experience or context. It shows, too, that racetrack handicapping involves complex reasoning and judgment. Experts, as Ceci and Liker reveal, "*go beyond the raw data in the racing program*, assigning 'weights' to each variable, systematically combining the various variables in complex, *nonadditive* ways, and computing a rough odds/probability equivalent for each horse. If this approach sounds cumbersome and time consuming, it is. Experts typically devote six to eight hours handicapping ten eight-horse races" (1986, p. 132; my emphasis).

This is an important line of research. Yet it is at this point comparatively undeveloped. If the exercise of judgment is to a large extent contextual, we must extend studies of this kind to a large variety of contexts in which we are called upon to employ practical knowledge and intelligence. What about the judgments required in the practice of law, medicine, politics, counseling, or teaching? What about judgments made in the course of everyday living such as selecting a mate, raising one's children, handling one's personal finances, and so on? And what about the exercise of moral judgment in any of these contexts? Further research should eventually shed more light on these and related questions. Some people, it is clear, have better judgment in some of these contexts than do others. And a person may have astute judgment in one area of life (for example, in practicing a certain trade or profession) and quite poor judgment in another (for example, as a parent or with respect to personal finances). A more adequate understanding of the psychological characteristics that contribute to successful judgment in various contexts is vital if we are to foster the relevant forms of practical knowledge and the capacity for sound judgment that is their manifestation.

In the meantime, however, we must make do with a number of very general but nonetheless useful reminders. First, it is the beginning of wisdom on this topic to emphasize the distinction between technical and practical reasoning. We should not expect that more and more technical knowledge will obviate the need for informed, reflective judgment. So long as we remain "finite creatures who face an indefinite or infinite range of contingencies with only finite powers of prediction and imagination" (Wiggins 1980, p. 234), we shall need to make judgments. It is thus that we ought to cultivate in ourselves and in others the capacity and willingness to review and revise previously held positions in response to new information, insights, arguments, or understanding. "No theory," as Wiggins emphasizes,

> if it is to recapitulate or reconstruct practical reasoning even as well as mathematical logic recapitulates or reconstructs the actual experience of conducting or exploring a deductive argument, can treat the concerns which an agent brings to any situation as forming a closed, complete, consistent system. For it is of the essence of these concerns to make competing and inconsistent claims. (This is a mark not of irrationality but of *rationality* in the face of the plurality of ends and the plurality of human goods.) The weight of the claims represented by these concerns is not nec-

essarily fixed in advance. Nor need the concerns be hierarchically ordered. Indeed, a man's reflection on a new situation that confronts him may disrupt such order and fixity as had previously existed, and bring a change in his evolving conceptions of the point, or the several or many points of living and acting (1980, p. 233).

It is not yet clear how one acquires the disposition and capacity to reflectively review and revise previously held positions. Psychological investigations into practical knowledge and intelligence may provide detailed insight on this matter. Until then, however, it is reasonable to suppose that this and related dispositions and capacities are often fostered by example, encouragement, and criticism (Baier 1979, p. 64). We learn to make good judgments in various contexts first by emulating others who are regarded as having sound judgment, and then responding to their evaluations and guidance. The external dialogue we undertake both with those to whom we must justify our initial judgments and with our mentors is eventually internalized and we learn to "fly solo."

I return now, after what may seem like a long digression, to moral compromise. Having seen, first, that judgment is an ineliminable component of moral judgment and, second, that it is largely a matter of practical rationality, we are better prepared to examine the place of judgment in the circumstances of compromise.

JUDGMENT AND COMPROMISE

Deciding to seek, devise, or accept a compromise on a matter of rationally irreconcilable moral conflict is more a matter of practical than of technical reasoning, more the outcome of reflective judgment than of a rationalistic decision procedure. There are, however, certain values that structure, guide, and help to assess the exercise of judgment in the circumstances of compromise. A scientist's judgment that one comprehensive theory is, on balance, preferable to another is not, as we have seen, unconstrained. Accuracy, consistency, scope, simplicity, and fruitfulness, as Kuhn points out, "play a vital role when scientists must choose between an established theory and an upstart competitor" (1977, p. 322). But such considerations do not and cannot in themselves fully determine theory choice. Different scientists with differing personal backgrounds and scientific goals will interpret these values differently and, in cases of conflict, place more weight on some than on others. Moreover, psychological factors that are not yet well understood render some scientists more adept than others at making this kind of judgment.

The same is generally true, *mutatis mutandis*, when we turn to compromise. Whether parties to an ethical disagreement should seek or accept a compromise is at bottom a matter of judgment. As judgment, a decision to seek or accept compromise will be highly context dependent and turn in part on insight, imagination, and interpersonal sensitivity and skill. It will turn, too, on complex and often unpredictable interactions of particular historically situated individuals. Still, as in science, the exercise of judgment is not simply a matter of taste. Arguments must be given and defended. And underlying these arguments must be certain values—corresponding to accuracy, consistency, scope, simplicity, and fruitfulness—that, though imprecise and occasionally conflicting, frame and guide one's judgments.

The principal values framing or guiding the exercise of judgment in the circumstances of compromise are individual integrity, overall utility (including social integrity), and equal respect . We are concerned, first, for our integrity as individuals and the identity-conferring commitments that give shape and meaning to our lives. Next is utilitarian concern for social welfare. How, we must ask, will a particular compromise affect the overall good? Indeed, the overall utility of social (or institutional) integrity will in many contexts be as important as individual (or personal) integrity (Ryan 1972; Mitchell 1982). Finally, there is a Kantian concern for respecting the choices, decisions, and viewpoints of others and for securing their informed, uncoerced agreement to our proposals by providing reasons that they cannot, insofar as they are rational, reasonably reject (Scanlon 1982). Agreement of this kind is valued not only if it furthers the overall good but also because it expresses a form of social relationship—one of mutual respect—that, other things being equal, is valued for its own sake. We may therefore in some instances opt for an outcome secured by informed, uncoerced agreement even if it does not maximize overall welfare.

Consideration of all three of these values is required if we are to be true to ourselves as complex beings with the capacity to view the world from both personal and impersonal perspectives (Chapter 4, pp. 95–101). Individual integrity is largely a function of personal perspective and is highly contextual. Our identity and integrity as particular persons is determined by local and particular rather than universal and general considerations. Our concern for overall welfare and for equal respect are, on the other hand, a function of our capacity to assume a more external perspective. When, therefore, we find ourselves in the circumstances of compromise, integrity, utility, and equal respect play vital roles in guiding and grounding our judgments as we try to determine, first, if we should seek compromise, and, second, whether a well-grounded, mutually satisfactory compromise position is actually available. As with accuracy, consistency, scope, simplicity, and fruitfulness in science, however, these values underdetermine choice.

Taken separately, the notions of individual integrity, overall welfare, and mutual respect are imprecise. Parties to a particular ethical dispute may, for example, legitimately differ as to whether in a particular instance compromising at all or adopting a particular compromise constitutes an excessive threat to individual integrity. Parties to an ethical disagreement may also differently estimate and interpret the effects of a particular compromise (or the failure to compromise) on utility and respect. Taken together, considerations of individual integrity, overall welfare, and respect for persons will in certain circumstances conflict. Although the notion of an integrity-preserving compromise suggests that in some cases of conflict each of these values can be adequately accommodated, it will not always be possible to devise compromises that are for all parties sufficiently integrity preserving. Those who, though valuing utility and equal respect, believe that in a certain situation the integrity of their particular world view and way of life would be devastated by compromise may judge differently from those whose world view and way of life may in the same situation be more accommodating. Kristen Luker has, for example, suggested that the strength of such a threat to the world views and ways of life of both prolife and prochoice activists on the question of abortion makes compromise on this troubling issue unlikely (1984a, p. 10). We will examine this topic in greater detail in Chapter 6.

Though falling short of a methodist decision procedure, then, considerations of integrity, welfare, and respect frame the relevant arguments and debates and help to shape and support our judgments on whether to seek and accept moral compromise. To qualify and be respected as rational, our judgments about compromise must be framed in terms of these values and we must be prepared to respond to questions or criticisms based on differing interpretations or weighings of them. In making and defending such judgments, we affirm our identity as complex beings capable of viewing ourselves from a number of perspectives and at the same time we acknowledge the capacity and rights of others to do so as well.

Other matters are also important. As our consideration of practical knowledge and intelligence suggests, some people are likely to be better at making judgments in certain contexts than are others. Among the personal characteristics that aid in devising well-grounded compromises on matters of ethics are a fertile imagination and interpersonal sensitivity. In many contexts the best or only plausible moral compromise cannot literally split the difference between the contending parties. A well-grounded, integrity-preserving compromise will often require a good bit of creative imagination. Parties seeking compromise must also be sensitive to the situation and feelings of those involved. Accepting a moral compromise usually involves relinquishing, at least temporarily, part of one's world view and way of life. We should in negotiating compromise be sensitive to this loss by acknowledging and attempting to ameliorate it. It is because instruments for measuring academic intelligence are blind to such contributors to practical intelligence as moral imagination and interpersonal sensitivity that there is little direct correlation between conventional academic skill and achievement, on the one hand, and skill and achievement in devising and maintaining well-grounded moral compromise, on the other.

Finally, because compromise is largely a matter of judgment and because judgment is so highly context dependent, it is difficult to determine from a distance whether, and if so how, a particular ethical disagreement should be resolved by compromise. The best we can do in presenting illustrations is to identify what appear to be fairly clear cases or to reconstruct and carefully analyze highly detailed case studies of more complex situations.

The three examples presented in Chapter 2 (the case study involving the intensive care unit; the Warnock Committee's compromise on embryo research; and the compromise between the American Cancer Society and the American College of Obstetricians and Gynecologists on how frequently women should undergo Pap smears) show that moral compromise may adequately satisfy the demands of individual integrity, utility, and mutual respect. Although not immune to challenge (any moral compromise will by its very nature be more or less controversial), these compromises seem, on the basis of the information provided, to be the products of sound judgment.

In other situations it is equally clear that moral compromise is out of the question, though prudential or tactical considerations will occasionally weigh heavily for "compromising" in another sense. There is no ethical reason to accommodate conduct that flagrantly and seriously violates considerations of utility or equal respect or to accommodate the world view and way of life in which it is rooted. Moral compromise with Nazis, racists, sexists, or rapists should, for example, be rejected out of hand, even if in some circumstances prudential considerations lead one to "compromise"—or, more accurately, to capitulate—in the face of their greater power.

Many cases will not be so clear, but there will often be grounds for judgment. Consider, for example, controversy over the response of the West to Ayatollah Ruhollah Khomeini's call in 1989 for the assassination of Salman Rushdie, whose novel *The Satanic Verses* the Ayatollah and many other Muslims consider blasphemous. In an article entitled "Rushdie's Book Is an Insult," former president Jimmy Carter urges the West to be "sensitive to the concern and anger that prevail even among the more moderate Moslems" (*New York Times*, 5 March 1989). Preoccupation with Rushdie's right to freedom of speech, Carter contends, should be attenuated and balanced by a sympathetic understanding of how deeply his book offends the Muslim consciousness. Expressions of outrage and denunciation by the West would, he hopes, give way to "tactful public statements and private discussions" to "defuse this explosive situation."

The former president's suggestion was later contested in a letter to the editor. Underlying Carter's point of view, writes Jerome M. Balsam,

> is the naive belief that every conflict is susceptible of resolution by reasonable compromise. As Iran made clear . . . it will be satisfied by nothing short of censorship in the West, and even that would not lead to revocation of the call for Mr. Rushdie's execution. Ayatollah Khomeini's campaign, whatever its underlying motive, must be seen as a frontal assault on Western values. On this there can be no compromise.

"If the West cannot stand for freedom of expression," Balsam adds, "it cannot stand for anything at all" (*New York Times*, 19 March 1989).

Balsam's judgment, it seems to me, is basically correct. Rushdie's right of free expression is essential to our world view and way of life and does not, in any straightforward way, violate general principles of utility or equal respect. Indeed, considerations of overall utility and equal respect may plausibly be said to support his exercise of free expression. Here, then, we must dig in our heels, vigorously defending the right of free expression and vehemently exercising it ourselves in opposing peremptory death sentences for those who would dare to employ this right. Freedom of expression is, as Jeremy Waldron (1989) argues, seriously compromised when fantasy, irony, satire, poetry, word play, and so on are forbidden on deep and important questions of religion and philosophy. Surely we should attempt to understand Islamic religion and culture and to appreciate its offense at Rushdie's book. We should also do what we can to convey this understanding and to defuse the issue. But we cannot take the book off the shelves, promote it less aggressively, or even criticize Rushdie for his irreverent and offensive use of satire and fantasy (as opposed to criticizing the book and its use of satire and fantasy on their artistic merits) without immeasurable cost to our identity and integrity. Nor can we moderate the defense of principles of tolerance and free expression basic to our own world view and way of life. To do so would betray not only ourselves but also members of past generations whose personal visions and sacrifice have enabled us to enjoy the fruits of free expression and members of future generations to whom we must bequeath this cornerstone of our culture.

Other cases will be more complex. In an article describing and defending the structure and operation of the President's Commission for the Study of Ethical Problems in Medicine and Biomedical and Behavioral Research, Commission Chairman Morris B. Abram and Susan M. Wolf emphasize the practical importance of virtual unanimity or consensus among the commission's members:

> A commission such as this one has only the power of persuasion. A group performing ethical analysis with no coercive powers cannot be persuasive without internal agreement. Unlike a court or legislature, which is structured to have effect as long as a majority agrees, a commission requires agreement that is as close to una-

nimity as possible, to have any effect at all. Without such virtual unanimity, the commission members simply voice possible arguments; with it, the commission can persuade.

The commission method thus forces the commissioners to find areas of common accord (1984, p. 629).

The provisions governing membership on the commission, Abram and Wolf add, mandated that commissioners have diverse backgrounds and represent a variety of ethical viewpoints. The commission's situation closely approximated the circumstances of compromise. Many of the issues it was asked to address were characterized by moral complexity and factual uncertainty. As individuals, commission members may have had differing views on some of these issues, but as commissioners they were required to arrive at agreement and issue a series of reports by a certain date. It was highly likely, therefore, that some of the commission's recommendations would involve moral compromise.

In an analysis tracing the development of the commission's recommendations on health policy, Ronald Bayer identifies and sharply criticizes the "kinds of compromises that were necessary to bring the Commission's work [on this topic] to a successful conclusion" (1984, p. 314). His principal concern centers on whether calls for reform in the structure of the health care system were to be forcefully framed in terms of a person's right to health care or framed more weakly in terms of a general societal obligation to insure equitable access to health care for all. Some members of the commission's staff took the first position, whereas most commissioners and the staff's executive director took the second. Early drafts prepared by the staff, Bayer writes, "addressed the problems of access to health care in terms of the broad ethical requirements of distributive justice. Therefore, it was deemed important to fashion societal policies and practices to fulfill the right of Americans to have access to health care" (1984, p. 306). As time passed, however, a number of factors, including the replacement of more politically liberal commissioners initially appointed by President Carter by more conservative commissioners appointed by President Reagan, led to weakening this position in subsequent drafts.

For those on the staff who wanted to preserve the tradition of framing calls for reform in terms of a right to health care, it was clear that given the opposition of the Chair and Executive Director, as well as the outlook of the new Commissioners, little would be gained from pressing their claims. Framing the Commission's work in terms of a societal obligation was the best that could be hoped for (Bayer 1984, p. 311).

Although Bayer's subsequent interviews with disgruntled staff members reveal that they had at one point considered en masse resignation and even issuing an independent staff report, nothing of the kind actually occurred.

"The final report of the President's Commission," Bayer concludes, "represents a compromise between the staff commitment to greater equity in health care and the view of those Commissioners who were deeply distrustful of governmental activity" (1984, p. 317). It was to his mind an unfortunate compromise.

> The concept of positive or social welfare rights has emerged in recent American history as the most potent political language for those seeking to make claims against an inegalitarian social structure. By explicitly rejecting the concept of a right to health care, thus breaking with recent public discourse on this matter, the Commission deprived those poorly served by the current health care system of a language with which to express their discontent. In so doing, the Commission implicitly adopted a perspective that views social change as the consequence of the recognition of moral obligations by the socially powerful, rather than as a result of demands pressed from below as a matter of right (Bayer 1984, p. 320).

Did staff members and commissioners personally favoring the concept of a right to health care judge wisely in compromising on this matter? Or did they betray the poor (and themselves) by conceding too much for the sake of agreement? It is difficult to say.

On the one hand, the final report includes much to substantiate calls for a right to health care. As Bayer himself acknowledges, the chapters of the report that summarize the data on prevailing patterns of access provide "a striking portrayal of inequality and make the case for reform, despite the efforts at textual prevarication" (1984, p. 317). Indeed, the marshalling of this data and its prominent position in the final report was no small achievement for staff members urging governmental recognition of a right to health care. A number of the more ideologically conservative commissioners opposed including this data in the report. One of them went so far as to refuse to assent to the final draft, expressing concern that "the report's 'mass of negative evidence' would 'bring forth policies which involve further spending and increased control of health care service by the Federal government'" (Bayer 1984, p. 318). So the final compromise was not one-sided. Concessions were made by those opposed to the concept of a right to health care as well as by those in favor of it.

On the other hand, it may turn out that what John Arras has characterized as the commission's "retreat from the right to health care" represents "a significant retrenchment of our public commitment to provide health care to the needy" (Arras 1984, p. 322). If the concept of a right to health care is essential for stating the case for more equitable access for the poor, the publication of a report by a prestigious presidential commission explicitly rejecting it would be an impediment to progress. Yet as Arras subsequently admits, the report's invoking the language of a right to health care may also have been quite counterproductive given the ideologically conservative political climate prevailing when it was released (1984, p. 343). If this were so, the compromise may have been a wise one.

Whether commissioners and staff members favoring the concept of a right to health care should have compromised on this matter is unclear. What is clear, however, is that in cases like this there is no escaping the burdens and uncertainties of judgment. Judgments about compromise require complex interpretations and comparisons of individual integrity, overall welfare, and mutual respect. And in many instances morally sensitive and thoughtful individuals will interpret and balance these important values differently and in ways that do not clearly violate well-grounded and widely shared ethical considerations.

FACILITATING COMPROMISE

Devising a well-grounded moral compromise will often involve bargaining and negotiation. We may, therefore, have much to learn from empirical research in this area. In an illuminating review of the literature on bargaining, negotiation, and compromise, David Luban distinguishes a popular adversarial paradigm that conceives of negotiation as "strategic competition" from a more cooperative paradigm that emphasizes "reasoned collaboration" (1985, pp. 398–401). Whereas the adversarial paradigm construes bargaining and negotiation as a set of manipulative techniques for obtaining whatever it is one wants in a hostile world ("a purely instrumental *modus vivendi*"), the cooperative paradigm situates bargaining and negotiation in the context of cooperative problem solving, emphasizing common standards rather than psychological manipulation, joint rather than individual gains, and collaborative rather than adversarial relationships among opposing parties.

The second paradigm speaks more directly to moral compromise than does the first. Its emphasis on mutual respect and mutual satisfaction and on construing conflict situations as "positive-sum" games (in which each party can in some sense legitimately conceive of itself as a winner) as opposed to "zero-sum" games (in which one party wins and the other loses) presupposes a sense of community or solidarity motivating the contending parties (Luban 1985, p. 400). This sense of community or solidarity is represented in the circumstances of compromise not only by a continuing, cooperative relationship but also by the (eventual) recognition among the contending parties that each is motivated by plausible (albeit conflicting) ethical considerations. Parties acknowledging such relationships will be more inclined to construe bargaining and negotiation as cooperative problem solving rather than as a form of strategic competition.

The literature identifies interpersonal skills and various approaches and attitudes that are likely to result in a mutually satisfactory outcome. Many of these are rooted in common sense and have long been employed by successful negotiators. As the authors of one of the most popular and accessible how-to volumes conclude: "There is probably nothing in this book which you did not already know at some level of your experience. What we have tried to do is to organize common sense and common experience in a way that provides a usable framework for thinking and acting" (Fisher and Ury 1981, p. 153). The empirically validated and clearly illustrated suggestions assembled in this and related books and articles usefully tutor judgment, reminding us of considerations that are in the heat of conflict all too easy to overlook.

Consider, for example, what is called in the literature fractionating a conflict. In certain circumstances it may be mutually advantageous to explicitly reformulate a conflict over a single big issue into a number of smaller ones. Progress may then be made in some smaller conflicts that may contribute to agreement on the larger one. If what appears to be intractable disagreement over a large-scale issue, A, can be reformulated in terms of a fractionated set of smaller issues, l, m, n, and o, it may then be possible to arrive at an agreement over l and m if one party feels very strongly about l and less strongly about m and the other party feels the opposite. Although no agreement was directly possible as long as the issue was formulated simply in terms of A, a compromise may be possible over the subsets l and m. The goodwill and mutual trust and satisfaction engendered by this agreement may then lead to compromises over further subissues and eventually to a compromise on the entire fractionated version of the larger issue, A.

This is a useful strategy that seems to play a major role in negotiations over arms reduction.

Fractionating conflict should avoid the stalemate that comes from a nation-to-nation confrontation in which neither country feels that it can make any concession without losing part of an over-all war. To the extent that issues are decided separately there is an increased chance that they are decided on their merits, that is, in light of their particular facts and circumstances. In this sense, agreements reached might be objectively better. Piecemeal settlement also recognizes that everything cannot be done at once and permits progress in certain areas while others are being worked out (Fisher 1964, p. 103).

Fractionating would seem applicable as well to at least some complex ethical conflicts. In Chapter 6 I explore the possibility of fractionating the large and bitter moral and political conflict in the United States over abortion. I also indicate how the division of labor characteristic of representational democratic politics contributes to the development of more "integrative" compromises (Carens 1979, pp. 126–29).

Although research into the cooperative paradigm of bargaining and negotiation will contribute to the development of mutually satisfactory agreements on various issues, it does not speak as directly as it might to ethical conflict. Wrongly assuming that conflict formulated in explicitly ethical terms is inimical to compromise, those working within the cooperative paradigm of bargaining and negotiation either ignore ethical conflict or attempt to reformulate it in terms of conflicting (equally legitimate) interests (Chapter 1, pp. 15–20).

That this is so is supported by the fact that much of the empirical research on bargaining and negotiation presupposes that agreement is the principal criterion of success (Luban 1985, p. 403). This in turn presupposes that the opposing positions or interests are always equally legitimate and that the opposing parties are equally well-situated. But these assumptions are at best questionable. Consider a contrived situation (adapted from Luban) in which an extremely rich person ("Rich") and a desperately poor person ("Poor") are together given $1,000 on the condition that they agree on how to divide it between them. Rich proposes that she take $900 and Poor $100 and then (credibly) refuses to consider any other outcome. "Take it or leave it," she tells Poor. After some deliberation, Poor swallows his pride and grudgingly agrees to the proposal. Agreement has, to be sure, been reached. But whether the outcome is satisfactory depends on explicitly normative considerations.

To a doctrinaire libertarian or a social scientist ideologically committed to agreement as the sole criterion of a successful negotiation, the outcome may be a good one. Moderate egalitarians, however, might argue that the outcome should instead be a $500/$500 split. The parties are after all moral (but not financial) equals and the money was given to them jointly; therefore it should be split equally between them. Rich's take-it-or-leave-it offer of a $900/$100 split exploits Poor's more restricted bargaining position. Rich takes advantage of a de facto power imbalance to extract agreement on her terms. Those taking a more radically egalitarian position may go so far as to argue that Poor should receive a larger share of the money than Rich. Poor's need for the money is certainly much greater than that of Rich. Poor's receiving a significantly larger share than Rich would thus make a contribution to overall economic equality. Utilitarians appealing to the principle of declining marginal utility might come to a similar conclusion; other things being equal, the money will make a larger contribution to overall happiness if most or all of it is allotted to Poor. Indeed, if Poor were to be replaced in the example by a different party, "Modest Means," and Rich were to make the same proposal she makes to Poor, Modest Means might well reject agreement (and the money).

Construing "best interests" quite broadly so as to include self-respect, it might well be in Modest Means's best interests not to settle in such a situation. If she is not desperate for the $100 she might, all things considered, be better off by refusing to accept it on the (only) terms satisfactory to Rich.

"Clearly," as Luban says of the presumption of agreement as the criterion of success, "we have here an unarticulated and undefended idea of what good negotiation is" (1985, p. 403). It is also upon inspection inadequate. Its ostensible value neutrality is, as the foregoing example reveals, specious. In circumstances approximating the situation of Rich and Poor, using agreement alone as the principal criterion of success stacks the deck in favor of the better situated and more powerful, explicitly favoring weaker (libertarian) over stronger (moderate or radical) conceptions of moral equality. "Only a full-fledged normative theory of dispute-resolution," as Luban adds, "can tell us whether a negotiation succeeded because it reached an outcome; perhaps, after all, it succeeded precisely because it failed to" (1985, p. 404).

We do not at present have anything approximating such a theory. A full-fledged normative theory of dispute resolution should, among other things, address explicitly ethical conflicts characterized by what we have called the circumstances of compromise and pay special attention to matters of integrity, utility, and equal respect. These normative considerations are often compatible with negotiation and compromise. Subsequent historical and empirical research should include explicitly moral compromise and try to determine what forms of bargaining and negotiation are most likely to contribute to the development of well-grounded, integrity-preserving compromises in these circumstances. Historical accounts of various efforts to ameliorate conflicts through moral compromise would, for example, prove most useful. In the meantime we can increase the likelihood that ethical disputes will be ameliorated by well-grounded, integrity-preserving compromises, first, by fostering and extending the sense of community presupposed by the cooperative paradigm of bargaining and negotiation and, second, by encouraging the cultivation of the relevant skills, understanding, and judgment.

Confronted with rationally irreconcilable moral conflict, we should remind ourselves of what we have in common with those with whom we disagree without at the same time ignoring deep and important differences. This requires more explicit recognition of the circumstances of compromise and the extent to which our identity as moral beings presupposes the more impersonal as well as the personal perspective. In so doing we acknowledge that despite important differences, as beings capable of taking a more reflective or impersonal perspective of moral conflict there is at least as much that joins us as divides us.

Public institutions—especially schools—can foster the capacity of citizens to seek and devise moral compromise. Structuring the classroom as a "community of inquiry" and including appropriately pitched philosophical discussion from the beginning are likely to cultivate the child's capacity to devise and maintain well-grounded, integrity-preserving compromises (Lipman et al. 1980; Matthews 1984). Indeed, there is a strong resemblance between what we have called the personal and impersonal standpoints in ethics and the nature of philosophical inquiry. "Philosophical argumentation," as Nicholas Rescher emphasizes, "is . . . *nonpreemptive*: the existence of one cogent resolution of an issue does not block the prospect of an equally cogent basis for its alternatives; by positive argumentation an excellent case can be built up in substantiation of each of several mutually incompatible theses" (1978, p. 220). At the same time, Rescher argues, this does not (or should not) lead to wholesale skepticism, relativism, or indifference. We should attempt to work out solutions to philosophical problems from a particular point of view while acknowledging the plausibility of a number of competing perspectives. "This two-tier approach requires us to do our philosophical work at two levels: (i) the basic level of substantive philosophical ideas, and (ii) the higher level of metaphilosophical deliberations" (Rescher 1978, p. 239). Philosophical thinking requires commitment at level (i) and tolerance at level (ii). Insofar as deep ethical disagreement is a form of philosophical disagreement, exposure to and cultivation of disciplined give-and-take discussion and philosophical thinking in the classroom is excellent preparation for devising well-grounded compromise.

In addition, investigations of students' understanding of and skill in compromise formation at various age levels provide insight into relevant empirical factors. One study, for example,

> confirmed the prediction that compromises were more likely to be formulated in peer relations than in authority relations. In fact, many students, in describing conflicts in authority context[s], explicitly stated that the adults would win the conflict merely be-

cause they were in a power position. In peer relations, however, since no one was in the power position, compromise strategies were more likely to be developed to resolve conflicts. To state it positively, peer context was more favorable to an equal exchange of ideas, and to a trust that one's view would be heard and respected (Leyva and Furth 1986, p. 450).

The extent to which compromise is not only fostered by perceptions of equality but also requires that parties to a compromise, despite differences in power and authority, actually be regarded and treated as equals leads directly to the question of ethics in compromise.

ETHICS IN COMPROMISE

Bargaining and negotiation in well-defined contexts involving conflicting (nonmoral) interests are often explicitly gamelike. Tactics and strategies that would in other contexts be unethical are permitted so long as participation is genuinely voluntary and the ground rules clearly understood and scrupulously followed. This is especially true of deception. Like faking a punt in football, being less than fully candid in buying or selling a house or automobile is part of the game. In this setting the usual objections to deception do not, as Sissela Bok points out, apply:

> In a bazaar, for instance, false claims are a convention; to proclaim from the outset one's honest intention would be madness. If buyers and sellers bargain knowingly and voluntarily, one would be hard put to regard as misleading their exaggerations, false claims to have given their last bid, or words of feigned loss of interest. Both parties have then consented to the rules of the game (1978, p. 131).

As with games generally, however, there are stringent ethical prohibitions on what one may do to achieve one's desired end.

We may bluff (or deceive) our opponents while playing poker, but not threaten to kill them if they do not allow us to win; we can fake left and then go right in basketball, but not gain an advantage by hitting (fouling) our opponents when they are taking a shot. Similar restrictions apply to rule-governed bargaining and negotiation. We cannot, for example, threaten to fire an employee if she is selling a car we have long desired and will not agree to what we consider a fair (and final) offer. This, like threatening to beat up the opposing pitcher if she strikes us out in a softball game, goes beyond the rules or conventions governing the social practice and to which participants have consented.

As game players or bargainers, consenting participants regard each other as equals. Though some players or teams will be wealthier, more powerful, or stronger than others, the rules are neutral between them. No deference or privilege is accorded to players or teams based on considerations external to the game itself. Each player or team is given the same number of opportunities to score; each batter in a baseball game is allowed three strikes regardless of wealth, fame, or political power and influence. So, too, in rule-governed bargaining or negotiation. Although buyer and seller may be unequal in overall wealth or power, so long as their interaction is genuinely and mutually voluntary and the ground rules clearly understood and jointly followed, there is nothing ethically untoward in their negotiations (though we remain free to criticize the institutions and practices contributing to or maintaining the initial distribution of wealth and power or, as in the case of Rich and Poor in the previous section, the very structure of the bargaining situation itself). Efforts to employ external considerations so as to force a more favorable settlement are, like similar moves while playing a game, unfair and unethical. Ethical considerations cannot, of course, by themselves insure that bargainers or negotiators will comply with them. But that the notion of fair or unfair bargaining or negotiation is part of our everyday language indicates that ethical considerations play a role in these practices.

As with games, most negotiations are not simply competitive; participants pursue ends that they believe can best or only be achieved jointly. We cannot, for example, take satisfaction in winning a game or making a particularly good competitive play without the rule-governed (competitive) cooperation of a worthy opponent. Achieving goods internal to and defined by excellent play requires the cooperation of an opposing player or team of sufficiently high calibre. Systematic violations of the written and unwritten rules of the game that eventually induce an opposing player or team to withdraw is a loss to both parties. Insofar as such violations weaken the integrity of the game itself, the ill effects are even wider. Similarly, negotiations frequently make possible gains that are independently unachievable. Neither party to a commercial or similar negotiation can as a rule achieve its aims without the other. It is thus in the interests of all of us to see that rules internal to valuable practices involving bargaining and negotiation are scrupulously followed.

Although the analogy with games is useful and revealing, there are important limitations. It is more difficult to determine whether participation is mutually voluntary and the ground rules mutually understood in less restricted settings. Games are, in addition, only games. We may elect to play them or we may refrain. It is not so easy, however, to withdraw from a labor negotiation or from buying or selling a house or an automobile if one needs to move or is desperate for money. It is also more difficult to determine and enforce the "rules of the game." A full account of these and related problems requires careful examination of detailed case studies (Bok 1978, pp. 130–31; Raiffa 1982, pp. 344–55). Our main concern, however, is with compromise involving conflicting values and principles, and it is to the ethics of bargaining and negotiation in this context that we now turn.

Situations in which the subject of disagreement is itself a matter of ethics and is recognized as such are importantly different from situations involving conflicting but equally legitimate nonmoral interests. If the conflicting parties are motivated to seek compromise it is in part because their understanding of the interpersonal conflict has created in each of them a related intrapersonal conflict (Chapter 2, 34). Each party to the disagreement wants its favored view to prevail. At the same time, however, each wants to come to some peaceful, mutually satisfactory accommodation or agreement with the person holding the opposing view. As the debate is internalized (Midgley 1985, pp. 452–55), the parties become as concerned with preserving their own integrity as they are with preserving the integrity of their relationship. Once this is acknowledged it becomes clear that the likelihood of arriving at a maximally integrity-preserving, mutually satisfactory outcome will be improved by candor and hindered by coercion or deception.

As parties to a rationally irreconcilable ethical conflict acknowledge their common predicament and attempt to negotiate a compromise, the overriding desire, grounded in part by a concern for their own integrity as moral persons, is for an "informed, unforced, reasonable agreement" (Scanlon 1982)—being able to justify one's proposed compromise on grounds that those with whom one is bargaining or negotiating could not reasonably reject. If this is their goal, the more honestly both parties express their actual convictions on the matter in question, the more likely it is that they will be able to devise a creative, mutually satisfying, optimally integrity-preserving, well-grounded compromise. Thus insofar as direct negotiators are in such circumstances as interested in integrating, or making peace with, themselves as they are with the opposing party, deceiving opposing parties is tantamount to deceiving themselves.

We cannot, then, acknowledge that an ethical conflict is characterized by the circumstances of compromise and at the same time attempt to secure a competitive edge by exploiting power advantages or employing deception or other forms of manipulation in seeking a solution more satisfactory to ourselves than to opposing parties. Compromise in ethics requires ethics in compromise. This in turn requires that parties to ethical disagreements in the circumstances of compromise respect each other as full moral equals, being completely candid and refraining from taking advantage of de facto differences in power and authority.

6
Compromise and Integrity in Politics

> Politics is a strong and slow boring of hard boards. It takes both passion and perspective.
>
> —*Max Weber, "Politics as a Vocation"*

> Conscience crucifies conscience unless the saints are protected from each other by political sinners who arrange the compromises of consciences and thus constitute the law which private consciences can agree to call "the public conscience."
>
> —*T. V. Smith, "Compromise: Its Extent and Limits"*

Compromise is part and parcel of democratic politics (Cohen 1971; Crick 1972; Carens 1979). Although devising and negotiating a well-grounded political compromise is a complex and delicate undertaking, it raises no special philosophical problems, at least when restricted to conflicts of legitimate interests. The art of political compromise becomes more problematic, however, when conflicts are rooted in opposing ethical convictions—especially those involving principled commitments to incompatible world views and ways of life. Politicians personally committed to one of two conflicting ethical positions who agree to a political compromise are frequently charged with betraying their principles or compromising their integrity. Is that always the case? For example, may politicians who are morally opposed to abortion devise or endorse a political compromise on this bitterly divisive issue without compromising their integrity? More generally, may one remain committed personally to a particular moral position while committed vocationally, as a politician, to a compromise that involves this same position?

Politicians whose personal opposition to abortion is based on deep and abiding moral considerations but who ground their search for compromise in political considerations are frequently criticized for hypocrisy or a lack of courage. "It is sad," writes prolife social critic

139

Mary Meehan, "to see politicians abandon their [prolife] convictions [on abortion], especially when the issue involved is one of life or death. A little expediency on something like tariffs or farm subsidies may be understandable. But when politicians do not draw the line where human life is involved, where can they draw it? What is left of their principles, and why should anyone trust them" (1984a, p. 24)? The controversy over abortion presents a particularly difficult and revealing test for the notion of integrity-preserving compromise.

POLITICS AS COMPROMISE

A political system of government is one that, first, acknowledges interpersonal and group conflict as an ineliminable feature of social life and, second, regards negotiation, compromise, and conciliation as preferable to force or violence as a means of ameliorating such conflict. Politics, as Bernard Crick observes, rests on both a sociological generalization (that advanced or complex societies "contain a diversity of interests—whether moral, social, or economic") and an ethical commitment (that "there are limits beyond which a government should not go in maintaining or creating a unity") (1972, p. 175). Politicians are those whose governmental roles include maintaining a modicum of social unity and singular overall direction while acknowledging diversity and eschewing violence. They are, in other words, our mediators.

Politics is also, however, a messy and morally ambiguous business. There is no science of politics, nor is there a singular political ideal or method that will spare us as politicians (or as those who elect politicians) the complexities, the confusion, and the exasperation of political debate and the reluctant compromises required both by conciliation and by the renunciation of violence (Crick 1972). Units of political rule, like individuals, must often balance tradition against the demands of rapidly changing, often unprecedented situations. Differences among groups and individuals committed to more and to less conservative world views and ways of life assure disagreement about particular issues, even with agreement on more abstract, general principles. Politics, then, is essentially dialectical; political decision is more a matter of practical judgment than of technical reason or logical deduction.

Not everyone has what it takes—the particular combination of temperament, analytical ability, knowledge, social intelligence, sensitivity, integrity, and judgment—to be a decent and effective politician. Some of us are unsuited for politics just as others are for various reasons unsuited for scientific investigation, child raising, teaching, accounting, selling, or racetrack handicapping. Some have part but not all of what it takes to be a decent and effective politician. A person may, for example, have the requisite desire and decency but lack the temperament for the social and, in some respects, seamier side of political activity. One who cannot abide the glad handing and the various "compromises" (the evasions, exaggerations, and dubious promises) often required to get elected or who takes no enjoyment from the rough and tumble of political bargaining and negotiation is probably not cut out for the life of a democratic politician. Others may be astute vote getters and effective political operators but be motivated mainly by personal aggrandizement, opportunism, or doctrinaire ideology at the expense of their constituents and the larger and nobler aims of political government. Although in many respects cut out for political life, they are best cut from it.

Unfortunately, a number of politicians are unscrupulous, inept, or both. Yet our response should not be to wash our hands of the entire business but rather to insist upon better politics and more decent and effective politicians. As Elizabeth Drew's illuminating account of ten days in the life of former Senator John C. Culver of Iowa reveals, politicians can be both honorable and effective, and we ought to do what we can to insure that there are more like them. "Culver," she writes,

> is not a saint and he is not an ideologue. He is an unusual combination: a man with firm principles and beliefs who is also a practical politician—one who gets in there and does the hard work of legislating, of putting together coalitions, of mediating among the conflicting interests in this country, of making the whole thing go. Anyone who tries to do this has to keep in mind a lot of roiling objectives and somehow work it all out. Those who can do this thoughtfully, carefully, and courageously are rare—*and essential.* Among the other senators, Culver soon developed a reputation for brains, tenacity, integrity, shrewdness at picking his issues and skill at pushing them, and an ability to work with his colleagues (Drew 1979, p. 12; my emphasis).

Anyone who attempts to walk such a series of personal and vocational tightropes must, as Drew's compelling portrait reveals, know when and how to compromise.

In a series of conversations with Drew, Culver conveys his conception of the politician's art. A number of his remarks are worth quoting at length, both for what they say about the vocation of politics and for what they reveal about him as an individual and as a politician. His first-person perspective provides useful insight into the complex relationships among compromise, judgment, and integrity in the world of politics. In discussing the presidency, Culver identifies the delicate balance the chief executive must strike between a consistent and coherent commitment to a particular "philosophical course," on the one hand, and the political means necessary to achieve it, on the other. "The major role of a President," Culver says,

> is to set the agenda—priorities, or whatever you want to call it—and then set out to mobilize the essential elements of a constituency that is congenial in a basic way, that is sustainable and will give you a chance of achieving the larger goals. That approach presupposes that in choosing your issues and in choosing your fights and *determining your compromises* you are acting in the context of holding together those larger elements of your constituency. There are trade-offs to be made. You have to decide what you want to make a matter of principle, what you want to do with it. You have to decide where you want to compromise, where you're willing to alienate some part of the constituency—keeping in mind that you need at least fifty per cent to get there, and if you dissipate so much of the basic core of support in the quest for exquisite rationality, or, on the contrary, try to make everybody happy, to get ninety per cent by some kind of ad-hoc appeal on an issue, then you run the risk of total disarray. You fragment your base to the point where there is no base (Drew 1979, pp. 87–88, my emphasis).

Too much concern for popular support, in other words, is as detrimental to political effectiveness as too little. And it is a matter of informed, astute political judgment to determine exactly where in particular situations the balance lies. "Politics," Culver adds, "is the resolution of conflicting and competing interests and values and goals in a complex society, and it seems to me you have to be prepared to make, and even enjoy making, such decisions" (Drew 1979, p. 88).

With respect to the demands of the Senate, Culver says,

> The hard thing is to stay with something—to cope with the fatigue of fighting for something and the psychological pressure not to do so. You're working with peers, and it's easier to have everything be pleasant. The difficult thing is to do something constructive and retain your relationships: it's another version of Sam Rayburn's "If you want to get along, go along"—a more sophisticated version. You could sit back and enjoy it and accept the perks and the psychic gratification, such as it is, but then no public purpose is served. And there *is* a little need for the "You scratch my back, I'll scratch yours." So you have to develop a reputation for integrity in your opposition and for being fair and keeping your word—but within that context you have to be willing to take on some uncomfortable things and still go to work every day. The whole thing is cutting edge: you can't worry too much about being loved; at some time, you have to decide, "Let's go! Bang!" If the others know that it's not a cheap shot, that often you might be right, they'll still respect you (Drew 1979, pp. 97–98).

If, to remain effective, senators must be able to work with and gain the respect of their senatorial colleagues, they must also retain the respect of those who elected them to office, those whom they represent. The distinction and tension between a political representative's roles as delegate and trustee are well known. As delegates, politicians are to represent directly the wishes and interests of their constituency, acting, as it were, as its conduit. As trustees, however, politicians are directed to use their judgment in making what they regard as the best decisions on particular matters even if in certain cases this means taking a position different from that of the majority of their constituents. "Obviously," Culver says in discussing this issue,

> officials who consistently vote against the wishes of their constituents will not and should not be returned to office. But we should be expected to do more than simply mirror the momentary mood of the public. We hear so much today about people wanting strong

leaders, but there's a certain contradiction in at the same time demanding leaders who do not lead but follow (Drew 1979, p. 114).

Elected officials, Culver maintains, have a dual responsibility: "to represent and reflect the interests and attitudes of the electorate, and even their prejudice on occasion, and also to educate public opinion" (Drew 1979, p. 116). In short, one must be able to devise compromises with constituents as well as with political colleagues and at the same time be respected for one's integrity by both. This can be accomplished only by the exercise of good judgment.

Culver astutely weaves these three strands of political life together when, after criticizing the conception of public officials as simply mirroring the views of their constituents ("then it's clear it doesn't matter who[m] you elect to the job"), he adds,

> One should have settled principles and convictions. Otherwise, you're on a slippery slope and there's no end to it. It has been my experience that if you just vote any way you think is right and you have your reasons and you can defend that vote, and defend it with conviction, the people will respect that. Similarly, in Congress you live by your reputation just as much as anywhere else. People turn to those they trust and those they respect, and if you're known as someone who has thought about a problem before you reached a decision you're not going to be subjected to all kinds of pressures and threats. They know you're not the kind of person who will respond to that. They don't think less of you for it; they think more of you. We all understand that people in Congress have to represent the interests of their districts or states and that Congress is a cockpit where you bang heads and try to reconcile all the competing interests. However, if people aren't willing to also lead and take risks, I don't really see why they are there. If they're there only to get reelected, what's the purpose of it? If you aren't going to contribute your own judgment, anybody can do the job and there isn't any real issue as to which person could do it better, or is more qualified, or has higher personal character or integrity, or anything else (Drew 1979, pp. 116–17).

The politician's vocation becomes even more difficult—some would say impossible—when we turn from conflicts of more or less equally legitimate interests to conflicts of deep and abiding moral conviction. How can politicians retain their integrity if they are vocationally required to devise and endorse compromises on issues that involve identity-conferring moral commitments?

PERSONAL ETHICS AND POLITICAL COMPROMISE

Politicians personally opposed to abortion but reluctant to transform these personal convictions directly into law or public policy are frequently criticized for a lack of integrity. "Far from being profiles in courage," writes Mary Meehan, "most politicians are profiles in jello on this issue" (1984a, p. 15). It is hard to imagine, she adds, how courageous, principled figures like Sir Thomas More and Andrew Jackson could have taken this separation between the personal and the political seriously:

> "Do you mean to say that our deepest personal convictions should have no influence on our public positions?" There would have been a look of polite disbelief from Thomas More, and one of withering scorn from Andrew Jackson. They would not have been able to understand how persons of integrity could separate their private and public convictions and then live at peace with their consciences. This would have seemed to them a great wrong and a matter of personal dishonor (Meehan 1984a, p. 16).

If compromising one's deepest convictions on this and similar matters is what it takes to be a competent or successful politician, Meehan suggests, then politics is not a vocation for one seeking to lead an integrated life. This is a serious charge. If we want to attract decent as well as effective men and women to political life we must be able to show that the vocation of politics is compatible with individual integrity. And we must do this without either trivializing political conflict (by restricting it to nonmoral interests) or falsifying it (by attempting to reformulate all conflicts of principle into conflicts of interest).

Governor Mario Cuomo of New York, a Catholic personally opposed to abortion, has responded to the charge leveled by Meehan in a speech to the Department of Theology at the University of Notre Dame in September 1984. He begins by pointing out that the Catholic who holds political office in a pluralistic democracy—who is elected to serve Jews and Moslems, atheists and Protestants, as well as Catholics—bears special responsibility. He or she undertakes to help create conditions under which *all* can live with a maximum of dignity and with a reasonable degree of freedom; where everyone who chooses may hold beliefs different from specifically Catholic ones—sometimes contradictory to them; where the laws protect people's right to divorce, to use birth control and even to choose abortion (Cuomo 1984, p. 32).

Catholic politicians do this, Cuomo adds, not because they lack conviction or endorse divorce, birth control, or abortion but rather because it is necessary to guarantee the Catholics' right to be Catholics—to pray, to use the sacraments, to refuse birth control devices, to reject abortion, not to divorce and remarry, and so on.

As a Catholic, Cuomo says, he has quite definite positions on the questions of when life begins and when it may be ended. But as a governor he is involved in "defining policies that determine *other* people's rights in these same areas of life and death" (1984, p. 33). And the political question—the question of how best in certain circumstances in a pluralistic society to translate personal conviction into public policy—is not fully settled by what one regards as the correct answer to the moral question.

Cuomo's position on this matter closely approximates the account of compromise and integrity developed in Chapters 2 and 3. There is a difference, he emphasizes, between what one regards, as an individual, as morally correct and what one regards, as a politician in a pluralistic society, as the most integrity-preserving course of action. No Church teaching, he adds, mandates the best political course for disseminating Catholic moral conviction. How best to do this is a matter of political judgment: In some instances, pressing for legal prohibition or requirement may be best; in others, Catholics would be advised to seek political compromise while continuing to advance their positions by moral argument, witness, and personal example.

As for abortion, Cuomo concludes that in his judgment as a Catholic politician, neither a prohibitory constitutional amendment nor returning the question to the states (either through constitutional amendment or by overturning *Roe* v. *Wade*) represents the best way to deal with the issue. Even a denial of Medicaid funding for abortion for poor women would not, he argues, further the Catholic objectives of reducing, if not eliminating, abortion. Instead he recommends a number of other avenues for achieving this end.

Underlying Cuomo's outlook is a political variation of what Nicholas Rescher has called orientational pluralism (1978). Philosophers, Rescher points out, often combine partisan commitment to particular positions or doctrines with metaphilosophical tolerance. Although strongly attached to various positions on particular issues, philosophers do not as a rule dismiss competing positions or those who maintain them as entirely wrong-headed. On the contrary, they draw an important distinction between "the task of the individual inquirer and the mission of the enterprise at large in its historical and communal aspect."

> The individual philosopher must do the best he can to elaborate and substantiate his solution to a philosophical issue. Nevertheless when he "steps back," so to speak, and detaches himself from his own methodological commitments by "bracketing" them, he can and should recognize *at the metaphilosophical level* that his own position is merely one alternative among others (a very privileged alternative to be sure, in being—as he sees it—the *correct* one). The work of the individual is *monistic*, that of the community *pluralistic*. We must needs recognize (and perhaps rejoice in) the fact that "the communal mind" of philosophical inquiry will and must press beyond our own positions, that the market is too big to be cornered (Rescher 1978, p. 241).

Insofar as ethical controversies rooted in conflicting world views and ways of life are also philosophical controversies, we can adapt Rescher's account of philosophical disagreement to illuminate the relationship between personal ethics and political compromise.

Of central importance is Rescher's reference to the mission of the philosophical enterprise in its historical and communal aspect. In addition to the philosopher's quest for personal understanding and solutions to various problems there is also her participation in a longstanding and ineluctably social (because it is dialectical) project. To seriously undertake philosophical inquiry is to engage in a series of conversations with the great figures of the past as well as with a large number of contemporaries. In acknowledging the legacy of the likes of Plato, Aristotle,

Hume, and Kant as well as the limitations of one's views as identified by thoughtful contemporaries, the individual acknowledges the "communal mind" of philosophical inquiry and the extent to which the enterprise as a whole transcends the self. Indeed, it is partly because of philosophy's historical and communal nature that identifying with the enterprise of philosophy is one (but only one) way of shaping and enlarging the significance of one's life (Chapter 3, pp. 60–62). In identifying with the communal mind of philosophical inquiry and its historical dimension while retaining their personal positions on particular issues, philosophers modestly transcend their limited spatial and temporal selves without relinquishing them.

A person's identity and integrity as a philosopher is, therefore, essentially dialectical. The vocation of philosophy requires that one develop and defend the truth on various issues "as one sees it" while furthering the historical and communal aspects of the enterprise as a whole. Philosophers qua philosophers do not betray their integrity if they acknowledge the limitations of their own views as well as the strengths of opposing views, both historical and contemporary. In identifying with the complex enterprise as a whole, a philosopher assumes an identity and a corresponding conception of integrity that makes room for such ambivalence and regards it as essential for the progress of the discipline. And insofar as the individual's identity (and capacity to outlive the self) is connected to the overall historical and communal project, she has a personal interest in contributing to its overall progress, even if it requires tolerance of positions she thinks mistaken or wrong-headed. Those who cannot abide the creative tension between identifying and defending what they may regard as the best position on a particular issue while acknowledging that it is only one among a number of plausible (and apparently incompatible) contenders are not cut out for the vocation of philosophy.

What is true of philosophy as a historical and communal undertaking is, in many respects, also true of democratic politics. Like the philosopher, the democratic politician's identity and integrity are determined in part by the historical and communal enterprise of political government. Those whose political communities have a history become part of the complex political conversation of the relevant community. To become a member of the United States Senate or House of Representatives, for example, is to commit oneself to the longstanding overall aims and principles of these communal bodies. Indeed, to assume office in any unit of political government or even to run unsuccessfully for political office is to become a member of the more abstractly conceived community of politicians and to contribute to the aims of political rule.

The vocation of politics, like that of philosophy, requires a creative blend of commitment to particular positions and tolerance of opposing positions. Like the philosopher, the politician's identity and integrity are essentially dialectical. A competent politician, as Culver emphasizes, is one who manages to retain an independent moral identity while also, in the interests of the integrity of the community as a whole (its continuity with the past as well as its future welfare), acknowledging the positions of those whose world views point in a different direction. The notion of single-issue politics is, therefore, an oxymoron—a contradiction in terms. Politicians who are obsessed with a single issue at the expense of all other issues or who fully surrender to the adamant will of powerful single-issue interest groups are not genuine politicians. Their position denies the mediating and communal nature of politics as a social institution.

There are, however, two important differences between politics and philosophy as historical and communal activities. First, with the notable exception of normative ethics, most areas of philosophy allow and encourage the thoughtful inquirer to remain agnostic until confident that the truth has been reached. We advance our own positions with modesty and tolerate opposing positions in the hope that continued investigation and conversation will eventually yield consensus on such issues as free will, the relationship between mind and body, the conditions of knowledge, and so on. Compromise on these more or less abstract theoretical questions is as a rule neither necessary nor appropriate. Politics, however, is born of the circumstances of compromise, specifically those involving an impending nondeferrable decision and a continuing cooperative relationship. Thus in politics, as with many questions of normative ethics, we are required to act—often in concert with others whose positions on certain matters are radically different from our own. (By "radically" I mean quite literally rooted in world views and ways of life opposed to and incommensurable with ours.) In such circumstances, to suspend judgment is politically irresponsible. Where agreement is required on a single course of action and consensus is unlikely (at least in the foreseeable future), we look to compromise.

The second important difference between philosophy and politics centers on the politician's ambiguous position as representative and colleague. Politicians, as Culver emphasizes, have obligations both to their constituents and to other politicians. To remain in office they must satisfy a sufficient number of constituents; to accomplish anything while in office they must gain the cooperation of a sufficient number of political colleagues. Achieving both requires skills, sensitivity, and judgment largely foreign to the pursuit of philosophical truth and understanding.

The willingness to compromise, together with the requisite skills and judgment, is part of the very identity and integrity of those who are by vocation politicians. "Political activity," Crick emphasizes, "is important not because there are no absolute ideals or things worth doing for themselves, but because in ordinary human judgment there are many of these things" (1972, p. 159). Like philosophy, the enterprise as a whole is best served by a creative, dialectical tension between various ideals and visions rooted in particular world views and ways of life, on the one hand, and political mediation of these conflicting ideals and visions, on the other. A speech by Abraham Lincoln in which he articulated the political position of his party on the question of slavery provides a useful illustration of a political approach to a moral conflict on which one has deep and abiding personal convictions:

> The real issue in this controversy—the one pressing upon every mind—is the sentiment on the part of one class that looks upon the institution of slavery *as a wrong*, and of another class that *does not* look upon it as a wrong. . . . The Republican Party . . . look upon it as being a moral, social and political wrong, and while they contemplate it as such, they nevertheless have due regard for its actual existence among us, and the difficulties of getting rid of it in any satisfactory way, and to all the constitutional obligations thrown about it. . . . I repeat it here, that if there be a man amongst us who does not think that the institution of slavery is wrong in any one of the aspects of which I have spoken, he is misplaced, and ought not to be with us. And if there be a man amongst us who is so impatient of it as a wrong as to disregard its actual presence among us and the difficulty of getting rid of it suddenly in a satisfactory way, and to disregard the constitutional obligations thrown about it, that man is misplaced if he is on our

platform. We disclaim sympathy with him in practical action (1858, pp. 312–13).

"This," Crick declares, "is true political morality—indeed political greatness. If anyone is not willing to walk this kind of path he might be happier to realise that he has in fact abandoned politics" (1972, p. 160).

Is this account of the relationship between personal ethics and political compromise applicable to the abortion controversy? Can politicians retain integrity while being personally opposed to abortion on moral grounds but politically tolerant (or even supportive) of more moderate or permissive policies? Is there a plausible compromise position on abortion that will lead to a truce between prolife and prochoice activists? The question of abortion provides an interesting illustration of the complexities of compromise and integrity in politics.

THE PROBLEM OF ABORTION

At the heart of the abortion issue is the question of the moral status of the fetus. A being has full moral standing, let us say, if it is protected by laws against killing (Feinberg 1986). If at some stage of development the fetus acquires full moral standing, then abortion can be permitted, if at all, only under very limited circumstances.[1] Arguments based only on a woman's right to privacy or self-determination, though certainly important, pale in comparison to arguments based on the prohibition against killing. If, on the other hand, we can show that the fetus does not acquire full moral standing until some point late in pregnancy or perhaps not even until birth, arguments based on a right to privacy or self-determination will, prior to that point, carry much more weight. The question of the moral status of the fetus is, however, one of the most complex and highly contested questions in contemporary philosophy.

There are three main positions on this issue: the extreme conservative position; the extreme liberal position; and the moderate position. The extreme conservative emphasizes the value of human life as such. For the extreme conservative, human life begins at conception and all living human beings are (or should be) equally protected by laws against killing (Noonan 1970; Wertheimer 1971).[2] If therefore taking

innocent postnatal human life is murder, then so too is taking innocent prenatal human life. The extreme liberal, on the other hand, argues that a necessary condition for having a right to life is a personal
interest in continued life, which requires developed capacities for self-
awareness and a sense of the future. These capacities, the extreme liberal maintains, emerge at or sometime after birth (Tooley 1983; Warren 1973; P. Singer 1979). The moderate position falls between the
other two. For the moderate, the fetus acquires independent moral
standing some time after conception but before birth (Langerak 1979;
Sumner 1984). Although each of these positions has something to recommend it, none is free of serious difficulty.

Taken literally, the extreme conservative position would, as Joel
Feinberg points out, require us to do as much to preserve the life of a
newly fertilized ovum as for anyone else whose life is in danger (Feinberg 1986, p. 290). Over 40 percent of fertilized ova fail to survive until
implantation, and the spontaneous abortion rate after implantation
ranges from 10 to 20 percent. If we seriously believe that the life of an
embryo or a zygote is as valuable as that of any postnatal human being, we will have to commit as much money to preventing this loss of
human life as we now commit to preventing the deaths of persons after
they are born. Yet this seems absurd. Consider, too, that even if we
were able to discover an inexpensive wonder drug that would save all
of these human lives, because most of them would be seriously handicapped the incidence of incapacitating congenital disease in the population would grow from approximately 2 percent to over 20 percent.
Finally, defenders of the extreme conservative position are hard
pressed to provide a plausible secular justification as to why all human
life is as such equally valuable. The most likely secular argument
would combine an emphasis on the consequences of our actions with
a concern about embarking on a slippery slope: "Once we allow the
taking of any innocent human life," the argument might go, "respect
for the value of all human life will be eroded and no one will be safe."
But the empirical evidence necessary to substantiate this worry has
not been forthcoming. Extreme conservatives are more likely, in fact,
to rely on explicitly or implicitly held theological world views that
place special value on human life as God's creation. These outlooks
are often quite attractive and worthy of respect (Callahan 1984;
Meehan 1984b), but inasmuch as other religious and secular world
views, equally plausible and worthy of our respect, differ with them

on this matter, such defenses by extreme conservatives cannot be morally or legally decisive in a secular, pluralistic society.

The main philosophical limitation of the extreme conservative position (its inability to provide a plausible secular justification as to why taking the life of a four-week-old fetus is as wrong as taking the life of a four-year-old child) becomes the main strength of the extreme liberal position. By focusing on the fundamental importance of our intentions and plans for the future, the extreme liberal can readily explain why as individuals we generally fear death and regard killing as the ultimate evil; death (or at least a premature death) deprives us of everything else that we want. But if we lack the capacity to formulate intentions and plans, death, which would at one stroke thwart them all, cannot be a wrong to us. Killing wrongs four-year-olds but not four-week-old fetuses because fetuses lack the cognitive and conative capacities for formulating intentions and plans and thus for having a personal interest in continued life. Because even irascible hermits can be supposed to have intentions and plans, killing them would be wrong even if no one would miss them or even learn of their deaths. Their interest in continued life is sufficient for their having a right to life even if there is no God or if they make no contribution whatever to the general good.

Like the extreme conservative position, however, the implications of the extreme liberal position are deeply counterintuitive. Without modification, it seems to license not only early abortion but also late-term abortion and even infanticide and the killing of the severely mentally disabled and senile, many of whom may lack sufficient cognitive capacities to frame intentions and make plans for the future. Proponents of the extreme liberal position are well aware of this difficulty and have responded to it in various ways (Warren 1973; Engelhardt 1978; P. Singer 1979; Tooley 1983; Kuhse and Singer 1985), but the cogency of their efforts remains in dispute (English 1975; Stevens 1984; Lomasky 1982; Williams 1985).

Moderates seize upon the counterintuitive consequences of both polar positions. According to moderates, the conservative grants a fetus moral standing too early and the liberal too late; the conservative's position on abortion is, therefore, too restrictive and the liberal's too permissive. The moral status of the fetus becomes weighty enough, the moderate maintains, somewhere between the two extremes. But exactly where? And for what reasons? Here the moderate view founders. Each of the most plausible criteria—for example, central nervous system activity, quickening, sentience, and viability—has been trenchantly criticized as morally arbitrary by liberals and conservatives alike (Noonan 1970; Wertheimer 1971; P. Singer 1979; Tooley 1983). It is hard to understand, the critics argue, why any of these changes is significant enough from an ethical point of view to constitute the difference between not having a right to life and having one. If, for example, one argues as does one of the most sophisticated moderates (Sumner 1984) that the appearance of sentience is the distinguishing feature, why should this ground a right to life rather than simply a right to be free of gratuitous pain and suffering? And how does this distinguish the moral standing of human persons having various plans from that of any sentient nonhuman animal? If being sentient is sufficient for having a right to life, does it not follow that any sentient nonhuman animal must also be acknowledged as having a right to life (P. Singer 1975, 1979)? Maybe so, but then what was initially offered as a moderate position takes on an increasingly extreme and controversial cast; apparently, to be a moderate on abortion one must be an extremist on the question of animal rights.

Thus the moral status of the fetus remains problematic. The debate is likely to continue, but prospects for a widely accepted, well-grounded philosophical resolution, at least in the near future, are dim. Matters become even more complicated when one takes into account the larger social and economic context in which the philosophical debate takes place. We cannot, for example, overlook the importance to political activists on both sides of the question of competing conceptions of the nature and role of motherhood in contemporary society and the conflicting world views and ways life of which they are a part.

In *Abortion and the Politics of Motherhood* Kristen Luker argues that a comparatively small number of activists on each side keep the controversy in the forefront of political consciousness. When these activists think about abortion, she points out, "abortion itself is merely 'the tip of the iceberg' " (1984a, p. 158). At stake are their conceptions of themselves and the world. To challenge their views on abortion, then, is to challenge their sense of what and who they are; it threatens their deepest convictions about the world and their entire way of life. "Each side of the abortion debate," Luker concludes, "has an internally coherent and mutually shared view of the world that is tacit, never fully articulated, and, most important, completely at odds with the world view held by their opponents" (1984a, p. 159). To challenge the activists' views on abortion is to challenge their identity as particular persons and hence the integrity of their lives.

Luker identifies a number of respects in which the world views and corresponding ways of life of prolife and prochoice activists differ. Prolife activists, for example, believe that men and women are intrinsically different and consequently have different roles in life. They endorse a division of labor whereby men, who are regarded as best suited for the world of work, spend much of their time outside the home while women, who are thought to be best suited to rear children, manage and nurture domestic life. Although prolife activists do not object to a woman's entering the labor force and agree that women should be paid at the same rate as men doing the same work, they believe that homemaking and child raising are full-time occupations and that if a woman elects to work outside the home she should not become a mother and vice versa.

Sexual relations are for prolife activists primarily for the purpose of reproduction, not pleasure or personal expression. Luker distinguishes "procreative love," the aim of which is reproduction, from "amative love," which aims at sensual pleasure and mutual enjoyment. Prolife activists believe that sexual relations are primarily procreative and that contraceptive devices, therefore, diminish the meaning of intercourse between husband and wife. Prolife attitudes toward teenage or premarital sex follow accordingly. Sex before as well as outside of marriage is wrong, as is providing contraception (and abortion) services for teenagers. Traditional moral standards and will power, not medical technology and surgery, are what are needed to stem the tide of teenage pregnancy in the United States.

Parenthood for prolife activists is mainly a biological rather than a social role. One becomes a parent by bearing or fathering children. Marriage, sex, and parenthood are intimately related.

Because pro-life people believe that the purpose of sexuality is to have children, they also believe that one should not plan the exact number and timing of children too carefully, for it is both wrong and foolish to make detailed life plans that depend upon exact control of fertility. Because children will influence life plans more than life plans will influence the number of children, it is also wrong to value one's planned accomplishments—primarily the acquisition of the things money can buy—over the intangible benefits that children can bring (Luker 1984a, p. 171).

A married couple who love each other and love children as well will generally have as many children as they can as soon as they can.

Underlying the world view of prolife activists is belief in God and the ultimate goodness of God's plan. "Morality, for them," Luker writes, "is a straightforward and unambiguous set of rules that specify what is moral behavior"; established by God, these principles are, they believe, "eternally valid regardless of time, cultural setting, and individual belief" (1984a, p. 174). Thus morality is located in the tradition of the Ten Commandments and the more literal renderings of the Judeo-Christian legacy. And, prolife activists maintain, this tradition forbids abortion. All human beings are equal before God and, as the commandment says, "Thou shalt not kill." In this view, abortion is the killing of one of God's most innocent and powerless creatures and must therefore be vigorously opposed.

The world view and way of life of prochoice activists, Luker shows, is diametrically opposed in each of these dimensions to that of prolife activists. Where, for example, prolife activists emphasize differences between men and women and recommend different but complementary roles for them, prochoice activists emphasize the similarity between men and women and urge that similar opportunities, especially in the world of work and career, be made available for each. In opposing sex role differentiation, prochoice activists argue that

> pro-life women who do not work outside the home are only "one man away from disaster." A death, a divorce, a desertion, or a disability can push a woman with no career skills or experience perilously close to the edge of penury—as shown by the ever-increasing numbers of "displaced homemakers"—widows and divorcées left with virtually no financial or employment resources (Luker 1984a, p. 176).

Prochoice activists add that if women are to be able to enter and advance in the labor force they must be able to exercise a large degree of control over conception and pregnancy. Such control is important to prochoice activists insofar as they regard sex as principally amative rather than procreative. Contraception and planning of pregnancy is thus of paramount importance. Not as vehemently opposed to teen-age sex as prolife activists, prochoice activists are equally, if not more strongly, opposed to teenage pregnancy. Consequently, they are more receptive to contraceptives for teenagers and, as a last resort, to abortion.

Underlying their opposition to teenage pregnancy is the prochoice conception of parenthood as a demanding social role, one that should not be assumed without sufficient financial resources, interpersonal and social skills, and above all emotional maturity. As a rule, teenagers are not prepared to meet the demands of raising a child. To love children, in the prochoice world view, is to plan for them, to make sure they are genuinely wanted, and to provide what they need to flourish. Thus whereas the prolife view suggests that if one loves children one will when married have many of them and as soon as possible, the pro-choice view implies that if one loves children one will have only as many as one has time, energy, and emotional and financial resources to provide for adequately. One should, then, defer having children un-til one is fully prepared to meet their complex needs.

The prochoice conception of morality is more secular and pluralis-tic than the prolife. Prochoice activists are less inclined than prolife activists to interpret the world as basically benign (as fulfilling God's infinite but mysterious plan). Prochoice activists therefore place more emphasis on the use of reason, planning, choice, and intervention in attempting to combat nature's less hospitable aspects if not to exercise as much control over them as they can. They are more concerned with this world than the "next" and are more concerned with what they re-fer to as the quality of human life rather than its quantity. Yet in at-tempting to struggle with the complexities of the world as they find it, prochoice activists have devised no singular code that will readily re-solve without remainder all of their moral choices. "They see moral-ity," Luker writes, "not as obedience to a set of inflexible rules, such as the Ten Commandments, but rather as the application of a few gen-eral ethical principles to a vast array of cases" (1984a, p. 184). And given the complexity of issues and plurality of values, the people most affected by various decisions must be the ones to make them. There-fore the difficult decision of abortion must be left, prochoice activists maintain, to the pregnant woman.

When one fully understands the nature and depth of these opposing world views and ways of life, one can see why the stakes for those holding them are so high and why, according to Luker, "the abortion debate is so heated and why the chances for rational discussion, reasoned arguments, and mutual accommodation are so slim" (1984a, p. 191). If those strongly wedded to one of these world views were suddenly forced to submit to the way of life of the other, the loss would, at least initially, be devastating to their sense of themselves as whole and particular persons. Hence many activists defend their respective viewpoints as if the nature and meaning of their lives depended upon it (Luker 1984b).

It is illuminating in this connection to compare part of what is at issue in the abortion debate with the challenges to human self-understanding presented by Copernicus in the sixteenth century and by Darwin in the nineteenth. In replacing the Ptolemaic, or geocentric, account of the heavens with a heliocentric one, the Copernican Revolution required a considerable revision in our picture of the cosmic importance of human life. If the earth were no longer the center of the universe—if it were just another planet going around the sun—then perhaps human beings, who were certainly the centerpiece of earth, were not the center of all creation. This was a profoundly shocking implication for those whose religious identity presupposed a geocentric conception of the universe, and consequently it was resisted by the Church for many years.

If this were not bad enough, some three hundred years later the theory of evolution seemed to require that we also deny any role for God's design or guidance in the development of the world's plants and animals, including what was now to be regarded as the human animal. The additional affront to human standing was for many intolerable. First Copernicus deprived us of our privileged place in the universe, and then Darwin took away our conception of ourselves as God's chosen species here on earth. Indeed, it is testimony to the strength of a pre-Darwinian world view that 130 years after the publication of *The Origin of Species*, "creation scientists" and others holding fundamentalist religious convictions continue to resist the theory of evolution.

It is against this background that we should understand the abortion controversy. To defenders of the extreme conservative position or to Luker's prolife activists, the proposals of extreme liberals or the prochoice activists are as revolutionary and as integrity- and identity-threatening as were those of Copernicus and of Darwin. Extreme liberals, for example, often develop and defend their position by insisting on a distinction between a living human being or organism and a "person" (Tooley 1983; P. Singer 1979; Engelhardt 1978; Warren 1973; Feinberg 1986). Being a living human being, they argue, is neither necessary nor sufficient for being a person. Personhood, as they understand it, requires having a conception of oneself as a continuing subject of consciousness, the capacity to deliberate and choose among alternatives, and the ability to plan for the future. This notion of a person as distinct from a living human being can be traced to Locke, who in his *Essay Concerning Human Understanding* characterized a person as "a thinking intelligent being that has reason and reflection and can consider itself as itself, the same thinking thing, in different times and places" (1690, p. 280). Whereas "person" is a moral and legal notion (Locke called it a forensic term), the notion of a living human being is to extreme liberals simply biological. According to this view, Karen Ann Quinlan, who remained in a persistent vegetative state (an irreversible coma) for over ten years, was a living, permanently unconscious human organism but not a living person. A living, permanently unconscious human being whose capacity for personhood has therefore been fully and irretrievably lost should, some argue, be considered dead (Feinberg 1974; Green and Wikler 1980).

If, then, as many extreme liberals maintain: (1) being a person is necessary for having a right to life, (2) not all living human beings (for example, fetuses, anencephalic infants, those in a persistent vegetative state, and perhaps some who are severely mentally handicapped or senile) are persons, and (3) some nonhuman beings (possibly extraterrestrials, super-duper robots of the future, or certain nonhuman animals) may qualify as persons, the importance and dignity of simply being human will once again have been dealt a significant blow as will the notion of fundamental human equality. It was bad enough to no longer be the centerpiece of the universe or even the chosen of the earth. But to have one's dignity and worth as a person turn on having certain cognitive capacities—capacities that some humans might lack and some nonhumans, including some animals, might possess—is for many a final and wholly intolerable assault on a world view and way of life in which personhood is "a 'natural,' inborn, and inherited right, rather than a social, contingent, and assigned right" (Luker 1984a, p. 157).

THE POLITICS OF ABORTION

The debate over abortion has moved to the forefront of domestic politics. Far from settling the matter, the Supreme Court's 1973 *Roe v. Wade* decision appears to have aggravated it. The emergence of the pro-life movement as a powerful political force is largely attributable to this legal landmark (Luker 1984a, pp. 126–57). A political candidate's position on abortion is now a relevant—in some cases, the principal—consideration for a large number of voters. During the 1984 presidential contest, for example, Archbishop Bernard F. Law of Boston called abortion "the critical issue in this campaign" and, together with seventeen other bishops from the New England states, issued a statement that "the holocaust of abortion" was more important than the possibility of nuclear holocaust (McBrien 1987, p. 145). This sort of single-issue thinking often affects political and judicial appointments as well. A prospective appointee's position on abortion is in many instances a litmus test of minimal acceptability for both prolife and prochoice activists. The overall effect on political judgment and its accompanying complexities has often been to distort or overshadow other considerations of equal or greater importance.

The abortion issue affects other areas of public life as well. In the spring of 1988 a prolife group called Operation Rescue initiated a well-organized, nationwide program of civil disobedience against abortion clinics. Modeled on the successes of the 1960s civil rights movement, Operation Rescue's nonviolent sit-ins were aimed not only at obstructing and deterring those seeking abortions but also at marshaling public support. By allowing themselves to be arrested and jailed, participants demonstrated the depth of their conviction and appealed to what they believed was the public's latent sense of justice. Their protest fit the standard definition of civil disobedience: "a public, nonviolent, conscientious yet political act contrary to law usually done with the aim of bringing about a change in the law or policies of the government" (Rawls 1971, p. 364). Whether their conduct also met the conditions justifying civil disobedience is more controversial (Rawls 1971, pp. 371–77; Bond 1988).

Other types of illegal opposition to abortion are more extreme. Bombings of abortion clinics have become more prevalent in recent years. And arson is suspected in the fires at three abortion clinics in

Dallas that broke out within an hour early on Christmas Day 1988 (*New York Times*, 27 December 1988). Although prolife political organizations and members of Operation Rescue condemn violent action and take pains to distinguish such means from their own, the bombings and arson indicate the intensity and depth of conviction on the part of some who are opposed to abortion. And they have understandably exacted a financial and emotional toll on those operating the clinics.

The course of health policy and the development of medicine have also been affected by the politics of abortion. For example, in 1988 the Department of Health and Human Services issued regulations withholding federal financing from family-planning clinics that offer abortion counseling (*U.S. News & World Report*, 3 October 1988).[3] Part of a comprehensive effort to prohibit the use of federal funds for any activities that might further abortion, these rules if implemented would not only limit access to abortions for many (mostly poor) women, but they would also prevent them from acquiring the birth-control information that would help them from becoming pregnant in the first place. The regulations would also corrupt the doctrine of informed consent, a cornerstone of contemporary medical ethics. If doctors in these clinics are forbidden from informing a woman of all legal methods for family planning—including abortion as a last resort—they limit her capacity for informed choice. Doctors practicing under such conditions would thus be forced to compromise (or betray) the ethics of their profession.

The question of research and experimentation on human embryos, which promises to contribute to the prevention and treatment of a number of developmental disorders, has also been affected by the abortion debate (Warnock 1985a, 1985b), as has the more recent question of fetal tissue transplantation. There is some reason to believe that the transplantation of fetal brain tissue into the brains of patients suffering from Parkinson's disease, diabetes, and perhaps other serious disorders may be of significant therapeutic benefit (Fine 1988). Those opposed to abortion also oppose further research in this area because they fear its success would eventually encourage and legitimize abortion. A federal panel assembled by the National Institutes of Health has given qualified endorsement to the ethical legitimacy of such research, but the issue remains unsettled (*New York Times*, 17 September 1988). The politics of abortion led the Reagan administration to consider an executive order that would prohibit the use of fetal tissue in any federally financed scientific experiments or medical treatments if obtained from an induced rather than a spontaneous abortion (*New York Times*, 9 September 1988).

That the American prolife movement is a political force to be reckoned with was reinforced in 1988 when it threatened to prevent the manufacture in France of RU 486, a new abortion-inducing drug that promises to reduce the cost, trauma, and complication rate of abortion, especially in parts of the world where safe surgical facilities are unavailable. Shortly after announcing the drug's availability, the French manufacturer, Groupe Roussel Uclaf, decided to suspend distribution under intense pressure attributed in part to the American right-to-life movement (*New York Times* 28 and 29 October 1988). Immediate and concerted opposition to the company's decision by physicians attending a meeting of the World Congress of Gynecology and Obstetrics, together with counterpressure from the French government, which owns part of Groupe Roussel Uclaf, led the company to reconsider its decision. Two days after announcing it would suspend distribution, Roussel did an about-face—it would now, it said, manufacture the drug after all. The question of whether RU 486 will be approved for use and manufacture in the United States—in particular whether any American pharmaceutical company, threatened with the prospect of a boycott of its other products by the prolife movement, will make it available—is uncertain (*New York Times*, 30 October 1988). The prolife movement may thus have the power to prevent what appears to be a safe and effective drug that would lower the cost and surgical risks of conventional abortion from becoming available to American women.

In a related matter, the prolife movement has gone so far as to threaten the availability of treatments for other illnesses. A new drug, Cytotec, developed by G. D. Searle & Company to prevent ulcers in arthritis patients, is believed also to induce abortion in pregnant women. The National Right to Life Committee is therefore urging the Food and Drug Administration (FDA) to withhold approval of the drug. Although FDA approval would only be for the treatment of ulcers, once a drug receives FDA approval it may be prescribed by licensed physicians as they see fit. The National Right to Life Committee is threatening to organize a boycott of all Searle products if the drug is approved and marketed (*New York Times*, 29 October 1988). Thus, in the present climate, even arthritis sufferers are hostage to the politics of abortion.

Given the distorting effects of the abortion controversy in so many areas of public life—from the oversimplifications of single-issue politics to the limitations imposed on medical research and development—is it conceivable that a well-grounded political compromise could contain the debate while allowing it to continue? And could politicians who are personally committed to one or the other of the polar positions devise and negotiate such a compromise without compromising their integrity? Ignoring for the moment that *Roe* v. *Wade* has effectively shifted the focus from the legislative to the judicial branch of government, let us explore the plausibility of an integrity-preserving political compromise on the abortion issue.[4]

Luker is pessimistic about the prospects for compromise. "The abortion debate," she predicts, "is likely to remain bitter and divisive for years to come. Beliefs about the rightness or wrongness of abortion both represent and illuminate our more cherished beliefs about the world, about motherhood, and about what it means to be human. It should not surprise us that these views admit of very little compromise" (1984a, p. 10). Yet the activists, we must keep in mind, are only a minority, and a well-grounded compromise may not require their whole-hearted endorsement to be politically effective. A recent Gallup Poll indicates a 57 percent majority favoring some sort of moderate or compromise position on abortion (legalized abortion, but only under certain circumstances) with 24 percent rejecting any legal restrictions and 17 percent supporting an absolute prohibition (*Minneapolis Star Tribune*, 23 October 1988). These figures, Gallup reports, have changed little since the 1973 *Roe* v. *Wade* decision. A compromise position understood and explicitly accepted as such by a significant majority might then be sufficient to defuse the extreme rhetoric and tactics of those at either pole. If it could restore a more complex and balanced politics, increase civility among the disputants, and allow other areas of medical research and therapy to proceed without threat of abortion-related veto, such a compromise would contribute significantly to public life.

ABORTION AND COMPROMISE

The abortion debate is situated in the circumstances of compromise
(Chapter 2, pp. 26–32). First, the facts are uncertain. What, for example, is the metaphysical—and hence moral—status of the fetus?
What will be the long-term consequences of either a significantly
more permissive or more restrictive policy on abortion than the
present one? Second, the issue is morally complex. Each party to the
debate bases its position on plausible moral considerations, none of
which clearly violates the principle of utility or the principle of respect for persons (Chapter 4, pp. 101–6). Third, the parties are involved in a continuing, cooperative relationship. All of us, whether
extreme conservatives, extreme liberals, or some type of moderate, are
members of a single nation requiring a uniform policy on matters of
life and death. And fourth, we face what appears to be an impending,
nondeferrable decision. The continued moral and political impasse on
this issue is now spilling over and adversely affecting many areas of
public life.

Prudential considerations give additional, though not decisive, motivation for activists on each side to consider the benefits of compromise. The polar positions are, and in the near future are likely to
remain, those of distinct minorities. The logic of the extreme conservative position, for example, forbids exceptions even for pregnancies resulting from rape or incest. Although sympathizing with the victim,
doctrinaire prolife advocates cannot endorse what the logic of their position regards as murder to remedy the situation. Yet only 11 percent
of the population disapproves of abortion in such circumstances (Gallup Poll 1988). Given the unlikelihood of their achieving a total prohibition of abortion, at least in the foreseeable future, right-to-life
activists may have more to gain by compromising their demands to
obtain a political consensus on a policy more restrictive than the
present one. Extreme liberals seem equally unlikely to marshal nationwide support for their favored position. Prochoice advocates, for
example, endorse legalized abortion for any reason whatever, including
not being able to afford a child. Yet apparently only 19 percent of the
public endorses this as a justification for legal abortion. The doctrinaire prochoice position thus attracts little more popular support than
that of doctrinaire prolife activists.

Those at either pole also run certain risks by refusing to compromise. The development of RU 486 may, for example, eventually render the sort of legal prohibition sought by prolife activists wholly unenforceable. Better perhaps for advocates of the extreme conservative position to settle for "half a loaf" in the form of a somewhat more restrictive, yet highly popular, policy than to risk losing everything. Those advocating more liberal positions may also decide to moderate their demands. Supreme Court Justice Harry Blackmun, author of the *Roe* v. *Wade* decision, has suggested that political pressure to replace retiring Supreme Court justices with those more sympathetic to the prolife position presents "a very distinct possibility [of *Roe* v. *Wade's*] going down the drain" (*U.S. News and World Report*, 3 October 1988). Better perhaps for prochoice advocates to seek some sort of political accommodation or truce with the prolife movement than to risk reopening the constitutional question.

Although there is something to be said for the terms of *Roe* v. *Wade* as a political compromise (Putnam 1983, p. 5), its status as a well-grounded constitutional solution is more questionable (Frohock 1983, pp. 63–74). Indeed, accounts of the development of the decision reveal not only its shaky constitutional foundation but also the personal and historical contingencies that contributed to its development (Woodward and Armstrong 1979, pp. 193–207, 215–23, 271–84, 491–93; Schwartz 1988, pp. 3–27, 83–151). Supreme Court decisions, as Bernard Schwartz's annotated collection of the successive draft opinions reveals, "are basically collaborative efforts in which nine individualists must cooperate to bring about the desired result. Before the final opinions are issued, there may be politicking, vote switches, and horse trading to secure them; ultimately, there are usually compromises to obtain the necessary working majority" (Schwartz 1988, p. 4). It is, perhaps, no surprise, given the moral and metaphysical complexity of the issue, that a constitutional justification for any position on the abortion issue is less than rock solid.

Indeed, apart from the quirky contingencies of the reasoning leading to *Roe* v. *Wade*, abortion seems more suited to political accommodation than Constitutional law. As our analysis of the problem suggests, reason, evidence, and argument yield no decisive solution to the abortion problem. The extreme positions, though philosophically coherent, have counter-intuitive implications. Efforts by proponents to blunt these implications have not been generally persuasive. Moderate positions, though intuitively more plausible, lack philosophical coherence. The moderate is unable to identify any morally significant change in fetal development—one that will justify permitting abortion prior to the change, but forbid it thereafter.

Inasmuch as the consistency and independent validity requirements for an adequate political solution are not as stringent as those in philosophy or constitutional law, it might be best, if historical conditions were to make it possible, to shift the focus from the Supreme Court to Congress. If a moderate position cannot be shown to be morally or philosophically superior to either of the polar positions, it may be defensible as a legislative compromise—one that at the congressional level acknowledges our national ambivalence and divisions rather than papering them over.

A plausible compromise position ought to require concessions by both sides and be able to be seen by the opposing parties as somehow splitting the difference between them. One possibility is to permit early abortions—during the first trimester perhaps or, more restrictively, some earlier portion thereof, such as the first ten weeks—and to prohibit later abortions except in unusual and extreme circumstances (for example, serious threats to the mother's life or health; pregnancies resulting from rape or incest that are either undetected or psychologically denied by the pregnant women until after the "no questions asked" cut-off point; determination that a fetus is anencephalic; and so on). Under this proposal extreme liberals would retain full freedom of choice during the period within which the majority of abortions are performed, but they would have to agree to a prohibition on second and third term abortions except in certain specifically determined circumstances. Extreme conservatives would gain a strong prohibition on second term abortions (and perhaps late first term abortions as well) but would have to concede the legal (though not moral) permissibility of abortion during the first term (or some significant part thereof).

An abortion law that is permissive during the earliest stages of pregnancy but increasingly restrictive somewhere around the beginning of the second trimester may thus be regarded as splitting the difference between the polar positions and providing the basis for a mutually acceptable, integrity-preserving compromise. Although similar to *Roe* v. *Wade* in its attempt to balance the competing viewpoints, it would redraw the line to give more weight to the prolife position. Further details would have to be negotiated by the affected parties or by their political representatives.

Variations on this proposal have been suggested in the literature (Frohock 1983, pp. 158–91; Berger and Berger 1984, pp. 73–82). The basic idea was even incorporated into an early draft of *Roe* v. *Wade* by Justice Blackmun. He eventually altered it, however, after receiving a letter from Justice Marshall, who proposed that "drawing the line at viability accommodates the interests at stake better than drawing it at the end of the first trimester. Given the difficulties which many women may have in believing that they are pregnant and in deciding to seek an abortion, I fear that the earlier date may not in practice serve the interests of those women, which your opinion does seek to serve" (Schwartz 1988, p. 149). In a letter to Blackmun dated one day earlier, however, Justice Douglas had written, "I favor the first trimester rather than viability."

Even if a political dialogue can be initiated around this or some similar compromise proposal, many difficulties remain, including questions about public funding (Sher 1981), enforcement (Luker 1984a), and abortion for fetal deformity. The latter could turn out to be an insurmountable barrier. Amniocentesis, the principal form of prenatal diagnosis, cannot be performed until late in the first trimester or early in the second. Abortions for various defects detected by amniocentesis are therefore performed in the second trimester and would, on this compromise proposal, henceforth be prohibited. Allowing abortion of fetuses with various detectable anomalies is just as vital to the world view and way of life of prochoice activists as forbidding it is to that of prolife activists. Moreover, the latest Gallup poll indicates that 60 percent of the population approves of abortion "if the baby will be born deformed" (Gallup Poll 1988). Respondents must, of course, have interpreted "deformed" in a variety of different ways, but however interpreted, restricting abortion to the first trimester may be too extreme for a sizable majority if it were to prohibit abortion for *all* prenatally detected fetal defects.

Could prolife activists be persuaded to allow an additional exception to the prohibition against second trimester abortions for prenatally detected fetal anomaly? Probably not. Abortions for "fetal indications," as Luker observes, are among those least tolerable for prolife activists:

Abortions for fetal deformity cut to the deepest level of prolife feeling about "selective abortion." Because the logic of abortion in this case depends upon a judgment that the embryo is "damaged" in one respect or another, it suggests to pro-life people an acceptance of the idea that humans can be ranked along some scale of perfection and that people who fall below a certain arbitrary standard can be excluded. . . . Already for example, the movement is vigorously opposing amniocentesis. . . . The present surgeon-general of the United States, [C.] Everett Koop, an active pro-life supporter, has called amniocentesis exams "search and destroy missions," and the movement itself has labeled amniocentesis "selective genocide against the disabled" (Luker 1984a, p. 236).

A similar outlook can be found among some advocates for the disabled who, though generally supporting *Roe* v. *Wade*, are opposed to abortion for "fetal indications" because, they maintain, it suggests that the disabled are less valuable as human beings than other people.

Differences over this matter would have to be addressed by those charged with negotiating the detailed terms of any compromise on the abortion issue. One possibility might be to allow postamniocentesis abortion for some but not all genetic anomalies. This is suggested by Catholic theologian Richard McBrien, who, although not endorsing the compromise proposed above, acknowledges the possibility of leaving "*legal* room for abortion in the cases of rape, incest, danger of [sic] the mother's life, or radical deformity of the fetus" (McBrien 1987, p. 166). Whether this suggestion would win sufficient support is likely to turn on the interpretation of radical deformity. The problem might, however, be circumvented by the development of new types of prenatal testing—for example, chorionic villus sampling as an alternative to amniocentesis. Whereas a diagnosis of fetal abnormality by amniocentesis cannot be made until the second trimester, chorionic villus sampling can be performed during the ninth or tenth week of pregnancy. Indeed, a newly reported variant of chorionic villus sampling may enable doctors to perform prenatal diagnosis as early as the sixth week (*New York Times*, 29 December 1988). The development of chorionic villus sampling would, therefore, move the entire process of prenatal diagnosis and abortion for fetal anomaly into what would, under the proposed compromise, be the protected area of the first trimester (Rhoads, Jackson et al. 1989; Mennuti 1989).

Another, perhaps deeper, difficulty remains. Even if prochoice advocates were to make the concessions identified above, one might think that prolife activists would never agree to this or any other proposed compromise on the abortion issue. For there is a fundamental difference between the prolife and prochoice outlooks. The prochoice outlook is by its very nature pluralistic. The secular pluralism of prochoice advocates allows them to regard their own particular world view and way of life as one among many. They would concede that had they been born in different times or raised in different social and cultural circumstances, their world views and ways of life might have been quite different. Indeed, they should be able to conceive of contingencies that would have resulted in their now holding prolife views.

Prolife activists, on the other hand, do not see their world view and way of life as contingent, as only one among many. Theirs is not *a* world view and way of life; it is, rather, *the* (only true) view of the world and way to live. It is not part of their world view and way of life to conceive that had they been brought up in radically different circumstances by radically different parents, they might hold correspondingly different views. One cannot, then, persuade them to compromise without changing them into different people. Thus reason, evidence, or argument are of limited effectiveness. All such efforts beg the question, for they presuppose a plurality of legitimate world views and ways of life with respect to abortion, and that is exactly what most prolife activists deny.

There are two ways of addressing this difficulty, one philosophical and the other political. The philosophical response is essentially my argument in Chapter 4, which provides a philosophical foundation for a pluralistic moral epistemology. I maintain, first, that there is no single world view and way of life that can claim to be uniquely supported by abstract reason or the "facts"; and, second, that rationally irreconcilable conflict rooted in opposing world views and ways of life is a feature of social existence that must be acknowledged by any adequate conception of ethics. Drawing on the importance of both the personal and impersonal perspectives for an integrated human life, I conclude that compromise is sometimes both necessary, because of conflicts between personal perspectives, and possible, because of our capacity to assume a more impersonal perspective. This latter perspective with regard to abortion allows us to acknowledge the contingency of our own world views and ways of life and the equal legitimacy of some others with which ours may occasionally conflict. Fully and carefully spelled out, this argument may be persuasive with some prolife activists. Yet those who continue to resist compromise cannot be shown by this argument alone to be irrational (Nagel 1987). And even if we could convince ourselves that they were being irrational, this would be small consolation if their continued resistance were sufficient to obstruct efforts to devise a satisfactory compromise.

Political considerations may in this event achieve what philosophical argument alone cannot. Governor Cuomo, for example, has pointed out that conscientious people of good will on both sides of the abortion issue are often allies in other areas: "In many cases, the proponents of legal abortion are the very people who have worked with Catholics to realize the goals of social justice set out in papal encyclicals" (1984, p. 34). Efforts on the part of politicians to emphasize this and other similarities between the opposing camps may eventually lead to lowering the heat on the abortion issue. As Cuomo suggests,

> Without lessening their insistence on a woman's right to an abortion, the people who call themselves "pro-choice" can support the development of government programs that present an impoverished mother with the full range of support she needs to bear and raise her children, to have a real choice. Without dropping their campaign to ban abortion, those who gather under the banner of "prolife" can join in developing and enacting a legislative bill of rights for mothers and children, as the bishops have already proposed (1984, pp. 35–36).

The larger problem might also be "fractionated" (Chapter 5, pp. 130–31), and progress made on various subissues. Both prolife and prochoice activists are, for example, concerned about the high rate of teenage pregnancy. Joint conferences that focus on this problem might reveal points of agreement that could lead to concrete collaborative efforts to address it. This in turn might induce each side to refrain from demonizing the other and eventually lead to compromise on larger issues.

Finally, even if those holding polar positions cannot be induced to accept some sort of compromise, a clear and articulate political appeal to the significant majority favoring a more moderate position with respect to the law may be sufficient to defuse the issue. Both prolife and prochoice activists must, if they are to be politically effective, court the significant majority of individuals favoring either moderate moral positions or compromise political positions. If a well-conceived political compromise is explicitly understood and endorsed as such by a significant majority, the bitter, polarizing efforts of activists on each side of the issue will eventually fall on deaf ears. Further efforts at civil disobedience, restricting various types of research, single-issue politics, and so on would become antagonistic or counterproductive. Thus even if a political compromise cannot in the end gain the support of the activists or those holding extreme positions, it may nonetheless be effective.

The moral debate would in this event continue. The question of whether a right to life is a matter of being human or being a person is as central to self-understanding as questions of whether the earth or the sun is at the center of our universe or whether the Book of Genesis or *The Origin of Species* provides a more accurate account of our beginnings. A political compromise would, however, allow us to contain the debate until one side or the other acquires considerably more popular support than it now enjoys. And this would be no small achievement.

Certainly there are many difficulties with this proposal. It is offered not as a blueprint or the last word on the issue but rather as a starting point for political discussion of the merits and possibilities of a legislative compromise. A full-blown argument for a political compromise on abortionwould require more space and detailed consideration than I can here provide. My principal aim is not to show that compromise on this vexing and divisive issue is actually achievable but rather to show that it is conceivable and that politicians of strong and diverse moral convictions who seek compromise on this and similar issues can do so with integrity.

COMPROMISE AND INTEGRITY IN POLITICS

If a well-grounded political compromise is available on the abortion question, it should be possible to devise plausible compromise positions on many less controversial moral issues as well. It is one thing, however, to identify a reasonable political compromise on paper and quite another actually to negotiate and implement it. The first can be done from afar and by a single individual; the second is a complex political undertaking requiring commitment, long hours of skillful coalition-building and negotiation, astute judgment, and a receptive social climate. The philosopher may be able to show that it is possible to compromise with integrity on a complex moral issue, but it is the politician who must persevere in the hard work of transforming possibility into reality.

Some years ago, T. V. Smith, an Illinois legislator and academic philosopher, proposed a division of labor for political compromise:

> Arrangement of compromise, like many another good practice, belongs today to specialists. We have such specialists, the politicians. Let these moral middlemen do this dirty work for you. They are paid to do it, and trained to do it. Moreover, they cannot do it well if you pull your punches. It is their business to find a middle course between two sincere and tangible positions. To locate the middle they must reckon from stationary banks (1942, p. 13).

Though overstated (the difference between politicians and the rest of us is less a difference of kind than a difference of degree), the recommendation is basically sound. On complex matters like abortion we will usually do better to allow partisans on each side to state their position in its strongest form and encourage politicians to negotiate the compromises. Empirical research suggests that the best compromises—those most well grounded, stable, and mutually beneficial—often come when each party to the dispute is able to state and defend its position in its strongest form. Guided by these "stationary banks," skilled politicians will look beyond more mechanical compromise positions to those that imaginatively respond to as many of the partisans' concerns as is possible. These so-called integrative compromises are likely to be the most satisfying and stable (Carens 1979, pp. 126–29; Pruitt and Lewis 1975).

Yet politicians should not and need not be moral ciphers. Politicians without principled commitments to particular world views and ways of life are, as former Senator Culver suggests, unlikely to earn the respect and trust of either their constituents or their political colleagues. Without respect and trust they cannot be effective. The moral chameleon is no more welcome in politics than in other areas of social life. Yet a politician's identity and integrity are a function not only of her nonpolitical commitments but also of her commitment to effecting (and not simply accepting) political resolution of social, moral, and economic conflicts. Whereas we as citizens are generally prepared to accept the outcomes of political rule, the politician is charged with devising and negotiating these outcomes. Thus we cannot without hypocrisy impugn the integrity of politicians who negotiate such compromises if we accept and endorse the products of their endeavors.

The vocation of politics requires a creative and complex blend of personal commitment and professional tolerance. These are integrated in part through identifying with the historical and communal aspects of political rule. Even here, however, there is nothing to prevent a politician from expressing deep personal allegiance to positions she is nonetheless willing, albeit reluctantly, to compromise in the political arena. Politicians personally opposed to abortion may, for example, express and act upon prolife convictions in a wide variety of ways. Governor Cuomo points to programs put in place in his state that make continuing a pregnancy and giving birth a much more attractive option to women than it was in the past: "One program in particular we believe holds a great deal of promise. It's called 'new avenues to dignity,' and it seeks to provide a teen-age mother with the special service she needs to continue her education, to train for a job, to become capable of standing on her own, to provide for herself and the child she is bringing into the world" (Cuomo 1984, p. 36). Mary Meehan and others challenging the integrity of politicians who refrain from directly transforming their personal moral convictions into political action fail to understand and, indeed, pose a threat to political government. They are opposed not only to certain politicians but also to the political resolution of deep moral conflict.[5]

Elizabeth Drew reports on a speech given by Senator Culver on single-issue politics in which he expressed concern that "strident and self-righteous groups of voters are proliferating in number and narrowing in focus." He said, Drew writes,

> that in the past politicians could count on the support of groups not each of which would agree with them every time, and "being right" on most of the issues most of the time was more than enough. Now, he went on, "for each narrow, self-defined lobby . . . the worth of every public servant is measured by a single litmus test of ideological purity. Taken together, the tests are virtually impossible for any officeholder who hopes to keep both his conscience and his constituency" (1979, p. 45).

Interestingly enough, Drew considers this line of argument not in connection with pressures placed on Culver from the political right but from the other side of the spectrum—a lobbyist for the Equal Rights Amendment.

We cannot reasonably expect our politicians to practice the art of compromise—that is, to be politicians—if we do not acknowledge that, though we want them to be people of integrity and have particular views on controversial issues, they cannot (and should not) as politicians advocate them as strongly as we can (and should). This is the division of labor between citizen-partisans and citizen-politicians proposed by T. V. Smith and overlooked by Ralph Nader in his attack on Joan Claybrook after she left her position as a lobbyist for his organization to accept a position as head of the National Highway Transportation Safety Agency (Chapter 3, pp. 64–66). The polity, like the individual, works best by tacking between two perspectives (Chapter 4, pp. 98–99). We go back and forth between the outlooks of partisans and those of the politicians, who represent and must provide direction and integrity for the community as a whole.

In a democracy the integrity and effectiveness of our politicians are determined in part by the electorate. To attract and retain decent and effective men and women to the vocation of politics, citizens must acquire a better understanding of compromise and integrity as they relate to both ethics and politics. Requiring the impossible of our politicians—that they retain the highest degree of ideological or philosophical purity while fulfilling their political roles—is to create a vacuum in our politics that will cheerfully be filled by the incompetent and the unscrupulous. We can avoid this by recognizing that politics requires compromise between voters and politicians as well as among politicians. In both cases, however, an appreciation of and identification with politics as a historical and communal undertaking allows us to make these compromises while still preserving our integrity.

Notes

CHAPTER 1.
THE MEANINGS OF COMPROMISE

1. In some cases, a compromise outcome will be limited to a particular situation; in others, it will be more permanent or "structural." Article III of the U.S. Constitution provides a good example of a structural compromise. It mediates a dispute between federalists, who wanted constitutional establishment of a large federal judiciary, and antifederalists, who, apart from a federal Supreme Court, wanted only the various state courts. Article III eventually settled the matter by allowing for a system of lower federal courts but investing ultimate power in determining whether and how to establish them to Congress. The result was a compromise in the sense that it established the possibility of a large federal judiciary (thereby placating the federalists) while leaving its ultimate fate to Congress (which being subject to local control placated the antifederalists). The Judiciary Act of 1789 was the first piece of major legislation to begin to work out the details of the federal judiciary under this structural compromise (Nowak et al. 1978, pp. 26–30). I am grateful to Stephen L. Esquith for calling the notion of structural compromise and this particular example to my attention.

2. A procedure that closely approximates splitting the difference is what Joseph Carens calls compromise by succession (1979, p. 134). Assuming a continuing relationship among the contending parties and that the conflict in question will recur, the compromise may take the form of one party obtaining everything it wants the first time, the second party getting its way the second time, the first party getting its way the third time, and so on. A simple example is the alternate possession rule in college basketball. In situations in which two opposing players simultaneously acquire possession of a loose ball, the matter is settled by awarding the ball the first time to the team that lost the game-opening tip off and the next time to the other team, and so on by succession.

3. It is, I acknowledge, sometimes difficult to distinguish moral from nonmoral conflicts and moral values and principles from nonmoral interests. Moral and nonmoral considerations do not fall into two demarcated categories. Moreover, as Williams (1985) cogently argues, systematic or doctrinaire employment of the distinction oversimplifies and distorts ethical reflection. Yet there are, it seems, clear or paradigm cases of each type of conflict and I

175

have wherever possible tried to use them in my illustrations. For example, a disagreement whether to go to one restaurant or another involves only non-moral interests. A disagreement about the permissibility of abortion, however, is a function of conflicting moral values or principles.

Questions remain about exactly what makes a dispute moral or nonmoral and what makes one conflict a conflict of interests and another a conflict of moral values and principles. I discuss this in Chapters 3 and 4 but provide nothing resembling a comprehensive response. Moreover, many cases are much less clear than the two I have just cited and raise difficult questions about whether, and if so how, we may draw the line.

I generally restrict the discussion to comparatively clear cases of moral and nonmoral conflict. Just because we have twilight, as Samuel Johnson once said, does not mean that there is not a clear distinction between noon and midnight. Certainly the task of exploring the differences and relations between moral and non-moral conflicts is of greater consequence than trying to determine exactly when day turns to night; but I trust that for present purposes it can be put aside. My principal argument will, I believe, be compatible with a more complex understanding of the relationships between moral and nonmoral conflicts.

4. Here and elsewhere I use the notion of a conflict of principles to designate any deep and (apparently) rationally irreconcilable conflict of moral values or principles. Such conflicts may be rooted in abstract, highly general, and impersonal considerations such as the principle of utility or Kant's categorical imperative, or they may involve principled commitments to local and particular world views and ways of life (Chapter 4). Any conflict that can be traced to incompatible, highly cherished ethical considerations, whether derived from abstract principle or principled commitment to a particular way of life (for example, being a practicing Catholic or a devout Muslim), will for convenience be designated a conflict of values or principles (Chapter 3).

5. The notion of an internal compromise is, of course, metaphorical. The self does not literally divide. Nor are there opposing parties who literally debate or make concessions to each other. An internal compromise most closely resembles an external compromise between two (or possibly more) parties that is mediated by a third.

CHAPTER 2. MORAL COMPROMISE

1. This fictitious case, which is based on an actual situation, was prepared by Joy Curtis and is presented and analyzed in a much briefer form in Benjamin and Curtis (1986, pp. 105–108) and Benjamin and Curtis (1987, pp. 441–48).

2. It is important to note, however, that both arguments rest in part on difficult determinations of fact. In addition to the problem regarding autonomy, there are questions about how much other patients would benefit if the staff were not doing so much for Marsha Hocking, how much her care is costing, who is paying the bill, whether the party paying the bill believes that the possible benefits outweigh the costs, and so on.

3. Of course this is not the only relevant standpoint. A resolution that preserved overall team effectiveness at the expense of other, more important moral considerations would be highly questionable.

CHAPTER 4. COMPROMISE
AND ETHICAL THEORY

1. Hampshire is, however, mistaken in adding Rawls's name to this list. As Rawls's later writings make clear, his theory of justice assumes that most interesting and important ethical questions are rationally irreconcilable: "Our individual and associative points of view, intellectual affinities and affective attachments are too diverse, especially in a free democratic society, to allow of lasting and reasoned agreement. Many conceptions of the world can plausibly be constructed from different standpoints. Diversity naturally arises from our limited powers and distinct perspectives; it is unrealistic to suppose that all our differences are rooted solely in ignorance and perversity, or else in the rivalries that arise from scarcity. Justice as fairness tries to construct a conception of justice that takes deep and unresolvable differences on matters of fundamental significance as a permanent condition of human life" (Rawls 1980, p. 542). In "Justice as Fairness: Political Not Metaphysical," he contrasts his (political) theory with the more comprehensive moral theories of Kant and Mill (Rawls 1985, pp. 245–51).

2. For purposes of her research, Luker defined prolife activists as those spending at least ten hours a week on prolife activity and prochoice activists as those spending at least five hours a week on prochoice activity. The different levels of activity were chosen in part because of the different historical phases of the two movements (Luker 1984a, pp. 250–54). The prochoice movement was most active and visible before 1973, whereas the prolife movement was so after 1973. Few prochoice activists, if any, worked more than five hours a week on prochoice activities in the early years (1977–80) of Luker's study.

3. This argument is developed at greater length in Chapter 6.

4. Other controversies rooted in conflicting world views and ways of life have, for example, to do with the rights of homosexuals and the independent moral standing of both nonhuman animals and nature. Thomas Nagel suggests that the same may be true of differing moral perspectives on nuclear weapons. "Whatever they may say," Nagel writes, "most of the defenders of these weapons are not suitably horrified at the possibility of a war in which hundreds of millions of people would be killed." Perhaps this is because a significantly greater proportion of them hold world views that include an afterlife (for virtuous anticommunists) than do those strongly opposed to nuclear weapons (Nagel 1986, p. 230n4).

5. William G. Perry, Jr., has written thoughtfully of the challenges posed by a good liberal arts education to college students' world views and ways of life. As students' simple and doctrinaire world views are discredited by new information and ways of thinking, educators are responsible "to hear and honor, by simple acknowledgment, the students' losses." Students must be allowed to

grieve and mourn the loss of their former selves if they are to go on and, with reasonable confidence and hope, develop more complex and less stable ways of viewing the world. "It may be a great joy to discover a new and more complex way of thinking and seeing; but yesterday one thought in simpler ways, and hope and aspiration were embedded in those ways." In allowing "a little time for the guts to catch up with such leaps of the mind" by acknowledging the student's loss, the responsible educator makes it more likely that the transition will be stable (Perry 1981, p. 108).

6. Our ambivalence and the tension between these perspectives generally is traceable to the free-will problem (Beardsley 1960).

7. The day may soon come when "speciesism" (P. Singer 1975) and "heterosexism" come to play the same sort of role in our language—and in effecting social and political change—as "racism" and "sexism."

8. An additional difficulty with the Kantian principle of respect for persons is disagreement over what constitutes respect. Does a man show respect for a woman by holding a door open for her? Do doctors show respect for their patients by calling them by their first names? People continue to argue about these and similar matters.

9. "Sometimes, and with some moral concerns, the complex description of a whole way of life, and of its history, do fill the place occupied in other moral contexts by general principles of utility and justice: that is, the justification stops when the interconnections of practices and sentiments within a complete way of life are described" (Hampshire 1983, p. 5).

10. See, for example, Hampshire (1983), Putnam (1983), Williams (1985), Nagel (1979, 1986), Baier (1985), M. G. Singer (1986), and Berlin (1969, 1988).

CHAPTER 5. JUDGMENT
AND THE ART OF COMPROMISE

1. Michael Walzer (1987, pp. 30–32) retells a Talmudic story that bears quite nicely on this point:

The story involves a dispute among a group of sages; the subject does not matter. Rabbi Eliezer stood alone, a minority of one, having brought forward every imaginable argument and failed to convince his colleagues. Exasperated, he called for divine help: "If the law is as I say, let this carob tree prove it." Whereupon the carob tree was lifted a hundred cubits in the air—some say it was lifted four hundred cubits. Rabbi Joshua spoke for the majority: "No proof can be brought from a carob tree." Then Rabbi Eliezer said, "If the law is as I say, let this stream of water prove it." And the stream immediately began to flow backward. But Rabbi Joshua said, "No proof can be brought from a stream of water." Again Rabbi Eliezer said: "If the law is as I say, let the walls of this schoolhouse prove it." And the walls began to fall. But Rabbi Joshua rebuked the walls, saying that they had no business interfering in a dispute among scholars over the moral law; and they stopped falling and to this day still stand, though at a sharp angle. And then Rabbi Eliezer called on God himself: "If the law is as I say, let it be proved from heaven." Whereupon a voice cried out, "Why do you dispute with Rabbi Eliezer? In all matters the law is as he says." But Rabbi Joshua stood up and exclaimed, "It is not in heaven!"

"Morality," Walzer emphasizes, "is something we have to argue about. . . . There is a tradition, a body of moral knowledge; and there is this group of sages, arguing. There isn't anything else."

2. If, for example, a radically new scientific concept were predictable, it would have to be articulable; if it were articulable, it would not be radically innovative (MacIntyre 1979, p. 5).

CHAPTER 6. COMPROMISE
AND INTEGRITY IN POLITICS

1. In a well-known article (1971) Judith Jarvis Thomson argues that in certain circumstances (for example, rape or contraceptive failure), abortion would be justifiable even if we grant the fetus full moral standing. Although agreeing with Thomson's general point, Feinberg (1986, pp. 275-88) shows that these circumstances may be more limited than she suggests.

2. Although Wertheimer does not endorse the extreme conservative position in this article, he formulates one of the most compelling arguments for it.

3. Although scheduled to be implemented in March 1988, the rules were challenged in court and enforcement temporarily blocked by a federal district judge in Colorado (New York Times, 17 February 1988).

4. Mary Ann Glendon's comparative analysis of abortion laws in other western nations suggests that political compromise on this issue is not only possible but also quite common. She indicates, for example, that the legal situation in France "provides strong support for the proposition that a divided society can compromise successfully on the abortion issue" (Abortion and Divorce in Western Law [Cambridge, Mass.: Harvard University Press, 1987, pp. 18-19]). I regret that I discovered Glendon's analysis too late to incorporate it into the text.

5. The same is true, for example, of Terrance McConnell's argument that Catholic politicians who value their integrity "should abandon either their support of permissive abortion laws or their Catholicism" (1987, p. 106). McConnell is more concerned with the individual's integrity as a Catholic than he is with the individual's integrity as a Catholic politician. The world of politics and political accommodation is for McConnell subordinate to the world of religion and religious conviction. On my account, however, both may be of equal importance, giving rise to a more complex conception of integrity and ethics than either McConnell or Meehan are prepared to acknowledge (Chapter 3, pp. 53-59; Chapter 4, pp. 101-6).

Selected Bibliography

Abram, M. B., and Wolf, S. M. 1984. "Public Involvement in Medical Ethics," *New England Journal of Medicine* 310: 627–32.

Arras, J. D. 1984. "Retreat from the Right to Health Care: The President's Commission and Access to Health Care," *Cardozo Law Review* 6: 321–45.

Auerbach, J. S. 1983. *Justice without Law*. New York: Oxford University Press.

Baier, A. [1979] 1985. "Mind and Change of Mind." In *Postures of the Mind*, edited by Annette Baier, pp. 51–73. Minneapolis: University of Minnesota Press.

———. [1980] 1985. "Secular Faith." In *Postures of the Mind*, edited by Annette Baier, pp. 292–308. Minneapolis: University of Minnesota Press.

Bayer, R. 1984. "Ethics, Politics, and Access to Health Care," *Cardozo Law Review* 6: 303–20.

Beardsley, E. 1960. "Determinism and Moral Perspectives," *Philosophy and Phenomenological Research* 21: 1–20.

Beiner, R. 1983. *Political Judgment*. Chicago: University of Chicago Press.

Benditt, T. 1979. "Compromising Interests and Principles." In *Compromise in Ethics, Law, and Politics*, edited by J. Roland Pennock and John W. Chapman, pp. 26–37. New York: New York University Press.

Benjamin, M. 1987. "Rethinking Ethical Theory: Suggestions from and for the Classroom," *Teaching Philosophy* 10: 285–94.

Benjamin, M., and Curtis, J. 1986. *Ethics in Nursing*. 2d ed. New York: Oxford University Press.

———. 1987. "Ethical Autonomy in Nursing." In *Health Care Ethics*, edited by Donald Van De Veer and Tom Regan, pp. 394–427. Philadelphia: Temple University Press.

Benjamin, M., and Weil, W. B., Jr. 1987. "Ethical Issues at the Outset of Life." In *Ethical Issues at the Outset of Life*, edited by William B. Weil, Jr., and Martin Benjamin, pp. 3–40. Boston: Blackwell Scientific Publications.

Berger, B., and Berger, P. L. 1983. *The War over the Family*. Garden City, N.Y.: Anchor/Doubleday.

Berlin, I. [1958] 1969. "Two Concepts of Liberty." In *Four Essays on Liberty*, edited by Isaiah Berlin, pp. 118–72. Oxford: Oxford University Press.

———. 1988. "On the Pursuit of the Ideal," *New York Review of Books* (17 March): 11–18.

Bok, S. 1978. *Lying: Moral Choice in Public and Private Life*. New York: Pantheon.

———. 1982. *Secrets*. New York: Pantheon.

181

Bond, J. 1988. "Dr. King's Unwelcome Heirs," *New York Times* (11 December).

Brewin, T. B. 1985. "Truth, Trust, and Paternalism," *Lancet* (31 August): 490–92.

Broyard, A. 1983. "Review of *The Butcher of Lyon: The Story of Infamous Nazi Klaus Barbie* by Brendan Murphy," *New York Times* (19 November).

Callahan, S. 1984. "Value Choices in Abortion." In *Abortion: Understanding Differences*, edited by Sidney Callahan and Daniel Callahan, pp. 285–301. New York: Plenum Press.

Camus, A. [1947] 1972. *The Plague*. Translated by Stuart Gilbert. New York: Vintage.

———. 1956. *The Fall*. Translated by Justin O'Brien. New York: Vintage.

Caplan, A. 1983. "Can Applied Ethics Be Effective in Health Care and Should It Strive to Be?" *Ethics* 93: 311–19.

Carens, J. H. 1979. "Compromise in Politics." In *Compromise in Ethics, Law, and Politics*, edited by J. Roland Pennock and John W. Chapman, pp. 123–41. New York: New York University Press.

Ceci, S. J., and Liker, J. 1986. "Academic and Nonacademic Intelligence: An Experimental Separation." In *Practical Intelligence*, edited by Robert J. Sternberg and Richard K. Wagner, pp. 119–42. Cambridge: Cambridge University Press.

Cohen, C. 1971. *Democracy*. Athens: University of Georgia Press.

Cranford, R. E. 1988. "The Persistent Vegetative State: The Medical Reality (Getting the Facts Straight)," *Hastings Center Report* 18 (February–March): 27–32.

Crick, B. 1972. *In Defence of Politics*. 2d ed. Chicago: University of Chicago Press.

Cuomo, M. 1984. "Religious Belief and Public Morality," *New York Review of Books* (25 October): 32–37.

Dennett, D. 1976. "Conditions of Personhood," In *The Identities of Persons*, edited by Amelie Rorty, pp. 175–96. Berkeley: University of California Press.

Dostoevsky, F. [1880] 1950. *The Brothers Karamazov*. Translated by Constance Garnett. New York: Random House.

Drew, E. 1979. *Senator*. New York: Simon & Schuster (Touchstone edition, 1980).

Engelhardt, H. T. 1978. "Medicine and the Concept of Person." In *Ethical Issues in Death and Dying*, edited by Tom L. Beauchamp and Seymour Perlin, pp. 271–84. Englewood Cliffs, N.J.: Prentice-Hall.

English, J. 1975. "Abortion and the Concept of a Person," *Canadian Journal of Philosophy* 5: 233–43. Reprinted in *The Problem of Abortion*, edited by Joel Feinberg, pp. 151–60. Belmont, Calif.: Wadsworth, 1984.

Feinberg, J. 1974. "The Rights of Animals and Unborn Generations." In *Philosophy and Environmental Crisis*, edited by William T. Blackstone, pp. 43–68. Athens: University of Georgia Press.

———. 1986. "Abortion." In *Matters of Life and Death*, 2d ed., edited by Tom Regan, pp. 256–93. New York: Random House.

Fiedler, L. 1984. "The Tyranny of the Normal," *Hastings Center Report* 14 (April): 40–42.

Fine, A. 1988. "The Ethics of Fetal Tissue Transplants," *Hastings Center Report* 18 (June–July): 5–8.

Fingarette, H. 1969. *Self-Deception*. London: Routledge & Kegan Paul.

Fisher, R. 1964. "Fractionating Conflict." In *International Conflict and Behavioral Science*, edited by Roger Fisher, pp. 91–109. New York: Basic Books.

Fisher, R., and Ury, W. 1981. *Getting to Yes: Negotiating Agreement without Giving In*. Boston: Houghton Mifflin.

Frankfurt, H. 1971. "Freedom of the Will and the Concept of a Person," *Journal of Philosophy* 68: 5–20.

Frederiksen, N. 1986. "Toward a Broader Conception of Human Intelligence." In *Practical Intelligence*, edited by Robert J. Sternberg and Richard K. Wagner, pp. 84–116. Cambridge: Cambridge University Press.

Frohock, F. 1983. *Abortion*. Westport, Conn.: Greenwood Press.

Gaita, R. 1981. "Integrity," *Aristotelian Society*, supplementary vol. 55: 161–76.

Gallup Poll on Abortion. 1988. *Minneapolis Star Tribune* (23 October).

Gardner, H. 1983. *Frames of Mind: The Theory of Multiple Intelligences*. New York: Basic Books.

Gewirth, A. 1960. "Positive 'Ethics' and Normative 'Science,' " *Philosophical Review* 69: 311–30.

Gorovitz, S. 1982. "Can Physicians Mind Their Own Business and Still Practice Medicine?" In *Who Decides? Conflicts of Rights in Health Care*, edited by Nora K. Bell, pp. 83–93. Clifton, N.J.: Humana Press.

Green, M. B. and Wikler, D. 1980. "Brain Death and Personal Identity," *Philosophy & Public Affairs* 9: 105–33.

Hampshire, S. 1983. *Morality and Conflict*. Cambridge, Mass.: Harvard University Press.

Hare, R. M. 1981. *Moral Thinking*. Oxford: Oxford University Press.

Janofsky, M. 1988. "The Judges' Subjective Yardsticks," *New York Times* (21 February).

Jennings, B. 1985. "Legislative Ethics and Moral Minimalism." In *Representation and Responsibility*, edited by Bruce Jennings and Daniel Callahan, pp. 149–65. New York: Plenum Press.

———. 1986. "Applied Ethics and the Vocation of Social Science." In *New Directions in Ethics*, edited by Joseph P. DeMarco and Richard M. Fox, pp. 205–17. New York and London: Routledge and Kegan Paul.

Jonsen, A. R. 1983. "Ethics, the Law, and the Treatment of Seriously Ill Newborns." In *Legal and Ethical Aspects of Treating Critically and Terminally Ill Patients*, edited by A. E. Doudera and J. D. Peters, pp. 237–41. Ann Arbor, Mich.: A.A.U.P.H.A. Press.

Katz, J. 1984. *The Silent World of Doctor and Patient*. New York: Free Press.

Keneally, T. 1982. *Schindler's List*. New York: Simon and Schuster.

Kierkegaard, S. [1847] 1956. *Purity of the Heart Is to Will One Thing*. Translated by Douglas V. Steere. New York: Harper Torchbooks.

Kolata, G. 1988. "Medical Groups Reach Compromise on Frequency of Giving Pap Tests," *New York Times* (7 January).

Kotre, J. 1984. *Outliving the Self*. Baltimore: Johns Hopkins University Press.

Kuflik, A. 1979. "Morality and Compromise," In *Compromise in Ethics, Law, and Politics*, edited by J. Roland Pennock and John W. Chapman, pp. 38–65. New York: New York University Press.

Kuhn, T. S. 1970. *The Structure of Scientific Revolutions*. 2d ed., enlarged. Chicago: University of Chicago Press.

———. 1977. "Objectivity, Value Judgment, and Theory Choice." In *The Essential Tension*, edited by Thomas S. Kuhn, pp. 320–39. Chicago: University of Chicago Press.

Kuhse, H., and Singer, P. 1985. *Should the Baby Live?* Oxford: Oxford University Press.

Langerak, E. A. 1979. "Abortion: Listening to the Middle," *Hastings Center Report* 9 (October): 24–28.

Larmore, C. E. 1981. "Moral Judgment," *Review of Metaphysics* 35: 275–96.

Lenin, V. I. [1920] 1940. *"Left-Wing" Communism, An Infantile Disorder.* New York: International Publishers.

Leyva, F. A., and Furth, H. G. 1986. "Compromise Formation in Social Conflicts: The Influence of Age, Issue, and Interpersonal Context," *Journal of Youth and Adolescence* 15: 441–52.

Lincoln, A. [1858] 1953. "Speech during Last Debate with Douglas (15 Oct. 1858)." In *The Collected Works of Abraham Lincoln*, vol. 3, edited by Roy P. Basler, pp. 297–318. New Brunswick, N.J.: Rutgers University Press.

Lipman, M.; Sharp, A. M.; and Oscanyon, F. S. 1980. *Philosophy in the Classroom*. 2d ed. Philadephia: Temple University Press.

Locke, J. [1690] 1961. *Essay Concerning Human Understanding*, vol. 1, edited by John Yolton. London: J. M. Dent & Sons.

Lomasky, L. 1982. "Being a Person—Does It Matter?" *Philosophical Topics* 12: 139–52. Reprinted in *The Problem of Abortion*, edited by Joel Feinberg, pp. 161–72. Belmont, Calif.: Wadsworth, 1984.

Luban, D. 1985. "Bargaining and Compromise: Recent Work on Negotiation and Informal Justice," *Philosophy & Public Affairs* 14: 397–416.

Luker, K. 1984a. *Abortion and the Politics of Motherhood*. Berkeley and Los Angeles: University of California Press.

———. 1984b. "Abortion and the Meaning of Life." In *Abortion: Understanding Differences*, edited by Sidney Callahan and Daniel Callahan, pp. 25–45. New York: Plenum Press.

McBrien, R. 1987. *Caesar's Coin*. New York: Macmillan.

McConnell, T. 1987. "Permissive Abortion Laws, Religion, and Moral Compromise," *Public Affairs Quarterly* 1 (January): 95–109.

MacIntyre, A. 1979. "Seven Traits for the Future," *Hastings Center Report* 9 (February): 5–7.

———. 1981. *After Virtue*. Notre Dame, Ind.: University of Notre Dame Press.

Marris, P. 1975. *Loss and Change*. Garden City, N.Y.: Anchor Books.

Martin, M. 1986. *Self-Deception and Morality*. Lawrence, Kans.: University Press of Kansas.

Matthews, G. 1984. *Dialogues with Children*. Cambridge, Mass.: Harvard University Press.

Meehan, M. 1984a. "In Things Touching Conscience," *Human Life Review* 10 (Winter): 14–26.

_____. 1984b. "More Trouble than They're Worth?" In *Abortion: Understanding Differences*, edited by Sidney Callahan and Daniel Callahan, pp. 145–70. New York: Plenum Press.

Mennuti, M. T. "Prenatal Diagnosis—Advances Bring New Challenges." *New England Journal of Medicine* 320: 661–63.

Midgley, M. 1985. "Philosophizing Out in the World," *Social Research* 52: 447–70.

Mill, J. S. [1861] 1957. *Utilitarianism*. New York: Library of Liberal Arts.

Mitchell, C. 1982. "Integrity in Interprofessional Relationships." In *Responsibility in Health Care*, edited by George J. Agich, pp. 163–84. Dordrecht, The Netherlands: D. Reidel.

Murray, T. H. 1987. "So Maybe It's Wrong: Should We *Do* Anything about It? Ethics and Social Policy," In *Ethical Issues at the Outset of Life*, edited by William B. Weil, Jr., and Martin Benjamin, pp. 239–57. Boston: Blackwell Scientific Publications.

Nagel, T. 1979. "The Fragmentation of Value." In *Mortal Questions*, edited by Thomas Nagel, pp. 128–41. Cambridge: Cambridge University Press.

_____. 1986. *The View from Nowhere*. New York: Oxford University Press.

_____. 1987. "Moral Conflict and Political Legitimacy," *Philosophy & Public Affairs* 16: 215–40.

Navasky, V. [1980] 1981. *Naming Names*. New York: Penguin.

Neisser, U. 1979. "The Concept of Intelligence," *Intelligence* 3: 217–27.

Neuhaus, R. J. 1984. *The Naked Public Square*. Grand Rapids, Mich.: Eerdmans.

Noble, K. B. 1988. "Harvard's Chief Battles Union Drive," *New York Times* (16 May).

Noonan, J. T. 1970. "An Almost Absolute Value in History." In *The Morality of Abortion: Legal and Historical Perspectives*, edited by John T. Noonan, pp. 51–59. Cambridge, Mass.: Harvard University Press. Reprinted in *The Problem of Abortion*, edited by Joel Feinberg, pp. 9–14. Belmont, Calif.: Wadsworth, 1984.

Nowak, J. E.; Rotunda, R. D.; and Young, J. N. 1978. *Handbook on Constitutional Law*. St. Paul: West Publishing Company.

Oakeshott, M. 1962. *Rationalism in Politics*. London: Methuen.

Perry, W. G., Jr. 1981. "Cognitive and Ethical Growth: The Making of Meaning." In *The Future American College*, edited by Arthur Chickering, pp. 76–116. San Francisco: Jossey-Bass.

Plato, *Crito*. In *The Trial and Death of Socrates*, translated by G. M. A. Grube, pp. 43–54. Indianapolis: Hackett.

President's Commission for the Study of Ethical Problems in Medicine and Biomedical and Behavioral Research. 1984. *Deciding to Forego Life-Sustaining Treatment*. Washington, D.C.: Government Printing Office.

Pruitt, D. G., and Lewis, S. A. 1975. "Development of Integrative Solutions in Bilateral Negotiation," *Journal of Personality and Social Psychology* 31: 621–33.

Putnam, H. 1983. "How Not to Solve Ethical Problems," the Lindley Lecture, Department of Philosophy, University of Kansas, Lawrence.

Raiffa, H. 1982. *The Art and Science of Negotiation*. Cambridge, Mass.: Harvard University Press.

Rand, A. 1964. *The Virtue of Selfishness*. New York: Signet.

Rawls, J. 1971. *A Theory of Justice*. Cambridge, Mass.: Harvard University Press.

_____. 1980. "Kantian Constructivism in Moral Theory: The John Dewey Lectures," *Journal of Philosophy* 77: 515–72.

_____. 1985. "Justice as Fairness: Political Not Metaphysical," *Philosophy & Public Affairs* 14: 223–51.

Rescher, N. 1978. "Philosophical Disagreement: An Essay Towards Orientational Pluralism in Metaphilosophy," *Review of Metaphysics* 32: 217–51.

Reston, J. 1983. "How Reagan Does It," *New York Times* (9 November).

Rhoads, G. R., Jackson, L. G., et al. "The Safety and Efficacy of Chorionic Villus Sampling for Early Prenatal Diagnosis of Cytogenic Abnormalities." *New England Journal of Medicine* 320: 609–17.

Rorty, R. 1979. *Philosophy and the Mirror of Nature*. Princeton, N.J.: Princeton University Press.

_____. [1980] 1982. "Pragmatism, Relativism, Irrationalism." In *Consequences of Pragmatism*, edited by Richard Rorty, pp. 160–75. Minneapolis, University of Minnesota Press.

_____. 1982. *Consequences of Pragmatism*. Minneapolis: University of Minnesota Press.

_____. 1986. "The Contingency of Language," *London Review of Books* (17 April), pp. 3–6.

Ryan, J. D. 1972. "Integrity." In *War, Morality, and the Military Profession*, edited by Malham M. Wakin, p. 180. Boulder, Colo.: Westview Press.

Sacks, O. 1985. *The Man Who Mistook His Wife for a Hat*. New York: Summit Books.

Scanlon, T. M. 1982. "Contractualism and Utilitarianism." In *Utilitarianism and Beyond*, edited by Amartya Williams and Bernard Williams, pp. 103–28. Cambridge: Cambridge University Press.

Schwartz, B. 1988. *The Unpublished Opinions of the Burger Court*. New York: Oxford University Press.

Sher, G. 1981. "Subsidized Abortion: Moral Rights and Moral Compromise," *Philosophy & Public Affairs* 10: 361–72.

Simmel, G. [1908] 1955. "Conflict." In *Conflict and the Web of Group Affiliations*, edited by George Simmel. Translated by Kurt H. Wolff and Reinhard Bendix, pp. 11–123. New York: Free Press.

Singer, M. G. 1986. "The Ideal of a Rational Morality," *Proceedings and Addresses of the American Philosophical Association* 60: 15–38.

Singer, P. 1975. *Animal Liberation*. New York: New York Review.

_____. 1979. *Practical Ethics*. Cambridge: Cambridge University Press.

Singer, P., and Wells, D. 1985. *Making Babies*. New York: Scribner's.

Smith, T. V. 1942. "Compromise: Its Context and Limits," *Ethics* 53: 1–13.

Sophocles. *Antigone*. In Sophocles, *The Theban Plays*, translated by E. F. Watling. Harmondsworth, Eng.: Penguin, 1947.

Stern, L. 1974. "Freedom, Blame, and the Moral Community," *Journal of Philosophy* 71: 72–84.

Sternberg, R. J., and Wagner, R. W., eds. 1986. *Practical Intelligence*. Cambridge: Cambridge University Press.

Stettinius, E. R., Jr. 1949. *Roosevelt and the Russians*. Garden City, N.Y.: Doubleday.

Stevens, J. C. 1984. "Must the Bearer of a Right Have the Concept of That to Which He Has a Right?" *Ethics* 95: 68–74.

Strawson, P. F. [1962] 1968. "Freedom and Resentment." In *Studies in the Philosophy of Thought and Action*, edited by P. F. Strawson, pp. 71–96. London: Oxford University Press.

———. 1985. *Skepticism and Naturalism: Some Varieties*. New York: Columbia University Press.

Strong, C., and Schinfeld, J. S. 1984. "The Single Woman and Artificial Insemination by Donor," *Journal of Reproductive Medicine* 29: 293–99.

Sumner, L. W. 1984. "A Third Way." In *The Problem of Abortion*, edited by Joel Feinberg, pp. 71–93. Belmont, Calif.: Wadsworth. Revised from L. W. Sumner, *Abortion and Moral Theory* (Princeton, N.J.: Princeton University Press, 1981), pp. 124–60.

Taylor, C. 1971. "Interpretation and the Sciences of Man," *Review of Metaphysics* 25: 3–51.

———. 1976. "Responsibility for Self." In *The Identities of Persons*, edited by Amelie Rorty, pp. 281–99. Berkeley: University of California Press.

Taylor, G. 1981. "Integrity," *Aristotelian Society*, supplementary vol. 55: 143–59.

Thomson, J. J. 1971. "In Defense of Abortion," *Philosophy & Public Affairs* 1:47–66.

Tolstoy, L. [1886] 1960. "The Death of Ivan Ilych." In *The Death of Ivan Ilych and Other Stories*, translated by Aylmer Maude, pp. 95–156. New York: New American Library.

Tooley, M. 1983. *Abortion and Infanticide*. Oxford: Oxford University Press.

Vlastos, G. 1971. "The Paradox of Socrates." In *The Philosophy of Socrates*, edited by Gregory Vlastos, pp. 1–21. Garden City, N.Y.: Anchor Books.

Waldron, J. 1989. "Too Important for Tact." *Times Literary Supplement* (10–16 March): 248, 260.

Walzer, M. 1977. *Just and Unjust Wars*. New York: Basic Books.

———. 1987. *Interpretation and Social Criticism*. Cambridge, Mass.: Harvard University Press.

Warnock, M. 1985a. *A Question of Life: The Warnock Report on Fertilisation and Embryology*. Oxford: Basil Blackwell.

———. 1985b. "Moral Thinking and Government Policy: The Warnock Committee on Human Embryology," *Millbank Memorial Fund Quarterly* 63: 504–22.

Warren, M. A. 1973. "On the Moral and Legal Status of Abortion," *Monist* 57: 43–61. Reprinted with a postscript (1982) in *The Problem of Abortion*, edited by Joel Feinberg (Belmont, Calif.: Wadsworth, 1984), pp. 102–19.

Weber, M. [1919] 1958. "Politics as a Vocation." In *From Max Weber*, translated and edited by H. H. Gerth and C. Wright Mills, pp. 77–128. New York: Oxford University Press.

Weil, W. B., Jr., and Benjamin, M. 1987. *Ethical Issues at the Outset of Life.* Boston: Blackwell Scientific Publications.

Wertheimer, R. 1971. "Understanding the Abortion Argument," *Philosophy & Public Affairs* 1: 67–95. Reprinted in a shortened version in *The Problem of Abortion*, edited by Joel Feinberg (Belmont, Calif.: Wadsworth, 1984), pp. 43–57.

Whitman, W. [1855] 1973. "Song of Myself." In Walt Whitman, *Leaves of Grass*, edited by Sculley Bradley and Harold W. Blodgett, pp. 28–89. New York: W. W. Norton.

Wiggins, D. 1980. "Deliberation and Practical Reason." In *Essays on Aristotle's Ethics*, edited by Amelie Rorty, pp. 221–40. Berkeley and Los Angeles: University of California Press, 1980.

Wikler, D. 1988. "Not Dead, Not Dying? Ethical Categories and Persistent Vegetative State," *Hastings Center Report* 18 (February–March): 41–47.

Williams, B. 1973. "A Critique of Utilitarianism." In *Utilitarianism: For and Against*, edited by J. J. C. Smart and Bernard Williams, pp. 77–150. Cambridge: Cambridge University Press.

———. [1976] 1981. "Persons, Character and Morality." In *Moral Luck*, edited by Bernard Williams, pp. 1–19. Cambridge: Cambridge University Press.

———. [1978] 1981. "Introduction." In Isaiah Berlin, *Concepts and Categories*, edited by Henry Hardy, pp. xi–xviii. Harmondsworth, Eng.: Penguin Books.

———. [1979] 1981. "Conflicts of Values." In *Moral Luck*, edited by Bernard Williams, pp. 71–82. Cambridge: Cambridge University Press.

———. 1985. *Ethics and the Limits of Philosophy.* Cambridge, Mass.: Harvard University Press.

Winch, P. 1972. *Ethics and Action.* London: Routledge & Kegan Paul.

Wittgenstein, L. 1953. *Philosophical Investigations.* Translated by G. E. M. Anscombe. New York: Macmillan.

Wolff, R. P. 1965. "Beyond Tolerance." In *A Critique of Pure Tolerance*, edited by Robert Paul Wolff, Barrington Moore, Jr., and Herbert Marcuse, pp. 3–52. Boston: Beacon Press.

Wolin, S. 1972. "Political Theory as a Vocation." In *Machiavelli and the Nature of Political Thought*, edited by Martin Fleisher, pp. 23–75. New York: Atheneum.

Wollheim, R. 1980. "On Persons and Their Lives." In *Explaining Emotions*, edited by Amelie Rorty, pp. 299–321. Berkeley and Los Angeles: University of California Press.

Woodward, B., and Armstrong, S. 1979. *The Brethren.* New York: Simon & Schuster (Avon edition, 1981).

Index

189